LOST ARTS
OF WAR

LOST ARTS OF WAR

Ancient Secrets of Strategy
and Mind Control

DR. HAHA LUNG

CITADEL PRESS
Kensington Publishing Corp.
www.kensingtonbooks.com

CITADEL PRESS BOOKS are published by

Kensington Publishing Corp.
119 West 40th Street
New York, NY 10018

All Kensington titles, imprints, and distributed lines are available at special quantity
discounts for bulk purchases for sales promotions, premiums, fund-raising, educational, or
institutional use. Special book excerpts or customized printings can also be created to fit
specific needs. For details, write or phone the office of the Kensington special sales
manager: Kensington Publishing Corp., 119 West 40th Street, New York, NY 10018, attn:
Special Sales Department; phone 1-800-221-2647.

First printing: March 2012

10 9 8 7 6 5 4 3 2

Printed in the United States of America

CIP data is available.

ISBN-13: 978-0-8065-3506-7
ISBN-10: 0-8065-3506-7

To "Red" John F. Johnson

artist, friend.

DISCLAIMER

The information contained herein is meant to be used for *informational purposes only.* (They made us say that.)

Don't try this at home . . . *take the fight to your enemy's front door!*

Black science: Generic: Any strategy, tactic, or technique used to undermine a person's ability to reason and respond for themselves. Synonyms: Manipulation and mind control. Term originally coined by C. B. Black.

ACKNOWLEDGMENTS

Charts by Christopher B. Prowant

CONTENTS

LOST ARTS
OF WAR

INTRODUCTION:

"Beasts? Badmen?
or Buddhas of Battle?"

"The end and perfection of our victories is to avoid the vices and infirmities of those whom we subdue."
—Alexander the Great

WE STUDY HISTORY in order to make history. And by making history, we remake history in our own image. Ah, *memory*, that greatest of tricksters—Loki laughing with the long-nose.

And so we study the histories—the actions and *thoughts*—of those who have gone before, those singular, often solitary, all too often sinister souls who long ago forded forbidding rivers of personal doubt, who climbed over or squeezed around or else broke and blasted (and bribed?) their way past any boulder or bonehead blocking their way, dauntlessly—and *ruthlessly?*—carving paths through the dark wilderness of ignorance to the wisdom waiting in the clearing just beyond.

True, all too often these peerless and fearless "pioneers of personal empowerment" were destined to decisively—*ruthlessly!*—hack a clear swathe through acres of the worry-weeds and clinging vines deliberately planted in their path by fellow men both indolent and insolent.

But carve those paths they did. And now, whether we choose to follow in their footsteps—intrepid, insightful . . . *insidious?*—or, just as determined

1

as they, inspired by their examples and anecdotes, we instead choose to map out our own unique path, we can take comfort and further inspiration from the fact we have both *their thoughts* and *our own thoughts* to guide us—a two-edged sword if ever there was one.

Yet can our thoughts—of adventure, of glory, perhaps revenge—be enough to augment these elder teachings, and together vouchsafe us for the coming struggle?

The thoughts that tempt and test the mind of youth are not necessarily the same thoughts that trouble the sleep and waking moments of the older—hopefully wiser?—man.

Solomon, dubbed "the wisest man who ever lived," powerful king, with a *harem* of over 4,000 wives and concubines,[1] authored *The Wisdom of Solomon*—believed written when he was at the height of his youth and power and vigor.

Later he would also write *Ecclesiastes*, whose resigned almost fatalistic tone leads experts to conclude it was written nearer the end of Solomon's life, in his days of waning health, after he'd "been there, done that," and had grown—understandably?—more cynical: "Vanity of vanities, all is vanity! What does a man gain by all his toil . . ."[2]

In other words, it's not unheard of for the wide-eyed optimism and ambitions of youth to become—*succumb to*—the raised-eyebrow ambiguity and compromise of middle age to, ultimately, the cynical, narrow-eyed abandonment of dreams, pride, and principle in waning years.

All too often, for all too many, "age" becomes synonymous with "settling for less."

But not for all men, e.g., Hannibal, Spartacus, Yoritomo, and Vlad Tepes.

Cynical? Perhaps because three out of those four never lived to see a ripe old age.

A little more optimistic? Perhaps because these were men made of sterner stuff.

But, for so many, Spring gives way to Summer, futilely trying to fend off that inevitable Fall toward the finality of Winter.

---

1. And this was "BV" . . . *before Viagra!*
2. Ecclesiastes 1:2.

Thus, in the course of any man's life, we find enthusiastic Spring truths, still-optimistic Summer truths, more pragmatic Fall truths, and the inevitable harsh, cold reality of Winter truths.

Thus, when studying the words of great and powerful men—dare we say, "men for all seasons"?—we must not look at merely *who* penned this wisdom and wile before us, but *when*—the tempo and temper of the times—as well as *where*—whether written while wallowing leisurely in the lap of luxury, or hurriedly scribbled down in the heat of battle, its eve, or its aftermath.

Different times try men (and their souls?) differently. Events a man in one era decries as "crisis" another man in another time smilingly spies and sighs "opportunity."

Indeed, would even the same man pen the same words in the eternally hopeful Spring of life as he would in the Winter of his discontent? Didn't the example of Solomon lay that quandary to rest?

Might not even the same man viewed from various vantages in his own time be seen—and be recorded—differently by friend and foe?[3]

Perception creates reality. Thus to some we are "beast." To others merely "badmen." To still others, those viewing us from a clearer, perhaps kinder perspective, we are "Buddhas," beings who relentlessly pursue wisdom, apprehend it, and then freely share that bounty with our fellows.

So what of these men before us today: Hannibal the Conqueror; Spartacus the Gladiator-turned rebel; Yoritomo, Japan's first *Shogun*; and Vlad Tepes, the fearless Prince who succeeded in saving medieval Europe at the cost of his own kingdom?

To some they are "beasts." To others, "badmen." But to some, they are truly deserving of the Eastern accolade "Buddha"—an "Enlightened One," often translated "one who is awake."

When we examine what deviant, devilish, or simply *determined* DNA such men share, we must look beyond superficial influences: That Spartacus, so obviously inspired by Hannibal, that the gladiator-turned-slave Messiah walked the same Roman roads as the Carthaginian conqueror a hundred years before; that some 1,800 years after Spartacus was himself taken in

---

3. See Vlad Tepes's Certainty IV, in Part IV of this book. Better known to the world as "Dracula," this ruler of Wallachia suffered just such a fate: his enemies, Germans, having invented the *printing press* before his friends!

chains from the hills of his native Thrace, another rebel and guerilla fighter, Vlad Tepes, fought in some of those same hills, perhaps using the same hidden ways and warrens of Spartacus to escape *his* enemies.

And what of Yoritomo? If not sharing the same Mediterranean bloodline as Hannibal, Spartacus, and Vlad Tepes, if not spilling the same enemies' blood, still the Japanese commander surely shared the DNA of *determination* with his Carthaginian, Thracian, and Rumanian counterparts.

- Yoritomo knew, as did Hannibal, Spartacus, and Vlad Tepes, what it was like to have to hunker down in the hills with a price on your head while the greedy blades of a victorious enemy beat the bush.
- Yoritomo knew, as did Hannibal, Spartacus, and Vlad Tepes, *the pain of patience*, of having to bite your lips and bide your time, until frustration could finally be melted down and recast as razor-sharp revenge!
- Yoritomo knew too, as did Hannibal, Spartacus, and Vlad Tepes—however briefly—the pleasure of seeing your patience and planning and persistence finally pay off as your humbled enemy is brought before you—either on his knees, or else his head on a pole!
- Yoritomo also knew, as did Hannibal, Spartacus, and Vlad Tepes, that we are made as much by our sins and sufferings as we are by any sermons we hear. Even as the Samurai sword is forged only in the hottest of kilns, after with a thousand merciless hammerings, so too the worth of a man is not measured by how many times he falls, or even is driven to the ground by an enemy. No, Yoritomo learned early on in life, as had Hannibal and Spartacus, as would Vlad Tepes, that the measure of a man is how many times he rises again from his sufferings.

It's said the wise Buddha, Prince Siddhartha Gautama of India (563–477 B.C.), spent years wandering in the wilderness, practicing all forms of painful *yoga* austerities, finally fasting and meditating for forty days without letup, before ultimately entering a higher state of awareness and enlightenment known as *Nirvana*.

In this way, Siddhartha became a "Buddha" (Skt. "Enlightened being"). And while Buddhism worldwide is today known for its dedication to nonviolence, down through the ages many *very* violent groups have called themselves Buddhist, or else proudly claimed Buddhism in their sect's lineage: Chinese Shaolin monks,[4] Japanese *Yamabushi* warrior-monks,[5] as well as Samurai Buddhists,[6] and Ninja.[7]

Since, at its most basic, Buddhism fearlessly dives into the depths of the human mind in order to uncover the roots of our negative thinking patterns,[8] it's hardly surprising that such intimate knowledge of the inner workings of the human mind might offer some—plenty!—of opportunity for misuse.[9]

What's interesting to note, especially for the task at hand, is that Siddhartha found the "enlightenment" he needed to become The Buddha *through suffering*, which he then determined was the *very nature* of human existence. Buddha's First Noble Truth: All Life is suffering; it is the nature of man that he suffers.

During their lifetimes, Hannibal, Spartacus, Yoritomo, and Vlad Tepes likewise knew "suffering" . . . suffering that could not but have had an influence on both their *outlook* and, it has to be admitted, their own later *output* of "suffering" they willingly and willfully with malice aforethought directed against their enemies.

We don't need Sigmund Freud to remind us we're made as much by our sins and sufferings as we are by the sermons we hear.

Having "paid his dues" in suffering, Siddhartha gained enlightenment— or at least the method by which others might gain their own enlightenment.

Whether Hannibal's, Spartacus's, Yoritomo's and Vlad Tepes's individual sufferings—their lands violated, their people killed, themselves hunted and thrown into slavery—brought those men personal "enlightenment" . . . who knows?

But if not "enlightenment," then at least their "experience via suffering"

---

4. For a complete course in Shaolin training and philosophy see "The Rise and Fall of Shaolin" in Dr. Haha Lung's *Mind Penetration* (Citadel Press, 2007).

5. See Lung and Tucker's *The Nine Halls of Death* (Citadel Press, 2007).

6. See "Atari-Shin: Samurai Mind Strike" in Lung and Prowant's *Mind Assassins* (Citadel Press, 2010).

7. Lung and Tucker, ibid.

8. Yeah, kinda like how you're paying that shrink with the funny accent $150 an hour to figure out why you keep having that nightmare where you keep showing up in machine-shop class buck-naked!

9. See "Buddhist Black Science" in Dr. Lung's *Mind Penetration* (Citadel Press, 2007).

brought them "insight," perhaps even "revelation," increasing their ability to focus their anger—righteous or otherwise, hone their hunger for justice—*and* for revenge, then their suffering was worth it: doubling their determination, thereby halving the chances that the enemies that had brought them, their land, and their loved ones suffering, could ever themselves escape retribution!

The same dagger that does evil can do good. The same bullet that brings suffering, can also relieve that suffering. Such is the nature of things.

Did not the wise Buddha declare that "It is the *nature* of men to suffer"?

One might then argue that Hannibal, Spartacus, Yoritomo, and Vlad Tepes were simply "Buddhas of Battle" doing what came "naturally."

Let us, therefore, let them *enlighten* us.

> *"If you're* scared *to ask,*
> *you'll probably be* terrified *by the answer."*
> —C. B. Black

Part I
From the Ninety-nine Sayings of Hannibal

"A victim of injustice from infancy . . . I had created a view of life very different from other men's. . . . Oh, I concede, I became wicked and even cruel. Woe betide anyone who offended me if I could snatch a favorable moment. I was the more dangerous because I never avenged myself until I was certain of success; I never showed my hatred until the instant propitious for satisfying it."
—Lacenaire, French murderer, guillotined 1836

Introduction

IT HAS BEEN PROMISED US, "Time heals all wounds," and indeed, recent research seems to bear this out.

A 2007 study found that, barely three months after a betrayal, people were eight times *less* likely to report still having negative feelings toward their transgressors.[10]

Curiously, while women held grudges longer, men were four times as likely to actually seek revenge.[11]

It seems, sometimes you just *can't* let it go.

Nine-Eleven comes to mind. . . .

Still, it's never advisable to go off half-cocked, lest you too soon find yourself in over your head, in a protracted firefight you can't win, from which you literally return half-cocked!

Prudence, patience, and planning are the sturdy tripod upon which revenge sits.

By the way, if your sensibilities are offended by our use of the word "revenge," feel free to substitute the word "justice" every time you see "revenge." Beware, however; *lying* to yourself can get to be a very costly habit. . . .

---

10. "Time Heals All Wounds," *Men's Health,* March 2010.
11. Ibid.

The (in)famous advice that "revenge is a dish best eaten cold,"[12] would have pleased Hannibal, himself cautioning that revenge should only be undertaken after balancing patience with preparation.

Some historians argue Hannibal launched the Second Punic War (247– 183 B.C.) between his native Carthage and Rome in *revenge* for his father Hamilcar's defeat at the hands of the Romans during the First Punic War (264–241 B.C.).

The "revenge" angle of this is bolstered by the oft-told tale of Hannibal: how, when still a boy, his father took him into Carthage's greatest temple and made him swear on the sword of his ancestors never to make peace with the Romans.

However, when we examine Hannibal's life *in toto*, we find him a complex man. And, while not a man living up to today's "high" moral standards,[13] there is much about Hannibal that deserves our admiration: his sense of duty and honor, his bravery, and his use of intelligence—both the innate and the gathered varieties.

Hannibal's time demanded much of men: that they keep their word to friend and do their duty to family. Then again, perhaps not so much to ask of a man (though many today would argue it is far too great a burden!).

And revenge? In Hannibal's world, revenge was a given. And an *incentive* to do the job right the first time. As the Romans warned, "Slay the Sons of Brutus!" Don't allow the son to live long enough to take up his father's sword in vengeance.

> *"The weakest foe boasts some revenging power."*
> **—Ben Franklin**

If the Romans had listened to their own advice about the "Sons of Brutus," Hannibal wouldn't have seen his first birthday. But the Romans didn't "finish the job" on the Carthaginians in general, nor on Hannibal's father in the First Punic War in particular, and so they paid the price for thirteen years, as Hannibal rampaged up and down the Italian peninsula, literally taking the war to his enemy.

An act of revenge? Or a *necessary* survival operation meant to break the

---

12. Most often *mis*quoted as "a dish best *served* cold."
13. Yes, that *is* sarcasm you detect in Dr. Lung's voice!

increasing stranglehold of restrictive reparations demanded of Carthage following the First Punic War?

Perhaps a little of both.

Whatever his motivation, Hannibal has been accused of many attitudes and even more atrocities, but he has never been accused, even by his most virulent foes, of rashness.

For Hannibal, revenge was, indeed, a dish best *eaten* cold.

In the end, after years spent eluding Roman pursuers following his defeat in the Second Punic War, Hannibal fell on his sword[14] with his final words:

> It is time to end the great anxiety of the Romans who have grown weary of waiting for the death of a hated old man.

This was not revenge on the part of the Romans. No, they hunted Hannibal out of *fear* of the loyalty even "a hated old man" could inspire!

---

14. Recall, some researchers claim Hannibal took poison, others that he both took poison and fell on his sword rather than suffer the indignity of falling into the hands of his lifelong enemy.

Hannibal's Five Rules
for Revenge

WHILE SEVERAL OF the "99 Truths" Hannibal left us can, in one way or another, be applied to the subject of "revenge," five specific "truths" stand out as "Hannibal's Five Rules of Revenge":

1. *The wine of a true friend is fine indeed. But some thirsts can only be satisfied by the blood of a foe!* (Truth LIII)

This is the reply Hannibal gave King Prusias of Bithynia when the latter gave the former Carthaginian commander sanctuary from his Roman pursuers following his fleeing Carthage in the face of a Roman warrant for his arrest.

The king assured Hannibal he was welcome to spend the remainder of his days in peace in Bithynia if he so chose.

In hindsight, Hannibal's words ring ironic, given that Roman bloodlust (born of *fear*) of their aging Carthaginian foe could, in the end, likewise only be sated by blood.

Here then is the first reality (and so "rule") of taking revenge: Sometimes you *can't* "just let it go."

Nine-Eleven.

2. *Revenge should wait until both your sword and your wits have been sharpened.* (Truth LV)

Between the end of the First Punic War and Hannibal's deliberate launching of the Second Punic War, Hannibal and his brothers grew up, grew strong, and grew into their warriorhood, helping Carthage conquer the Iberian Peninsula—a rich but "barbaric" land not yet under Rome's heavy thumb.

All this time, thoughts of eventual revenge against hated Rome never left the sons of Hamilcar.

Nineteen hundred years later, on the other side of the world from Carthage, in 1701 Japan, Lord Kira, the Japanese Shogun's minister Master of Ceremonies devised a plot to rid himself of his longtime rival, Lord Asano. Knowing Asano to be a man easily brought to anger, Kira deliberately provoked Asano into drawing his sword while the two were guests on Imperial ground.

For this grievous breach of etiquette, Lord Asano was ordered to commit ritual suicide—*seppuku*.

At the time, Lord Asano had forty-seven Samurai knights serving him. As was Samurai custom at the time, many expected that at least some of Lord Asano's forty-seven knights would commit *hari-kiri* and follow their Master into The Void. At the very least, to "save face" and guard their honor, many argued that the forty-seven should have immediately launched a bold—albeit suicidal—attack against the numerically superior Samurai guarding Lord Kira.

But instead, the forty-seven went their separate ways, choosing to become *Ronin*, "masterless Samurai," akin to what in the West would be out-of-work gunslingers.[15]

For two years thereafter, wherever one of these forty-seven Ronin ventured in Japan, they were reviled as the scum of the earth. Fathers pointed out the forty-seven as examples to their sons how *not to be* a Samurai, of what happens to a Samurai when they lose their honor. . . .

But then, on the second anniversary of their Master's death, all forty-seven Ronin returned from all over Japan, secretly gathering outside the walls of Lord Kira's castle.

---

15. A trivia—but not *trivial*—fact, the Western standard *The Magnificent Seven* (1960), the story of out-of-work gunslingers, was a remake of the 1954 Japanese classic about seven Ronin, *The Seven Samurai*.

As one, the forty-seven Ronin breached the castle walls. Caught by surprise, Lord Kira's Samurai quickly fell beneath the blades of the forty-seven.

As dawn found them, all forty-seven Ronin knelt in silence as they placed the head of Lord Kira on the grave of their Master, Lord Asano. Then, one-by-one, all forty-seven Ronin committed *seppuku*, finally joining their Lord in The Void.

This example fits Hannibal's insight that revenge should not be taken until both your "sword" and "wits" are sharpened. In modern parlance, we'll call that your collecting the (1) means and (2) intelligence sufficient to accomplish the task.

3. *Revenge demands a steady hand and a steadier eye.* (Truth LVI)

A "steady hand" means the determination to carry through the act of revenge you have planned. Just as important, Hannibal advises we must have a "steadier eye."

Think of "steadier eye" as your intelligence gathering, i.e., the more information you have about your target, the easier it is to hit that target.

An excellent example of this principle is depicted in Edgar Allen Poe's *The Cask of the Amontillado* (1846), where, though not revealed until the closing lines of the story, the narrator reveals that decades before he had successfully taken revenge after suffering "a thousand insults" from his tormentor-turned-victim, and is only now finally sharing his "confession" with his readers. Patience indeed!

But what is of most importance is the fact that he successfully lures his enemy to his doom in the catacombs beneath the city by promising the one thing his enemy would be unable to resist—in this instance, a large cask of rare wine.

This kind of "insider" information comes only after studying your intended target with a "steady" eye.

Just as the dagger is nothing without the determination to use it, so too the greatest of genius comes to naught without the method and means to turn belief into a blade.

4. *Revenge demands a long blade . . . and a longer memory.* (Truth LVII)

Just because we can reach our enemy—a long blade—doesn't mean we have to do it *today*.

The forty-seven Ronin had "a long sword," the means by which to avenge Lord Asano. But, in the face of overwhelming odds, they would not have accomplished their mission had they rashly attacked on the day of their Lord's death.

The successful avenging of their Lord's death meant that "a longer memory" was called for.

It is often hard for Westerners to understand *the risk* those forty-seven Ronin took in waiting those two long years to get revenge.

Their greatest risk was not the possibility of their being killed. Death walks beside a warrior every day of his life. No, the greatest risk was to their *honor*. Had any of the forty-seven died—even by accident—during those two years, that man's honor—as well as the honor of his family, clan, and *ken*[16]— would have forever been besmirched.

But, for the forty-seven, their *giri* (duty) demanded that they risk waiting—that they place justice for their Master above even their own honor.

In the West, this is sometimes called "eating crow," backing down from an immediate challenge because bigger stakes are at risk. This is often a bitter pill to swallow but sometimes necessary . . . feathers and all!

The fledgling army of the newly declared Republic of Texas faced ridicule from both friend and foe for their failure to "actively engage" the enemy. In fact, Mexican Dictator Santa Anna chased Sam Houston all over Texas, trying to trap the "rebel" into a stand-up fight.

Houston would have none of that.

Following the successful examples of Hannibal refusing to fight Roman legions face-to-face, and the way American Colonials refused to give British "lobsterbacks" a "sporting" fight, so too Sam Houston knew his ragtag force would be no match in a toe-to-toe tussle with the veteran Mexican army. Instead, Houston continued his "strategic retreat" until finally—literally—he caught Santa Anna with his pants down at the telling Battle of San Jacinto.

Thus, this Rule for Revenge blends seamlessly into Hannibal's final Rule for Revenge:

5. *Revenge, like fine wine and royal blood, takes time to ferment properly.* (Truth LVIII)

---

16. Warrior Society.

Read *The Count of Monte Cristo* (1845), the best fictional revenge story this side of *Hamlet*.

Study Puzo's *The Godfather*, the book *and* the movie(s).

Look up a wily Sicilian Greek named Gelon of Gela.[17]

> *"The stupid neither forgive nor forget; the naive forgive and forget; the wise forgive, but do not forget."*
>
> —Thomas Szasz

---

17. See "What Would Gelon of Gela Do?" in *Mind Penetration* by Dr. Haha Lung (Citadel Press, 2007).

Hannibal's Six Movers of Men

HANNIBAL'S FATHER, HAMILCAR, who had been Carthage's much-heralded military commander during the First Punic War, not only taught his sons, Hannibal, Mago, and Hasdrubal, the art of war, but also instilled in them an abiding hatred for all things Roman. Reportedly, with the bitter taste of defeat from the First Punic War still fresh in his mouth, Hamilcar took young Hannibal to Carthage's main temple, where he made the boy swear on his father's sword undying enmity with Rome. Hannibal kept that vow till his last day.

> *"Revenge is the purest emotion."*
> **—Mahabharata**

Later in life Hannibal would also prove himself an able administrator, diplomat, and—when need be, though much to his disliking—politician.

But Hannibal is, of course, best known to history for his brilliant battlefield exploits and insights. Today he continues to impart his hard-won wisdom to us through *The Ninety-nine Truths*. Like Sun Tzu's masterwork *Ping-fa*, Hannibal's *Ninety-nine Truths* are universally applicable, capable of fitting into any time and place, capable of *dominating* any time and place, as applicable in the boardroom as they are on the battlefield. For example, in his Truth LX, Hannibal gives us "The Six Movers of Men," the six basic motivations he saw as (1) naturally influencing man's actions, and (2) basic motivations that could—in the right or wrong hand—all too easily and effectively be used by one man to influence—*control!*—his fellows. Truth LX reads:

> He who fights for blood soon finds it dripping from his own heart.
>
> He who fights for glory never lives long enough to hear the victory songs.[18]
>
> He who fights for gold is already blinded by the glitter and glare of his own greed, all too soon led astray by all things shiny.
>
> He who fights for sport seldom finds The Gods in a sporting mood.
>
> He who fights for love must leave the one he loves the most behind so he can dance with the one he hates the most.
>
> But he who fights for honor cannot be led astray.

The first thing we notice is that all six of *Hannibal's "Movers of Men"* possess the positive attribute of "focus." That's because these are all six prime motivators, those things—one or the other or several together—we all obsess over to some extent.

No surprise then that positive "focus" *in extremis* all too easily becomes negative "obsession." For example, while we might, especially in our modern, politically correct, oh-so-sensitive times, eschew fighting for morbidly attractive topics like "blood" and "glory," and "gold" and cruel "sport,"[19] few would or could successfully argue against fighting for such high-minded virtues as "love" and "honor."

Yet even when these two highly esteemed motivations (excuses often used to justify whacking our fellow man on the head with a rock!) are taken to extremes,[20] when we lose focus of our original chivalrous quest or, worse yet, when we allow love and honor—or any of the previous four "movers" for that matter—to become "obsessions," even they can become liabilities, and invite indictment:

---

18. It's obvious just from looking that, at least in the English translation, only a single, thin line separates "glory" from "gory"!

19. UFC, bullfighting, and national political conventions every four years being the exception.

20. Which simply means we get to liking the "whacking" part!

1. Blood

Blood attracts two types: (1) The revenge-minded (admit it, like we all were immediately following Nine-Eleven), and (2) serial-killer types who get off on seeing the red stuff. It's obvious Hannibal is speaking here of the former, though he undoubtedly ran into more than his share of the blood-thirsty latter during his admittedly sanguinary campaigning.

Hannibal was well aware that, like any good knife, revenge cuts both ways.

Down through the years revenge has gotten a bad rap. People try to soften it up by using euphemisms like "justice" and "karma," but the truth is, there's an innate desire/compulsion within us to seek "balance"—*lex talionis*, an eye for an eye. When we've been wronged, the Universe feels out of whack, off balance. The only way to right that balance is for the perpetrator of our suffering to suffer an equal (or perhaps greater) proportion of the suffering and loss he has inflicted on us. Admit it, we'd have all liked to see Osama bin Laden's head on prominent display on a pole at Ground Zero . . . after we'd had a really long—leisurely—"talk" with him.[21]

The desire—need—for "rebalancing" is basic to the human animal and is thus found in all cultures, as previously mentioned usually under the euphemisms as "justice," "karma," and, occasionally, "God's Will."

More personal, one-on-one, hands-on "rebalancing" we call "payback" and "vigilantism."

The man out for revenge, out for blood, is, if nothing else, *focused*. Since before Hannibal's time we've written ballads and told tales of wronged men (and women) who *focus* and take to the blood-trail, seeking righteous revenge—justice: Scotland's William Wallace (at least Mel Gibson's version) and Gotham City's Batman.

All societies condone revenge (under the heading of "justice") to one extent or the other. Though societies generally frown on vigilantism, preferring instead a general consensus, usually requiring a blessing by The Elders[22] before embarking on revenge, the following events would seem to contradict this consensus:

---

21. For a complete course on how to negotiate with terrorists, see: *Theatre of Hell: Dr. Lung's Complete Guide to Torture* (Loompanics Unlimited, 2003).

22. Today we call them "Congress."

- Dinah is raped and, days later, a group of Israelites first trick and then slaughter all the men of the rapists' tribe.[23]
- The assassination of the entire Romanov dynasty.
- The atomic bombing of Hiroshima and Nagasaki.
- The invasion of Afghanistan.

So, as a society, we do condone bloody vengeance, uh "justice," so long as at least 51 percent of[AM1] us are in agreement.

The other type of "blood" motivation—spilling blood simply because we like seeing "oh, the pretty color!"—is generally not sanctioned by civilization. When not fed by some "Mama made me wear her old dresses to school" psychological glitch, this kind of rogue "vampirism" usually bubbles up in someone already predisposed to anger.[24]

Once a Black Science adept recognizes that their targeted person is prone (i.e., *vulnerable*) to anger, they will either (1) fan the flames of the target's already existing anger, or else (2) engineer a scenario designed to "bring out the beast," i.e., deliberately enrage that person—timing/coordinating their target's outburst for the most inconvenient, most embarrassing, and career-damaging time possible for that person.

Whenever possible, further influence your already angry target by providing the enraged person with a convenient scapegoat to blame, thus encouraging (i.e., "justifying") the target's newfound thirst for revenge.

One might imagine that soldiers out for vengeance would make the best soldiers, but this is not necessarily the case. A wily commander like Hannibal understood there are times when inflaming your soldiers' anger and need for vengeance is useful for galvanizing them against the common foe. But, too much of a lust for vengeance can turn an otherwise disciplined force into a lynch-mob. Thus at other points in *The Ninety-nine Truths,* Hannibal touched on both the *need* for revenge, and the need to reign in—or at least more finely hone—one's need for revenge.

Recall how, fleeing from Carthage with a Roman bounty on his head at the conclusion of the Second Punic War, Hannibal was given asylum by King Prusias of Bithynia who, during a banquet, assured his honored guest that he

---

23. See Genesis 34.
24. One of our five "Warning F.L.A.G.S."

was welcome to live out his days in peace in Bithynia if he chose—even though both men knew the Carthaginian would never rest in his quest to bring down Rome. Reportedly Hannibal toasted his gracious host with what became Truth LIII:

> The wine of a true friend is fine indeed. But some thirsts can only be satisfied by the blood of a foe!

In hindsight, Hannibal's words ring ironic, given that Roman bloodlust (fueled by *fear*) of their aging Carthaginian foe could likewise only, ultimately, be satisfied by blood.

2. Glory

Stephen Crane's *The Red Badge of Courage* (1893) tells the universal tale of a young man who naïvely soldiers off to war in search of "glory" only to discover that the truth of war is men left broken and bloody and buried, the medals pinned to their chests scant recompense for the metal lodged in their hearts.

Black Science adepts know that many of the people motivated by dreams of "glory," of fame and recognition, probably never have, and probably never will, venture near an actual battlefield. As a result, we class "glory seekers" into two types:

- The young and naïve who crave to carve their place in society, to find themselves. These kind of naïve glory seekers are really "identity seekers" who lack focus and self-esteem and so are easy fodder for gangs, cults, and ruthless military recruiters.
- Those who crave "glory" out of all proportion to any potential of talent they actually possess. More often than not, such people are frustrated, angry, and resentful at a world that fails to recognize their "destiny" and "genius." How difficult are people like this to manipulate? Not very.

Offering a way for someone to achieve the "glory" (recognition, fame, etc.) they so crave puts the manipulator firmly in their favor, securely in the driver's seat.

The first type, the "identity seeker," can be dazzled with tales of past heroes, showing them how they too can be a "hero," a "winner," or one of "The Chosen"—all along the way being sure to constantly reassure the seeker how "special" they are.

This kind of glory seeker falls into the category Sun Tzu calls "Expendable Agents."[25] Send him on a one-way (i.e., suicide) mission "only he" can accomplish. This kind was (figuratively or literally) born to "die for a cause" . . . why not *your* cause?

The second type of glory seeker, those who feel frustrated the world doesn't recognize their talents, is easily drawn to *you* (and your cause) simply because you do appear to recognize their talent. In this way you adroitly string the glory seeker along with the promise of making them famous, until the glory seeker becomes dependent on you for his self-esteem.

3. Gold

Focused. Obsessed. Greedy. Reckless. Mercenary—his loyalty is contingent upon profit. Convince him you know where the Mother Lode of his particular brand of "treasure" is and he'll follow you anywhere . . . until he finds out different. See Bogart's *Treasure of the Sierra Madre* (1948).

However, "Dr. Lung's Altruism Rule" states: There's no such thing as "altruism." Everybody gets paid. If you want someone to do something, simply tell them what's in it for them.[26]

Where one gets paid in gold—cold hard cash—another gets paid in that warm feeling that they're a "good person" for stopping to help a stranded stranger. So "gold" in some instances doesn't mean the heavy, shiny stuff (though it's nice to have plenty of that too!).

Your particular "gold" (the apple, or rather *obsession*, of your eye) might be all kinds of things—from physical symbols of wealth (a fancy car, fancy girlfriend) to "knowing" in your heart you've done a good deed to your family and friends.

---

25. *Ping-fa*, Chapter XIII. See the chapter "Sun Tzu Storms the Gate!" in *Mind Warrior* (2010).

26. However, if the truth of the matter is that there isn't anything in it for them . . . you might want to invest in a couple more "Dr. Lung" books first!

It's simple push-pull: Find out what kind of "gold" a person wants and then either "pull" them in with promises of showing them where there's plenty of it to be found, or else threaten to withhold their "gold" from them:

> What a man loves, what he hates, what he needs, what he desires: These are the four pillars that support his house.
> (Truth IV)

4. Sport

Except for the expedient extraction of information in the face of a looming "dire threat situation" where life is in immediate peril,[27] cruelty has no place on the battlefield. Battle, by its very nature, is cruel enough, without our making "sport" of a defeated enemy. Okinawan Grandmaster Gichin Funakoshi, founder of *Shotokan* karate, taught his students, "Slay . . . but never humiliate a man."

Deliberately indulging in cruelty—*sans* justifiable excuse—making sport of those no longer able to defend themselves, marks us as petty and cruel. When conmen discover this sadistic "cruelty" trait in others, they immediately fan the flames, encouraging that person's obnoxious acts—in the case of a cult leader, or ruthless dictator, actually giving their "blessing" to such cruelty. This in turn sets up a "feedback loop" that only benefits the conman: The more obnoxious and offending the person's acts are (1) the more he will find himself shunned by other—normal—people, therefore (2) the more he will be drawn into the conman's Mind Slayer's camp (or cult) and the more he will take the conman into his confidence and, most importantly, (3) he will soon become dependent upon the conman for validation and vindication.

Many of this type are natural bullies (though they may lack the physicality to play out their bully fantasies). Such people are easily bored and easily led, especially when their *enabler* provides them an excuse, or better yet a whole venue (gang, cult, rebel army, etc.), in which to freely practice their perversions.[28]

---

27. Right, *Theatre of Hell: Dr. Lung's Complete Guide to Torture* (Loompanics Unlimited, 2003) again!

28. Read the Marquis de Sade's *120 of Sodom* . . . if you dare.

5. Love

No one is more focused than those motivated by the love of kin, kind, and country. Of Hannibal's six "movers," *love* is trump—as if that comes as a big surprise to anyone.

On the positive side, such people are loyal, attentive, caring, and self-sacrificing. However, in negative manifestation, love all too easily becomes myopic, obsessed, possessed, and overly possessive, and Othelloean jealous. The "self-sacrificing" aspect on the positive side of the equation, corrupted by *perceived* neglect, all too easily becomes "martyrdom" . . . and that martyrdom thing seldom ends well.

Machiavelli hit the nail on the head, telling his prince that (if forced to choose) between being feared or being loved, the prince should prefer the former, since fear is at least more constant than love. In other words, if someone truly fears you, there's little chance that fear is suddenly going to blossom into love. Love, on the other hand, can turn to hate in an instant, at just the drop of a former lover's name.

Manipulating a target is often as simple as finding the thing he covets and offering to help him obtain it:

> What a man loves, what he hates, what he needs, what he
> desires: These are the four pillars that support his house.
> (Hanibal's *Ninety-nine Truths*, Truth IV)

Or else finding the thing he treasures the most and threatening to take it away from him. Hannibal's first Truth:

> Enemy! When you look at me don't see something you
> hate . . . see the very thing you love the most. For that is what
> I will surely rip from you if you ever rise against me!

6. Honor

It is telling that Hannibal, by all accounts an honorable man himself, should reserve "honor" as the final, and by default, most worthy of things worth fighting for.

The man who fights for honor fights not only for himself, but for those things he loves outside himself, for his honor is intricately linked to the honor of his loved ones, those who call him friend, and the cause and country he fights for.

The honorable warrior is focused, truthful, and loyal to the clan, cause, and country to which he has pledged that honor.

On the negative side, too sensitive an honor can make a man hesitant when instead he should be hurling himself headlong into the fray.

His honor called into question, or otherwise trespassed, at the very least, steps are taken to reclaim that honor. *In extremis*, vengeance becomes the order of the day—as it was for the forty-seven Ronin.

A manipulator can play on "the honor" of only *a shallow mind*, one with an equally *shallow* sense of honor, by making it appear that person has lost his honor (or lost "face," if you will), further entrapping him by offering a way to regain that lost honor.

Shallow men often fail to see their own shortcomings, inflated and imagined entitlement, and their own lowness in attitude and inattention to detail as the true cause of their being dishonored, preferring instead to point their finger at other, more honorable men as the cause of their affront.

But, so long as we are honorable, no other man can ever make us lose that honor. Figuratively and literally, that honor is left to ourselves.

Only by our taking action when decorum and common sense call for counsel and quiet, or else through our inaction when it is time for honest and battle-honed men to step to the fore, only then can we ever cause our honor to be called into question.

> *"Duty flows out from my breast. Obligation pours into my ear!*
> *Skin cut a thousand times eventually heals. Honor wounded but*
> *once never heals. War always begins with deceit. This is why war is*
> *always the final recourse of an honorable man. War always ends in*
> *desperation and death . . . and the death of honor is the most tragic*
> *of these."*
> **—Hannibal**

When asked why the greatest of men prefer an honorable death to a life *sans* honor, King Leonidas of Sparta, leader of "The 300 Spartans" replied: Because they regard the latter as being a gift of nature, while the former is in their own hands.

Part II
The War Scroll of Spartacus

"When Spartacus spoke men listened. It wasn't just his prowess in the arena, or his experience in the Roman army, or his possible reputation as a bandit. It wasn't simply his royal-sounding name or his communications skills—although those were surely considerable. Something else, some X factor, multiplied his authority."
—Barry Strauss, *The Spartacus War*

Introduction

*"The Romans were nothing if not inventive when it came to killing
their fellow humans."*
—Robert Matthews, *The Age of Gladiators*

THERE IS MUCH we do not know about the *man* Spartacus. But there is much
to the myth, legend, lore, and ultimate legacy of Spartacus, the mercenary-
auxiliary to the conquering Romans turned guerilla chief who, captured,
becoming first a shackled slave, then a celebrated gladiator, before becoming
bane to the Roman tongue, an enemy the likes of which the Latins hadn't
known since the days of Hannibal.

It came about by way of these many personal tragedy–induced
transformations—a molding metamorphosis of man to menace to what many
would see as messiah—that tore a "lowly" Thracian from his country's own
war-torn hills, raising him first to notice then to glory, until he stood tall
enough to challenge the seven hills of Rome. Ultimately he would lead the
most (in)famous, largest, most successful slave revolt in ancient times, a revolt
that would first inflame all of Italy before ultimately engulfing a godly portion
of the peninsula.

Spartacus caught Rome with its pants down (or, its toga over its head, as
the case may be!). His was a revolt that saw the defeat and humiliation in at

least nine pitched battles and numerous skirmishes[29] of what was then the most powerful, most disciplined army in the world.

This is Spartacus's legacy. And, for our purpose of learning his art of war, that legacy will more than suffice.

What we must remember, however, while studying Spartacus's Scroll of War is that, as a species, we have an inclination—a bad habit—of elevating our enemies from the merely bothersome to The Boogeyman, from dire menace to admirable myth.

Had it not been for Sheriff Pat Garrett, we'd never have heard of the young, wet-behind-the-ears, gap-toothed killer dubbed "Billy the Kid."[30] Had not the ambitious Garrett, his eye fixed firmly on higher office, not hired a ghostwriter to pen The Kid's bloody biography—with especial prose and praise given the "heroic" lawman who finally put an end to the killer's rampage. In other words: the bigger and more scary your enemy is, the bigger and badder you look when you finally bring him down. Politics 101.

Fact: The Romans—like all empires worth their salt—first *demonized* their enemies (it's easier to kill "zombies" and "sub-humans" than it is your fellow man) before they then lionized them, most notable, their canonization of their former Carthaginian nemesis. And rightly so.

As we've already (hopefully successfully!) argued, Hannibal did more to "create" the Roman Empire than did any actual Roman. By the end of the Second Punic War—Hannibal's war—Rome was the undisputed cock-of-the-walk.

You're known by the company you keep—and your enemies as well.

FBI despot J. Edgar Hoover, upon being told he was being given a "distinguished service award" by his friends, corrected: "A man is *honored* by his friends . . . he is *distinguished* by his enemies!"

So it was with Rome and Hannibal. So too it became with Spartacus.

No "mere slave" could dare challenge regal Rome! It stands to reason therefore—in Roman-*think* at least!—that Spartacus *must have* come from royal stock himself—even if it was Thracian royal stock at best, "lesser Greeks."

And no "mere gladiator" could ever hope to stand toe-to-toe, besting trained legionnaires, not to mention slathering shame on Rome's wisest gen-

---

29. An ambush by any other name stinks just as bad!
30. Actually only wanted as "Kid Antrim" during his lifetime.

erals! This Thracian *must have* been a commander in his own right in his own country before becoming a slave. . . . Better still, a mercenary auxiliary *trained* by Rome. Certainly! That was the only *acceptable* explanation to account for both Spartacus's villainy[31] as well as his victories.

Of course this "embracing" of Spartacus by the Romans didn't come in the Thracian's own time—at least not openly.[32] *Disbelief* was more the order of the day when it came to thoughts of Spartacus there in the first century B.C.

Disbelief that mere slaves could even be inspired to revolt, let alone ever be organized by one man's charisma—*a slave himself!*; slaves taught to stand and fight, to take an impossible chance, against an invincible empire!

Indeed, Spartacus turned the Roman world upside down, spitting at the status quo, defying the will of The Gods—at least so far as the Romans of the time understood the will and whim and workings of "gods."

If there was a Latin word for "topsy-turvy," that would perhaps suit our purpose, helping to explain the dramatic and drastic reversal of fortune forced upon his Roman masters by their slave Spartacus: that it should come to bad slaves cutting down good Romans, that those fated to spill their life's blood in the arena for the pleasure of their keepers should themselves be kept awake at night troubling after the fate of their own throats!

That a mere slave could swing wide the gates of the arena to allow all manner of beasts—most deadly, that two-legged variety!—to riot and ravage the whole of the Italian peninsula. . . . No, no mere slave could accomplish so much with so little against so many.

No mere slave could openly defy the majesty that was Rome and live to gloat after his deeds. . . . No mere slave, *that* sort of bravado, *that* firm eye of open defiance would demand a Leonidas, an Alexander, a Hannibal . . . a *Spartacus!*

---

31. Ironically, our modern word "villain" comes from the Latin *villa,* an estate. This later became the English "village." *Villains,* serfs working and living in the lands surrounding a villa, were notorious for poaching and stealing from the master of the estate just to make ends meet, hence the word "villain" (i.e., villager) soon became synonymous with "thief" and "criminal."

32. Gaius Caesar (better known as the infamous Caligula), ruled 37–41 A.D., chose Thracian gladiators to officer his German bodyguard. This according to Suetonius's *The Twelve Caesars,* c. 99 A.D.

FROM MAN TO MESSIAH

"Italy historically has been the land of brigands and Spartacus is
the grand-daddy of all outlaws."
—Barry Strauss, *The Spartacus War*

The ancient land of Thrace, today roughly the modern country of Bulgaria, took its name from Thrax, the son of Mars, the Roman god of war. Ironic, given that Rome's treatment of Thrace at times bordered on child abuse!

A hardy people, fond of tattoos and their "ecstatic religion"[33] (more on this in a minute), Thracians loved hunting and drinking, were master horsemen, and were "born brawlers with a reputation for brutality."[34] Superb guerrilla fighters, adept at ambush, night fighting was their much-feared specialty.

The Thracians were trounced by Roman general-cum-dictator Sulla (138–78 B.C.) in response to Thracian raids into Roman-controlled Macedonia. These Thracian forays had been inspired by the revolt of Mithridates (120–63 B.C.), King of Pontus.[35] Some sources maintain Spartacus also served with Mithridates as an insurgent against Rome.

Of the early life of Spartacus growing up in Thrace, we know little. In contrast, we do know much of the historical background of the time, and it's not unreasonable to expect that events powerful enough to shake the very foundations of the known world would, most certainly, have been weighty enough to excite any young, able-bodied lad of the day, especially a young, able-bodied lad with dreams of warrior glory.

Truth be known, we can't even be sure that "Spartacus" was our Spartacus's birth name. In Roman Latin, *Sparadakos* means "famous for his spear" and could have been the name given him by the promoters (Lt. *editors*) of the Roman gladiatorial games, a name both indicative of his ability to effectively wield a spear, as well as a ribald allusion to the size of his penis, i.e., his "spear."[36]

---

33. Strauss, 2009:3.

34. Ibid.

35. Ancient country in NE Asia Minor on the southern Black Sea coast.

36. Not an unheard of promotional ploy. Consider the similar literary license (or is that *licentiousness?*) taken by fifteenth-century author/historian Sir Thomas Malory when writing about King Arthur's pal and bedroom rogue Lancelot, i.e., "a *lot* of *lance*."

The name "Spartacus" was reportedly found in the records of a Thracian royal family, testifying to (or at least suggesting) that our Spartacus might have been a Thracian aristocrat. Bolstering this are ancient sources reporting that a few Thracian "nobles" caught as "insurgents" against Rome ultimately found their misfortunate way to Rome as slaves.[37]

Again we must rely on the Roman post-game review that (like all post-game reviews!) always contains plenty of *rationalization* about why our team got its ass kicked. As previously mentioned, so far as the Romans were concerned, in order for Spartacus "the slave" to have kicked their ass (on *several* occasions!) he must have come from "royal" blood and have had previous military training—at least as an officer?

Indeed, after being conquered by Sulla, the Thracians, particularly the *Maedi* people believed to have been Spartacus's tribe, were required to serve as auxiliary troops to the Romans as "tribute" (Read: ransom/extortion). Spartacus could well have been one of these "conscripts" required to give service to Rome.

By 83 B.C. would-be dictator Sulla was gathering an army in Greece to invade Italy and start a civil war against Rome. To augment the force of Romans loyal to him he'd already assembled, he recruited both infantry and cavalry from Greece and Macedonia. It's possible a twenty-year-old Spartacus might have been among those recruited.

Was Spartacus part of Sulla's force? We may never know for certain. What we do know is that another main player—it could be argued *the main defensive player*—destined to win *MVP* in the two-minute warning to Spartacus's deadly game of "pin-the-tail-on-the-Romans" a decade later, Marcus Licinius Crassus, was allied with Sulla as he prepared to return to Italy.

Did young Spartacus and Crassus—the two men destined to one day decide the fate of Rome the way two hungry gamblers might wrestle for the better part of the last wishbone, meet one another ten years before the life of one would require the death of the other? If not the stuff of fact, then at least a scene demanded of fair fiction.

Spartacus was thirty years old when the revolt—soon a *war!*—of slaves that bears his name began in 73 B.C.

What happened between his service to Sulla in Greece—assuming

---

37. Strauss, 2009:25.

indeed that was the case—and his winding up a slave and gladiator in Italy isn't known for certain.

Somewhere between service to Sulla in 83 B.C. and showing up as a slave in 73 B.C., Spartacus became branded a *latro*, a word meaning "thief," "bandit," "highwayman" . . . but implying "guerrilla."[38]

One way or another, it seems Spartacus deserted Sulla's army and beat feet for the Thracian hills. Whether he did so simply because he didn't warm to the idea of being a "draftee," especially in the same army that had just a short time earlier made war on *his* people, or whether he held some strongly felt patriotism and decided to join the guerrilla fight against the Roman invaders isn't known.

What is known is that, somewhere over the next ten years, Spartacus was captured and placed (in chains) on the next thing smokin' (or, rowing, as the case may be) for Rome.

THE GLADIATOR

The first "gladiator games" began in Italy as far back as 264 B.C., as funeral rites (*munus*, literally "obligation") where two condemned prisoners or slaves were forced to fight atop the graves of prominent Roman citizens.

In time, and depending on just how prominent the deceased Roman had been (or how "prominent" his surviving family members wanted to make it appear he had been), these "funeral rites" grew ever more elaborate down through the years until, in Spartacus's time "gladiator games" had been taken over by the state, becoming not only big business but also a political device meant to (1) mold public opinion while (2) keeping the baser elements of "proper" Roman society distracted:

> The bloody games in the arena had, by 100 B.C., become a primary tool in the campaign of any ambitious politician. Winning votes meant pleasing the Roman mob and there was no better way to do this than to entertain them. (Rupert Matthews, *The Age of the Gladiators*)

---

38. "Terrorist" (or, in this case, "guerrilla") is what the big army calls the little army.

This is the philosophy of political expediency known as "Bread & Circuses," i.e., so long as the common people have enough to eat—bread—and something to keep their minds *off* politics—circuses like gladiator games—then the common people will never revolt against the powers-that-be.[39]

While Rome gave the beast a name—"Bread & Circuses"—Romans can't lay claim to have *created* the beast, although they do hold the dubious distinction of having taught the beast to jump through flaming hoops![40]

Worth noting are the two main types of gladiators used in Spartacus's time:

By all accounts, Spartacus himself was a "big" man. . . . Right: "Famous for his spear." Such heavy-weight gladiators were known as *murmillo*. Such men carried a large shield and, usually, a heavier, longer, straight sword and/or spear.

The second well-known type of gladiator was ironically called "The Thracian," sporting a smaller, round shield with a shorter, curved sword.

Big business demands bigger investment:

> By about 75 B.C., the men fighting in the arena were no longer cheap, second-rate slaves sent to die. They were highly trained, skilled fighting men at the peak of physical fitness. Only these men could put on the sort of show that would win favor with the crowd. (Rupert Matthews, *The Age of the Gladiators*)

This is important to understand, and worth repeating: By Spartacus's time, gladiators were *trained killers*, not a bunch of expendable ragamuffins. Common criminals were often summarily executed as "pre-show warm-up" entertainment *before* the main event of *trained* gladiators putting on a show.

In other words, so far as Spartacus and the men who would follow him into revolt against their former masters, *Rome had created its own enemy!*

Gladiators by this time had become popular, with the crowd siding with and rooting for their favorites. In case an opponent got the upper hand, sections of the crowd would demand that the *impresario* (producer) of the

---

39. NFL, NBA score points with you?

40. To simplify: Get the Blu-ray of Russell Crowe's *Gladiator* (2000). It will bring you up to speed on the kind of world Spartacus found himself—literally!—being dragged into.

games—later the Emperor himself—give their downed favorite the "thumbs-down" signal so the wounded gladiator could live to fight another day. (Contrary to popular depictions "thumbs-up" symbolized a drawn sword whereas "thumbs-down" symbolized sword in scabbard.[41]

And neither were the "skills" of the gladiators confined to the sands of the arena:

> Soon many leading patricians were acquiring and running gladiatorial schools. These gladiators did not do much in the way of actual fighting, and they were trained in some very unusual skills. They were taught how to move through city streets at night without attracting attention. They were taught how to administer poison and slit throats. They learned how to force a path through an angry mob, how to disarm attackers and how to break limbs.
>
> These slaves were big, tough men who were housed in gladiatorial barracks and lived by the gladiatorial code, but they were not gladiators as most people then or now understand the word. They were the private strong arm gangs of unscrupulous politicians. Romans were forbidden to recruit and train private armies, but in their gangs of gladiators the ruthless men of power had the next best thing.

Many of the men who would later join Spartacus's revolt undoubtedly brought these useful and lethal skills with them. Mary Shelley wouldn't pen *Frankenstein* for another couple millennium. Too bad, the Romans of Spartacus's time could have used the warning!

RISE OF THE SPARTACANS

"Ave Caesar, moritori te salutant!"[42]

The timing for Spartacus's revolt couldn't have been better.

At the time the Italian peninsula was nothing like today's unified Italy; instead Roman "Latins" ran roughshod over a patchwork of often coerced

---

41. "Thumbs-up" as a *good* thing actually came about during WWI when pilots needed to signal that everything was well, but couldn't be heard above the roar of their engines.

42. "Hail Caesar! We who are about to die salute you!"

socii (allies) that included Samnites and Etruscans in central Italy, as well as Lucanians and Bruttians further down "the boot." Keep in mind several of these same "allies" had wasted no time defecting to Hannibal during his decade-long campaigning up and down the peninsula.

Even within Rome itself, in both the Senate and in the streets, warring factions seemed capable of coming to a consensus only when absolutely convinced all of Rome was in danger.

Add to this chaotic mix close to one and a half million slaves (20 percent of the population of Rome at the time) as potential "Spartacans" and a recipe for disaster was already simmering on the stove!

Of course, Romans weren't completely blind to the potential of slave revolts—they'd weathered several serious slave insurrections before Spartacus, which was why, by this time, laws stipulated that no gladiators could permanently be housed within the city limits of Rome. As a result, Capua (130 miles south of the city of Rome) had become a major staging area for the training of gladiators. At one time Julius Caesar himself owned a school for gladiators there. And, ironically, during the Second Punic War, in 216 B.C., Capua had been one of the first cities "allied" with Rome to defect to Hannibal.

A hundred years later, 104 B.C., Capua was then Ground Zero for a slave revolt led by, curiously, a rich young *Roman* citizen named Titus Minucius Vettius.

It seems young Titus had fallen in love with a slave girl. On his estranged father's estate just outside Capua, Titus gathered around him an army of 3,500 slaves, whom he drilled into his own legion.

Unfortunately for Titus's budding "cult," Rome wasted no time sending a *real* legion of soldiers against him, under the command of a wily, no-nonsense Praetor named Lucius Licinius Lucullus.

Rather than resort to wholesale slaughter, Lucullus instead convinced Titus's freed slave "General," Apollonius by name, to betray him.

Trapped somewhere between desperation and despair, Titus and his lover committed suicide, inspiring a mass suicide amongst his followers. End of revolt.

Fortunately, the revolt of the Spartacans fared somewhat better.

As already mentioned, by Spartacus's time the slave-gladiators of Rome were a hardy, well-trained, disciplined, *and deadly* lot, composed mostly of

Spartacus's own Thracians and Illyrians from the Balkans, Celts from Gaul,[43] and Germans.

To their credit, Spartacus's keepers had made it a policy to deliberately mix-and-mingle the various slave nationalities, thinking this would discourage communication, ergo unified *revolt*. However, what the Roman slavemasters ultimately, unintentionally created was an ersatz "United Nations" where, if nothing else could be agreed on, common cause was found in the slaves' mutual hatred of all things Roman.

On a warm spring[44] night, whether from long planning or spontaneous riot, 216 men—Thracians, Illyrians, Celts, and Germans—rallied 'round Spartacus and a Celt named Crixus.

All 216 of these gladiators were determined to die free or die trying, to take a chance on dying while attempting to escape, versus the inevitability of dying in the arena.

Of Crixus the Celt we know little, save that he and Spartacus appear, for the most part, equals, as evidenced by their later co-commanding of divisions of what would eventually grow into a slave army estimated as many as 120,000 at its peak.[45]

Of Spartacus we know much—equal parts fact and fiction, as befits both a man and a myth that many thought a *messiah*.

THE MESSIAH FACTOR

Though 216 gladiators were initially in on Spartacus and Crixus's plan to escape, when the time came, only seventy-four people were able to fight their way out of captivity in Capua.

One of these was "The Thracian Woman," a mysterious and vitally important component *and catalyst* to the Spartacus legend.

Female slaves were routinely housed near and with male gladiator-slaves; women acting as servants and, often, as *rewards* to especially-prized gladiators.

---

43. Approximately modern France and Belgium.

44. In spring gladiators were traditionally trained for "The Great Games" held in September, games with an especially high mortality rate among gladiators. In other words, Spartacus and his followers were gettin' out while the gettin' was good!

45. See Strauss, 2009:80. It is not known if this high-end estimate includes women and children slaves attaching themselves to the gladiator army.

By all accounts, "Spartacus's woman" was a Thracian, perhaps even a priestess in her own land before falling into slavery in Rome.

The simplest rendition of the tale has the Thracian Woman cohabiting with Spartacus in his quarters at Capua when Spartacus was jolted awake one night by a snake that had somehow wrapped itself entirely around his face. Spartacus obviously survived this ordeal and most, upon hearing the tale, counted Spartacus "lucky" and quickly forgot the event.

But not the Thracians, and especially not the Thracian Woman.

To many of the time, especially Thracians, a snake was the symbol of the god Dionysus[46] who, to his worshipers, was the god of death, resurrection, and rebirth.

As they would later come to view Christianity, so too the Roman authorities of Spartacus's time viewed the worship of Dionysus as subversive to the State. So much so that in 186 B.C., Roman authorities launched a somewhat successful pogrom ("witch hunt," if you will) against the disruptive followers of Dionysus, until:

> After 186, only women, foreigners, and slaves were permitted
> to worship the god. . . . Dionysus was left to the powerless
> of Italy and they embraced him. (Strauss, 2009:34)

Among the Thracians enslaved at Capua (thanks in no little part to the deliberate efforts of the Thracian Woman), Spartacus began to be looked upon as the "Chosen" of Dionysus.

The importance of this cannot be underestimated. As Vlad Tepes has pointed out, "Men are moved as much by *symbols* as they are by *swords*."[47]

Roman nemesis Mithridates the Great (132–73 B.C.) had once declared himself "The New Dionysus" in order to rally support against Rome. Likewise, King Ptolemy, ruling Egypt from 221–205 B.C. had also invoked Dionysus, to the point of the god adorning his coins.

Now the Thracian Woman—a prophetess?—had declared Spartacus the "Chosen" (if not the very *incarnation*!) of the god himself.

To the Greeks, especially those who long ago had settled in southern Italy (what they called "Magna Graecia"), Dionysus was the god of wine and the theater. A symbol of kings in Greece, here in Italy where the Greeks

---

46. *Apollo* to the Romans.
47. See "Dracula's Dark Art of War" section that follows.

inhabiting the heel and toe of "The Boot" were often unwilling "allies" to Rome, Dionysus (especially after the 186 B.C. "purge") had become a symbol of the downtrodden and the slave.

How fitting then that, *when* the god Dionysus should again show his face, he should do so through a popular *slave* gladiator like Spartacus.

> By invoking Dionysus, The Thracian Woman stirred a chord among foreign-born gladiators and slaves as well as among Italians who remembered Mithridates. . . . By her prophecy, Spartacus' lady gave her man a holy duty. As a servant of Dionysus, Spartacus would be liberator.

Most important, strategically, as a Thracian (Greek) and as Dionysus's "Chosen One," Spartacus (and any who followed him) might hope to find allies in southern Italy.

Did Spartacus himself believe this? Never underestimate the power of a woman. Helen's face had launched a thousand ships. Delilah had shorn even the mighty Samson of his strength. . . .

The tale of the snake wrapping itself around Spartacus's face reminds us of the Hercules myth where he crushed two vipers placed in his crib by an assassin.

And we find similar tales of miraculous escapes (and "dubious" blessings) attached to heroes throughout history.

So we must ask again: Did Spartacus himself believe Dionysus—called Zagreus and Sabazius by his Thracians—had shown him favor? On the one hand it matters if such belief would further galvanize the Thracian to revolt (not that he *needed* any additional urging!). An intelligent man, a wily commander, even if not a "true believer" himself, he surely appreciated any tool—any additional motivator—he might use to rally his fellow slaves (not that they *needed* much additional urging!).

Of course, Crixus and his fellow Celts, not to mention the other nationalities of slaves represented in Spartacus's mushfake United Nations were *not* worshipers of Dionysus.

Still Crixus, by all accounts as savvy a student of human nature as was Spartacus, could not but recognize the . . . "usefulness," *propaganda*-wise, of having your revolt led by a "messiah."

And, for those less "spiritually inclined," both among his own countrymen and the myriad of other countries represented in the revolt, there were always baser rewards of revenge and loot!

Barry Strauss, in his excellent *The Spartacus War,*[48] explains that Spartacus's (and Crixus's) followers fought for various reasons: freedom, nationalism, religion, revenge, and riches.

Strauss, professor of history and classics at Cornell University, also isolates nine aspects of Spartacus's personality, giving us a clue as to the man's charisma, as well as a glimpse of why men (and women) might gladly follow him in revolt:

1. He was an orator.
2. He was a showman, at one point crucifying a Roman to "prove" to his men that Romans could die just like any other. When Crixus was killed, he staged "funeral games," forcing Roman POWs to fight to the death for the enjoyment of men who, a short time before, were themselves slated to die in the arena for the pleasure of the Romans.
3. He was a politician, holding together the various factions and nationalities by reminding them of their common cause.
4. He was a man of simple tastes: freedom, the *simplest* of tastes.
5. He was stoic. He shared the hardships of his men. Thus his command: "Bleed only where cut!"
6. He shared the wealth. Spartacus "the myth" is still a darling of socialists to this day. Adam Wieshapt, founder of the 1776 *Illuminati,* wrote under the nom de plume "Spartacus."
7. He was religious. Believing in The Gods, perhaps he believed his destiny already written. But what is "known" by one, must often be "shown" to another . . . *the hard way!*
8. He fought for freedom, realizing his own freedom hinged on the freedom of the man standing next to him.
9. He thirsted to kill every enemy commander by his own hand. You can't teach what you don't know, and you can't lead where you don't go. First over the wall, first in the breech. By our example and blood we teach. The Romans trained Spartacus to fight in the arena. . . . They had no idea that "arena" would one day be the whole of Italy!

---

48. Simon & Schuster, 2009.

THE REVOLT

"There is nothing impossible to him who will try."
—**Alexander the Great**

Fleeing Capua, Spartacus and the others fortuitously[49] encountered inbound carts loaded with weapons *destined to be used by gladiators*. Yeah, that's called *irony*.

Re-arming themselves with these new weapons,[50] they fled south toward Mount Vesuvius, 4,000 feet high and twenty miles south of Capua.

Fully aware of his growing "Messiah" celebrity, it's been speculated that the Thracian chose Vesuvius for its religious significance—think Moses and Sinai. Even if true, Spartacus, and the other ex-military amongst his men, couldn't help but recognize the importance of "taking the high ground," a defensible redoubt offering a smaller force both advantage and respite against what would soon be the inevitable arrival of much larger pursuing forces.

Predictably: No sooner had Spartacus's troops reached Vesuvius than they were overtaken by a police/militia force from Capua.

It's here we see the beginning of a pattern that would be repeated again and again over the course of the next three years: Romans *under*estimating the ability of "mere slaves" to fight back in general, even when led (and inspired) by a general of Spartacus's mettle—and metal!

Word of Spartacus's swift victory in beating back these initial pursuers brought hundreds more slaves to his cause. In short order, Vesuvius became a training center for Spartacus and Crixus's growing army. It was here that the slaves of Rome literally began melting down and reforging their chains into weapons. It was here too that Spartacus and Crixus began planning their strategy.

By all accounts Crixus was every bit the equal of Spartacus in courage, but perhaps not in common sense (Strauss, 2009:100). The two men often differed in their overall strategy for resisting and repaying their former Roman masters, with Spartacus's more guerilla-oriented *ch'i* attitude thank-

---

49. Chance favors the prepared mind.

50. Their initial escape plan betrayed, Spartacus's band had been forced to fight their way out of captivity using kitchen knives and skewers!

fully more often winning out over Crixus's more direct "Let's just charge down the hill and kill 'em all!" *cheng* approach.[51]

Realizing the *propaganda* advantages to be had by Spartacus's personal charisma and growing popularity with the slave masses now flocking to their cause, Crixus, while never shy about voicing his opinion, generally deferred to the Thracian's final decision. In the end, both men's strengths and weaknesses were balanced out by the other's.

For example, when Roman forces lay siege to Vesuvius (thinking to starve out the rebel slaves), Crixus busied himself with beating back Roman forays, while Spartacus coordinated slaves weaving ropes from the vines plentiful on Vesuvius. Using these ropes that night, Spartacus's slave army, cloaked in the night (recall Thracians were master night-fighters), they escaped down sheer cliffs left unguarded by the encircling Romans.

For a second time for Spartacus, *escape* proved the sweetest victory.

Escaping entrapment at Mount Vesuvius, Spartacus's rebels moved south, overthrowing several towns along the way, building up their supply of provisions and weapons, picking up thousands of recruits along the way.

Much is made of what appears to be *the* major disagreement between Spartacus and Crixus: According to most sources, Spartacus favored fleeing Italy by going north to the Alps, at which point, hypothetically, the slave army could then disperse, each faction to their respective nations—Gauls to the northwest, Germans to the northeast, Spartacus's Thracians and the Illyrians striking out for the Balkans.

Crixus, on the other hand, wanted to "punish" the Romans and showed no fear at the prospect of going toe-to-toe with Legionnaires. Besides, he told Spartacus, "If we run, they will chase us."

Another factor often listed as to why many of the slaves under Spartacus's command wanted to "stay and fight" was that they really had no place else to go. Despite being slaves, Italy was their home, many having been *born* into slavery, but born into slavery *in Italy*.

Tactically, Crixus was right: The odds of their slave army escaping north

---

51. For a complete understanding of the Chinese strategy of *Ch'i-Cheng,* when to use direct "orthodox" force and when to use an indirect "unorthodox" strategy, see "The Six Secrets of T'ai Kung Kung-fu" in Lung and Prowant's *Mind Assassins* and "Cao Cao's Nine Strategies" in their *Mind Warrior* (both books published by Citadel Press, 2010).

before being caught by pursuing Romans were slim to none.[52] Somewhere along the way Spartacus's army would be forced to turn and fight *at a place of the Romans' choosing.* By turning south to face the Romans before they could gather an even larger pursuit force, the slave army would have a chance of defeating the Romans.

Strategically, Spartacus was right: His followers would never be free so long as they remained in Italy. As an admirer of Hannibal, Spartacus knew the Romans would never stop fighting on their own soil and—by the first century B.C.—Romans arrogantly considered *all* the Italian peninsula *their soil!*

At this point, we can imagine Spartacus heaving a heavy sigh, realizing that Crixus was right: The Romans would never stop chasing them. And they would eventually—at the worst possible juncture—catch up to them.

Never let your enemy choose the battlefield.

Autumn 73 B.C., the Spartacan army turned back south, having decided to deal with the immediate threat of the pursuing Romans.

Slashing their way south, Spartacus's army fights several pitched battles: defeating a formidable Roman force at Campania, successfully ambushing a force under Consul Cossinius (KIA) near Pompeii, even making daring raids on the camps of Roman Legions sent to stop him.

Seemingly unstoppable, Spartacus invades the "arch" of Italy's boot inflicting "a terrible slaughter,"[53] eventually conquering the walled coastal city of Thurii. FYI: Thurii was taken after slaves within the heavily defended city opened the gates for the besieging slave army.

Spartacus now set up his "capital" at Thurii, using the brief respite allowed by this victory to further drill his army.

All too soon word reaches the Thracian that no less than four Roman Legions (20,000 men) are marching south to crush the slave army. At this point, Spartacus and Crixus differ as to how to respond:

Once again Spartacus favors striking north, battling their way to the Alps and to freedom.

Crixus favors fighting a more defensive guerrilla-style war concentrating on inciting riot and revolt in the south where they have more support.

In late 73 B.C., Spartacus and 30,000 of his followers head north while

---

52. Especially given the ever-increasing train of women and children swelling their slave "army."

53. Strauss, 2009:82.

Crixus remains in the south with upwards of 10,000 men, mostly Gauls and Germans.

While much is made of this "split," it may well be the case where Spartacus and Crixus gambled that by splitting their "army" into two forces, it would force the Romans to fight on two fronts. What is it Sun Tzu said? When my enemy doesn't know where I will attack, he must prepare everywhere. Forced to prepare *everywhere,* my enemy is strong *nowhere!*

Prudently keeping to Italy's mountainous Apennines spine, away from open flatlands where arrayed Roman Legions knew no equal, in these mountains Spartacus fights several successful battles with the army of Consul Lentulus Clodianus. But, while this is going on, Lentulus's co-Consul Lucius Gellius attacks Crixus with two Legions, killing him at the Battle of Garganus (modern Gargano). Two-thirds of Crixus's 10,000 are either killed or captured.

Prevented from reinforcing Crixus before it was too late, Spartacus now finds his own force trapped between the armies of Lentulus and Gellius.

Enraged at the death of Crixus, determination mixed with desperation—rather than wait for the two Consuls to converge, closing the trap, Spartacus immediately rushes to attack Gellius's army (actually, *what's left* of Gellius's army after tangling with Crixus!).

Still licking their wounds from their Pyrrhic victory over Crixus, Gellius's army acts as appetizer to Spartacus's army, which, hungry for revenge, immediately turns to chew up Lentulus's Legion, itself exhausted from rushing to Gellius's aid.

Other authorities have Spartacus first smashing through Lentulus's Legion (before it has a chance to set up) before then turning his full wrath on Gellius, the slayer of his comrades.

In the end, who died *first* hardly matters, even to the *last* man to die that day. . . .

Spartacus had just crushed two armies sent against him. A great victory, but one that came at such a high price: the death of Crixus, his good right arm.

While Roman survivors fled north to safety, in the south, Spartacus held funeral games for his fallen comrade. Whereas the gladiator games both he and Crixus had been fated to die in had started with the ancient custom of forcing two slave-gladiators to fight over the grave of a Roman, as much to honor his fallen friend as to help inspire both his own troops and those of

Crixus's Celts and Germans who had survived, Spartacus held his own "funeral games" gladiator fights, forcing 300 Roman prisoners to fight to the death around Crixus's funeral pyre.

Recorded Cicero (106–43 B.C.):

> What Spartacus did was to give gladiator games for slaves—a spectacle that Rome had heretofore reserved for the free. Spartacus added a bitter twist by reversing roles, making slaves spectators, making Romans gladiators.

Crushing the armies of Lentulus and Gellius would be the high point in the whole of Spartacus's revolt. Oh, there would be more battles, many skirmishes, with the Spartacans coming out ahead—if not unscathed—from most of them but, even as Spartacus's men were cheerfully handing Roman POWs swords with which to kill each other over the grave of Crixus, back in Rome a beaten and battered Lentulus and Gellius were—gladly!—handing command over to the one man who would—in the end—prove Spartacus's equal . . . and, ultimately, his conqueror.

THE COMING OF CRASSUS

Marcus Licinius Crassus took command from disgraced Consuls Gellius and Lentulus in late summer/early fall 72 B.C.

Recall that Crassus (115–53 B.C.) had returned to Italy in 83 B.C. as one of the usurper Sulla's supporters. Again we're left to speculate whether young Spartacus and Crassus might have crossed paths in Greece long before they crossed swords in Italy.

Early on in life Crassus had mastered the codependent skills of making money and making enemies. The former ability made him one of Rome's richest men, earning him the jealous nickname "Crassus the Rich," while his propensity to acquire the latter forced him to prudently flee political assassins, first to Spain, before ultimately joining Sulla in Greece.

In light of later political and military entanglement, it's necessary to note that Lentulus and Gellius were both allies of another powerful Roman general and statesman, Pompey "The Great" (108–48 B.C.).

It's never a good idea to piss off anybody named "The Great". . . .

Ever the opportunist, Crassus took advantage of Lentulus's and Gellius's humiliation at the hands of "a mere slave" to win (some say "buy") popular support, ultimately influencing the Senate to give him a special command tasked with bringing them Spartacus's head.

Defeating Spartacus was guaranteed to give Crassus the upper hand over Pompey and his allies.

Unlike many Roman Consuls given authority command of fighting Legions even though they had had little or no previous military service themselves, Crassus had not only studied guerrilla warfare and counterinsurgency while in exile in Spain, he'd also ridden beside Sulla as the conqueror marched on Rome.

With the blessing (and a little bribery!) of the Senate, in short order Crassus had raised six new Legions, over 45,000 men—twice the size of any Roman force yet sent against Spartacus.

But, from the beginning, Crassus's overall strategy was *not* designed to endlessly chase Spartacus's highly mobile slave army up and down the peninsula. Instead, Crassus's plan called for tightening the noose around Spartacus, slowly but surely cutting him off, cutting down his area of movement—starving and strangling his army to death![54]

But before you can "command" the enemy's men, you have to win the respect—or at least *fear!*—of your own men.

In later years, history would remember Crassus as "Crassus the Decimator," from "decimate," i.e., "one in ten."

Having discovered 500 men shirking their duty, Crassus had fifty men chosen from them by lot (one in ten). He then had each of these men clubbed to death by the remaining nine soldiers of each ten!

Crassus's lesson to his new command could not have been more crystal-clear: "Spartacus *might* kill you if you do your duty. I *will* kill you if you *don't!*"

With his new army's undivided attention, Crassus marched south.

---

54. Classic counterinsurgency strategy: (1) Locate the guerrillas/terrorists, (2) isolate them in ever-smaller areas of operation, cutting them off from supply and/or local support, (3) kill them! See *On Guerrilla Warfare* by Mao Tze-Tung.

ENDGAME

*"I am not afraid of an army of lions led by a sheep; I am afraid of
an army of sheep led by a lion!"*
—Alexander the Great

As Crassus moved south, Spartacus struck north to confront him near
Lucana.[55]

At this point, Crassus sends two legions commanded by a man named
Mummius with orders to circle around behind Spartacus's advancing army
but not to engage the enemy.

Mummius didn't listen and, in short order, Spartacus made short work
of him and his short attention span. It's worth noting here that wily Crassus
did not send his newest troops with Mummius but, rather the survivors of
the ill-fated Lentulus/Gellius expedition.

As the survivors of Mummius's insubordination limped back into Crassus's camp, The Decimator had one in ten of them slaughtered on the spot!

As Crassus's own force approached, wisely avoiding fighting Romans on
the open plain, Spartacus quickly retreated south, perhaps with a plan of
drawing Crassus into an ambush in the more slave army–friendly Lucanian
mountains.

Crassus and Spartacus did "skirmish" in north Lucania, but neither man
seemed ready for a fixed battle.

Spartacus continues south after Crassus succeeds in overtaking and
defeating a small, separate detachment of 10,000 Spartacans.

It's evident that, by this point, Spartacus recognized that the rules of
the game had changed. Most ominous, this new player Crassus didn't play by
any "rules," at least not the way Spartacus—up to this time—had been writing The Rules:

> What Spartacus had warned his men all along was now
> coming true. The men had spirit but Spartacus knew the
> odds. He understood Rome's overwhelming superiority in
> pitched battle. Earlier Roman soldiers had turned and fled
> but Crassus' men would fight. Against previous Roman com-

---

55. Think "the Ankle" of the boot of Italy.

manders there had always been room for ambushes and other tricks. Crassus, however, would not be easily fooled. (Strauss, 2009:127)

It was time to leave Italy by hook or by crook—and everybody knew the best crooks with the best hooks were the notorious pirates of Sicily.

Spartacus was now determined to escape to Sicily, where he gambled he could count on help from those traditionally anti-Roman pirates, the same pirates who had previously sided with Mithradates and with Rome's renegade general in Spain, Quintus Sertorius (at the time busy battling Crassus's rival Pompey for control of the Iberian Peninsula).

By 72 B.C., Sicily had become Rome's main supplier for both grain and cattle. Escaping (i.e., *invading*!) into Sicily would serve Spartacus thrice: first, putting some distance and a barrier—the Straits of Messina—between him and Crassus; second, gaining a toehold in Sicily would replenish his supplies—both in material as well as recruits from Sicily's sizable slave population[56]; and, finally, once embedded on Sicily, Spartacus would be in perfect position to threaten Rome's main food source—a potential bargaining chip?

Of course, all this hinged on Spartacus actually getting his army across the Straits of Messina . . . and that's where the pirates came in. Or, as history records, they *didn't* come in.

Spartacus reached Regium (toe*nail* of the boot) sometime in late 72 B.C. Now only two miles separated him from Sicily . . . two miles of treacherous water he needed those equally treacherous pirate "allies" for.

But the pirates refused to help the fleeing slave army, despite bribes of considerable wealth the Spartacans had pillaged along the way.

Spartacus's initial plan was to pay the pirates to ferry 2,000 of his best fighters across the Straits, where they would establish a "beachhead," allowing for the safe crossing of the remainder of his train. But this was not to be.

Recall that, long before he was the much-feared "Crassus the Decimator," Crassus had been the much-envied "Crassus the Rich." So, falling back

---

56. Sicily was no stranger to bloody slave revolts, having weathered the First Sicilian Slave War (135–132 B.C.) and the Second Sicilian Slave War (104–100 B.C.), both of which had involved tens of thousands of rebel slaves.

on this former persona, Crassus simply paid the pirates more money *not* to help Spartacus!

Spartacus's "Plan B" for crossing the Straits of Messina had his men attempting to build rafts to ferry his people across. Several drownings later, this too failed.

Realizing there would be no escape via Sicily, Spartacus immediately turned his army back north.

But while Spartacus had been busy bargaining with pirates, Crassus had been busy building a wall.

Thinking to keep Spartacus bottled up, Crassus had spent months constructing a thirty-five-mile defensive line of fortifications that effectively severed the "toe" from the rest of the boot of Italy.

Engineering a series of deep, stake-filled trenches and bulwark, taking full advantage of the natural features[57] of the already difficult-to-pass Aspromonte mountain range that cuts across the instep of Italy, Crassus created what he smirkingly referred to as his "Tuna Trap" (Lt. *tonnara*), so-called for the way its ever-narrowing path was designed to herd Spartacus's army onto the only half-mile-wide Melia Ridge where, strategically, the only road north from the ridge Crassus also fortified with a deep, heavily defended trench.

Crassus had effectively trapped the Thracian between the Devil—that would be Crassus!—and the deep blue—those uncrossable Straits of Messina.

Crassus was initially content to wait Spartacus out—actually *starve* him out—seeing as how "Crassus's wall" effectively cut Spartacus's army off from Lorci, the coastal town north of Crassus's wall the Spartacans had been counting on as their primary provisioner.

And to this, Spartacus soon received word that Pompey[58] (fresh from a victory over Sertorius) had been recalled from Spain to "help" Crassus, his rival, deal with the "Spartacus problem."

Knowing that Crassus and Pompey hated each other, Spartacus (undoubtedly stalling for time, but perhaps also holding out the hope that there might be a "negotiated" way for his followers to escape what seemed

---

57. "With regard to narrow passes, if you occupy them first, let them be strongly garrisoned and then await the approach of your enemy." (Sun Tzu, chapter X)

58. Pompey often wore a cloak once owned by Alexander the Great.

their inevitable fate) approached Crassus with the offer of a truce, even to the point of somehow offering to "aid" him against Pompey.

Crassus might have been tempted by Spartacus's offer but, with his eye on gaining even more power in Rome, Crassus realized that to even be seen "negotiating" with "a slave" would only serve to raise that slave in stature— being treated as an equal—while Crassus's own stature would be undermined should he "lower" himself to "discuss terms" with an inferior.

"Thanks but no thanks," Crassus told Spartacus. "Rome wants your *head*, not your *handshake!*"[59]

Another way of saying, "We don't negotiate with terrorists," thereby giving them legitimacy.

Some historians maintain that Spartacus never actually held out any realistic hope of coming to a negotiated settlement with Crassus, that the Thracian had only been playing for time, waiting for his cavalry to arrive.

Indeed, Spartacus *had* been waiting for the arrival of his often far-ranging cavalry. Once these reinforcements arrived, Spartacus wasted no time in launching a surprise night attack—a Thracian specialty, remember?

Tactical experts disagree as to exactly how Spartacus managed to cross the deep, stake-filled trenches Crassus had counted on as his main deterrent. Some claim pure dedication (desperation?) on the part of Spartacus as his men ultimately filled the trenches with slave dead, allowing the rest of the Spartacans to race across the bodies of their dead comrades on foot and even on horseback.

Others maintain a more ruthless ploy was used, arguing that Spartacus, never a commander to spend the lives of his men futilely, instead herded masses of captured Romans into the trenches until their corpses provided foothold for the Spartacan breach.

Still others theorize the Thracian commander constructed breaching ladder-bridges designed to span the trenches, a not unheard of tactic in Classical times.

Whatever the tactic, much to Crassus's chagrin, Spartacus succeeded in breeching the Romans' "wall," albeit at a high price: Only one-third of Spartacus's army survived the breakout from the Melia Ridge entrapment.

Stabbing north again, Spartacus now knew for certain, as did most of his

---

59. See Strauss, 2009:153.

followers, that leaving Italy was their only viable option. Yet once again he allowed 30,000 Celts and Germans under the command of two former gladiators named Castus and Gannicus to break away.[60]

No sooner did the Spartacans divide than Crassus—in hot pursuit— fell upon and routed the Celtic/German division. The Celts and the Germans were saved only by the timely arrival of Spartacus. Were it not for the report (by Roman historians, of course) of the severe thrashing Castus's and Gannicus's division took, one might suspect this whole dividing of his force to have been a ploy on Spartacus's part, i.e., dangling out "easy bait" for Crassus in the form of a smaller, easier to overcome Celtic/German force.

Not to be outdone, Crassus withdrew to set up not one, but *two* camps. Leaving his command tent obvious in one camp, taking a page from the Thracian's book of war,[61] Crassus slipped out with his men during the night. Dividing his cavalry into two groups, he then sent the first group to purposely draw Spartacus off, while Crassus successfully ambushed and destroyed the Celtic/German division, 35,000 men plus their commanders, Castus and Gannicus.

According to Strauss, Crassus "achieved more through one night of cunning than he had in weeks spent moving masses of earth" to build his supposedly impenetrable Melia Ridge defensive line.[62]

Spartacus, having read the writing on the wall, struck out for the Adriatic port of Brundisium, hoping to either buy or seize ships for his followers' escape.

Unfortunately, Crassus had anticipated this potential escape route, his ally Marcus Lucullus having landed a Roman force there. Former Governor of Macedonia, fresh from successfully suppressing the fierce *Bessi* tribe of Thrace, Lucullus held no fear of hunting down one more Thracian.

Spartacus once again found himself in a familiar spot: between a Roman

---

60. Most likely with Spartacus's "blessing"—smaller armies travel faster; besides, any infighting would only injure their cause further.

61. Escaping from Mount Vesuvius Spartacus had left tents, campfires burning, and had even set up the bodies of dead comrades as "sentries," all in order to distract from his followers escaping down the unguarded sheer cliffs at night.

62.Ibid., 166.

rock and a hard place. As he had done—successfully—two years before against the Legions of Lentulus and Gellius (following the death of Crixus), Spartacus now prudently decided it was better to fight one Roman army than two—at *his* own time, on the battlefield of *his* choosing.

April 71 B.C.: Spartacus turned back south. Crassus rushed north to meet him.

The Battle of Oliveto Citra took place on two miles of open plain dead center on the ankle of the boot of Italy. Best estimate, 40,000 rebel slaves stood behind Spartacus, while Crassus commanded the loyalty—read *fear!*—of 40,000 Legionnaires.

Legend has it Spartacus killed his own horse before the battle began, proclaiming that, if he died that day he would have no need of a horse. If he won, he would have his choice of *Roman* horses!

Classic Sun Tzu, Spartacus attacks *before* newly arrived Crassus has a chance to set up his camp.

Whatever Spartacus's overall battle plan, his personal mission? Fight his way to Crassus and kill the man! Cut off the head, the snake dies. Strategic simplicity.

Unfortunately, Spartacus and his "bodyguard," 100 or so elite fighters, were all ultimately killed before reaching the Roman commander.

The battle lasted five hours. At what point in this slaughter Spartacus fell isn't known, but it's reasonable to assume Spartacus's death would have had the effect of disheartening his followers, so he probably died closer to the end than the beginning of the fight.

The final count: 1,000 Romans dead, balanced against upwards of 10,000 rebels killed out of the 40,000.

With all due respect to Kirk Douglas's memorable "I am Spartacus. No, *I* am Spartacus!" scene in the 1960 *Spartacus* movie, Spartacus's body was never found. This, of course, has led to much speculation—all favorable to the already-growing "Spartacus the Messiah" legend.

Given the horrendous nature of warfare at the time, add to that blood-soaked ground, tens of thousands of men and horses stomping to-and-fro, and it's pretty easy for a human body to be trampled beyond recognition.

"But Spartacus was a *big* man!" it's argued. "Surely his body would have been identifiable?" Reasonable thought, giving birth to all manner of fanciful tales that (1) Spartacus actually escaped the battlefield alive, or (2) his body was carried off by his followers to prevent the Romans making a spectacle of his corpse.[63]

That Spartacus escaped is unlikely to unrealistic.

That his followers—perhaps even the Thracian Woman, if she survived?—would spirit away his beloved corpse, more a possibility. Yet had this latter been the case, surely we would have at least, in later years, seen the rise of a "cult" of Spartacus, perhaps witnessed his being elevated to "Son of God" status, in this case Dionysus . . . perhaps even God Dionysus himself incarnate?

So far as we can tell, this "cult" never manifested.

We do know that, predictably, after their leader's death, Spartacus's surviving followers scattered.

Crassus's subsequent "mopping up" operations netted 6,000, all of whom (as accurately shown in that sixties movie) he crucified on the road between Capua and Rome.

POSTSCRIPT TO REVOLT

Flare-ups of both the Spartacus-inspired rebels as well as a few actual Spartacus survivors sprouted up from time to time over the next few decades—dubbed *bandits*, none could hope to rally the kind of support Spartacus had.

Of Spartacus's enemies we know somewhat more:

Ironically, by 60 B.C., Crassus and his longtime rival (okay, *enemy!*) Pompey had grudgingly joined forces with Julius Caesar to rule Rome as the First Triumvirate.

Crassus was finally slain while campaigning in Parthia[64] in 55 B.C., while Pompey was killed in Egypt in 48 B.C. after a falling-out between him and Caesar.

Two years later, after the Thracians continued to revolt, in 46 B.C. Rome formally annexed Thrace.

But, with the exception of Julius Caesar, who other than die-hard historians really remembers the names of Crassus and Pompey?

But "Spartacus," that name we remember, thanks in part to director

---

63. A lesson Mussolini—himself a latter-day Roman—would have to learn the hard way!
64. Nowadays, NE Iran.

Stanley Kubrick's 1960 classic, or perhaps the unremarkable 2004 remake *Spartacus: The Complete TV Miniseries,* or, most recently, the 2010 Starz series *Spartacus: Blood and Sand* and the follow-up, *Spartacus: Gods of the Arena,* in 2011.

For the military-minded and students of politics, Spartacus's revolt holds many lessons—both successes and failures to be studied—with the former occasionally recalled and imitated, the latter all too often ignored . . . and then *repeated*!

LOST IN TRANSLATION?

> *"By now the rebels had taken his measure. They recognized a winning general and a favorite of the gods as well as a giant gladiator. His vivid gestures moved them. His austerity hardened them; his generosity helped them. His care for innocent civilians might have left them cold, but it underscored the quality that sums up Spartacus: Righteous."*
> —**Barry Strauss,** *The Spartacus War*

What are we to make of this "War Scroll" of Spartacus?

Not only "What," but "When and Where," and perhaps "Why" as well?

Should we accept these scant scrawls as that bold Thracian's legacy, his "last Will and Testament," perhaps hurriedly written that final night before the telling Battle of Oliveto Citra, written by Spartacus himself, else dictated to a close companion, perhaps even to his mysterious witch-priestess-lover-muse?

Or is instead Spartacus's War Scroll heathen *hadith*[65] collected by his friends and followers after his death, again, perhaps copied down by his "Thracian Woman"?

Experts today contend over these opinions as heatedly as did Legionnaire versus rebel-slave contend back in Spartacus's time.

In the end, it matters little off whose tongue fly war cries and wisdom. Mattering so much more: on whose ear war cries and bits of wisdom finally perch.

In the final analysis, are the words of Spartacus—or any such leader whose voice calls out to us across the years—*useful* to us today?

---

65. Supposed sayings of Muslim Prophet Muhammad spoken to his close "companions," collected after his death.

What truck does the man—or woman—of today have with first century slaves in revolt? At first glance . . . little to none.

But then the wise man always has a second to spare for taking a second look.

At first glance there indeed appears no overriding consistency[66] to the War Scroll of Spartacus. What we find are verses, vignettes, subtle and not-so-subtle vehemence directed toward those same subjects that have always troubled—and still today trouble—the minds of men: fear of failure; death and dying (hopefully well!); the power of words to motivate the minds of men; secrets of winning strategy (if only by successfully making your enemy *lose!*[67]); as well as some obligatory hat-tipping (or is that *toga-lifting*?) to the gods-that-be (that never seem to let men be).

Along the way Spartacus manages to slip in freestanding, seemingly off-hand comments on those things that most occupy a man's mind: hunger, honor, revenge . . . and the unfathomable nature of women.

More a collection of aphorisms than any major philosophical opus, hardly the equal of the systematic cynicism of Machiavelli's *The Prince*, nor comparable to the precise bulletpoint-by-bulletpoint treatises on mental control and martial arts of Eastern classics like Sun Tzu's *Art of War* or Miyamoto Musashi's *A Book of Five Rings,* Spartacus's literary legacy to us is more akin to, and on par with, Hannibal's *Ninety-nine Truths* and *The Seventy-two Certainties* of Vlad Tepes. The scroll's utilitarian use vies for our attention somewhere between *The Art of War* and *Poor Richard's Almanac.*[68]

Both the hammer and the sword find use only with the hand that grasps them.

So too words of wisdom find use only in the grasping mind of he who has an ear to hear.

I. Water is quick to quench our thirst . . . Quicker still to drown us.
Fire cooks well our food . . . Untended, it quickly consumes all a man values.

---

66. We are indebted to C. B. Black for helping translate Spartacus's timeless thoughts into modern voice and for his help organizing and titling sections of Spartacus's scroll, e.g., "Strategy," etc. for both clarity and brevity.

67. Hannibal, Truth III.

68. See "Poor Richard's Rich Wisdom" in Lung and Prowant's *Mind Warrior: Strategies for Total Mental Domination* (Citadel Press, 2010).

Wind cools the heated brow . . . Else it comes upon us a'sudden to collapse our shelter.

Earth remains firm beneath our feet . . . Until the day giants[69] stir, and the very ground opens to swallow us!

Water, Fire, Wind and Earth . . . If none of these first of things can be fully trusted, how much less the ways of men?

DIFFERENT PATHS

II. A man heavy-burdened with armor cannot hope to walk the same narrow mountain path as a woman bearing a light basket.

So too there are paths so narrow only one man at a time may tread there safely.

True again, though a path be wide enough for two men to pass abreast, still that path will be too narrow to allow for the passage of a fully-laden cart.

Where Hannibal[70] passes, his elephants may not.

Yet where one man steps safely, others may follow. Where one man falls, others must take warning.

Better to learn from the blood of others.

The roads of the Romans are straight and wide, allowing even two fully-laden carts to pass one by another.

The Roman way is not our way.

Our path is narrow, and much too unforgiving to allow even a single Roman to pass safely!

Beyond the obvious, we can discern a call for "unforgiving" vengeance against his and his followers' former masters.

III. The Gods do not punish a man for daring to cross a great mountain range in winter. The Gods know the ice and snow will do that for them.

Again, an inspiring reference to the boldness of Hannibal, his choosing to cross the "impassable" Alps in order to attack Rome on its less-guarded northernmost border.

---

69. "Titans," from Greek myth, thought responsible for earthquakes.

70. Early on Spartacus makes note of Hannibal, an obvious influence and inspiration for him.

Metaphorically, each action carries within it the potential for "punishment," just as every thought and action inherently harbors "reward." Farther East they call this "karma."

IV. A great boulder blocking our path is a bother to us. Yet even a small boulder, dislodged from a hilltop, is even more a bother to our enemy.

The boulder I hide behind I call "blessing." The same boulder falls upon him from above and my enemy screams "Curse!"

The largest boulder is the hardest to move. But once it begins rolling downhill, what fool dares stand in its way!

Beyond being sound guerrilla strategy, it's not hard to equate a boulder gaining momentum rolling downhill with the hopes Spartacus must have harbored as he watched more and more slaves flock to his "revolt."

V. It is said determined Hannibal broke the great rock blocking his way with but fire and piss. Can we do less with blade and blood?

Actually, history records that Hannibal and his men, faced with a boulder of massive proportions blocking their passage through the Alps, first heated the rock with fire before then pouring *vinegar* on it to cause it to crack into smaller, more manageable pieces. Other sources argue in favor of wine as the cooling agent used by Hannibal—since his men, by the nature of being men, were more likely to carry wine with them than vinegar. Of course, one might surmise that, given Spartacus's crude rendering, that Hannibal and his men first *enjoyed* the wine, before then *relieving* themselves *of* (or perhaps more accurately, *on*!) the bothersome boulder.

What was it Hannibal had declared when told there was no passage through the Alps?

I will either *find* a way . . . or I will *make* a way!

SLAVES

VI. All scholars study the words and ways of the wise men who came before them. No one takes notice of the pissings and passings of either the fool or the slave.

Beware! Lest you find both the fool and the slave studying you!

Miyamoto Musashi (1594–1645) advises us to "learn the ways of all professions." He didn't leave this advice behind for his students in his masterpiece *Go Rin No Sho* (A Book of Five Rings) just in case that whole being-a-bad-assed-Samurai gig didn't work out for them. No, Musashi knew that the more notice we take of the "little people" (e.g., "fools and slaves") around us, the better our chances of (1) learning tactics, tricks, and techniques *outside the box*, different from "traditional" and *predictable* operating parameters of both ourselves and our enemies, while (2) preventing ourselves from falling victim to an enemy who *is* smart enough to learn from and/or *employ* these "little people."[71]

VII. The King does not study to take glory from the Fool. Can the same be said of the Fool?

Sun Tzu promises that if you know yourself and know your enemy, in a hundred battles you will never taste defeat. Conversely, he warns that, even if you know yourself—capabilities, aspirations, resources available—but lack knowledge of your opponent, then your chances of winning are at best 50/50.

If your enemy has better study habits than you, he will pass, you will fail. He will get the gold star and you will end up with the orange jumpsuit.

VIII. When the Master orders you to kneel and tie his sandals . . . Tie them together!

Where muscle is lacking, mendacity, menace, and medicine *malefic* becomes the (dis)order of the day:

IX. A philtre[72] in a slave's hand is more dangerous than any spear in the hand of a Legionnaire.
X. The slave eats but a tenth portion of what his Master eats, yet that lean slave can work tenfold beyond that of his fat Master.
When the mountains crumble and the earth heaves, who will row the boats?

Here we hear Spartacus inspiring fellow runaway slaves, raising their self-esteem with a little "positive image" building.

---

71. See "Blood Tells: Dracula's Dark Art of War," Section IV of this book, "The 72 Certainties" XIX and XXXI. See also "Mastering the Tricks of the Little People" in Lung and Prowant's *Mind Warrior* (Citadel Press, 2010).

72. i.e., medicine, cure.

XI. The slave sees, but is seldom seen. He listens, but when is he ever heard?

We should not misinterpret this as mere lamenting of a slave's ignored lot in life. Quite the contrary. Here Spartacus alludes to the inordinate amount of knowledge *every* slave held of his Master and his Master's land: vital intelligence a savvy commander like Spartacus needed.

The same holds true today. Even without the obvious dangers inherent in leaving "digital DNA" behind you on the open Internet, take a moment to consider all the "little people" you deal with every day—from clerks to the cleaning lady, cab drivers to that lazy SOB down at the DMV—who "know" things about you, and who know where to find out even more information about you . . . for that right price your enemy waves in front of their face.

XII. In each Roman villa there are those who question slavery . . . They are the ones called "Slaves."

XIII. The Gods made us men. The Romans made us slaves. Whose word is law?

A century later, an obscure philosopher named Jesus of Nazareth would advise something similar: "Render unto Caesar what is Caesar's."

Spartacus's quandary is perhaps the same: If the Gods themselves place princes and principalities in power, and those divinely sanctioned princes and principalities choose to enslave their fellow man . . . who are those slaves to dare defy the whim of the Gods?

As we will see in later verses, Spartacus—just such a "slave"—has quite a lot to say about both the "powers-that-be" as well as the "whim" of the Gods.

XIV. When you put a spade in a slave's hand, do you not expect him to dig?

Why so surprised then when the cook's knife ends up in your back!

XV. How foolish the man so lazy he allows another man to sharpen his knife for him!

Following the defeat of Carthage in the First Punic War, mercenaries employed by Carthage revolted for lack of pay and laid siege to the city. Only fast thinking (read: patient, disarming negotiation followed by surprises swift and savage slaughter!) by Hannibal's father, Hamilcar, saved the city.

Another example of why you need to sharpen your own knife? For centuries, Egyptians maintained an elite officer corps of *white* warrior-slaves called *Mamelukes* (literally "one who is owned").

Recruited from the Caucasus mountain region, in order to better their lot in life and improve the fortunes of their families, these Mamelukes entered into something akin to indentured servitude. Converting to Islam, Mamelukes were then legally adopted into well-to-do Egyptian families who then paid to have them outfitted and trained to become professional military officers—basically the Egyptian equivalent of West Point.

Since it was mandatory that high-ranking Egyptian families present their own sons for military service, each family's Mameluke served as surrogate, taking that son's place on the firing line.

This worked well until the fourteenth century when, after successfully defeating an invading Mongol army, these Mamelukes, under their charismatic commander Baibara El Rukn (Arabic, "The Rock"), assassinated their Egyptian overseers and staged a coup, leading to their ruling Egypt for the next 300 years.

Had the Egyptians read Spartacus's warning, they might have had enough foresight to "sharpen their own knives" rather than enlisting Mamelukes to do it for them.

The trouble with the tried-and-true ploy of "Get a dog to eat a dog" is that, ultimately, the dog *you* take on to help you get rid of another dog (1) grows strong as he goes about doing *your* dirty work, and (2) once the job is done, "your" dog can become bored and begin looking around for another bone to chew on. . . .

XVI. The greatest of knights,[73] on the fiercest of mounts, is powerless so long as another man holds tight the reins.

XVII. Let the enemy grow drunk on the wine they've bought. Then we will help them drown in it!

In Spartacus's time, wine was the major commodity traded for slaves. In other words, he is equating the slaves of Rome with the wines of Rome . . . both of which Rome would pay dearly for in the end.

Another way of looking at this is "the Judo principle." Instead of match-

---

73. i.e., *equis.*

ing your enemy blow for blow, strength for strength (something a guerrilla army can scarce afford to do), pretend to give in, giving your enemy exactly what he wants, as a way of (1) making him weaker in the long run, and (2) as a way of leading him into ambush.

The best example of the former is the way in which the Chinese accepted domination by the invading hordes of the sons of Genghis Khan but, within a generation, by the time of Genghis Khan's grandson Kublai Khan, the ferocity of the Mongol conquerors had been all but castrated by the "civility" of the Chinese Imperial Court.

A great example of the latter is every ambush ever set where a "fleeing" guerrilla force is pursued by a larger force . . . straight into *ambush!*

It has oft been said that the easiest way to utterly destroy a man is to give him everything he wants.

MEMORY AND PATIENCE

XVIII. It matters not if the Romans know our names this day. For they will not soon forget the names of their brothers and sons and fathers whom we make them sacrifice this day!

XIX. All that we are is all that we remember.

All that we can become is what your enemies and The Gods remember of us.

Let us give both much to remember!

XX. Shout loud, brothers! Loud enough that if The Gods are not moved to help us, they will at least be disturbed enough to remember us in their dreams.

XXI. Patience is but memory well-guarded. And victory but memory put to good use.

XXII. Guard your memories well, that your memories may well guard you.[74]

XXIII. Chains on a man's ankles do not make him a slave. Only chains on his memories can accomplish that.

XXIV. A wronged man balances the shortness of his spear against the length of his memory.

---

74. See Dracula's "72 Certainties," XXVIII, in the following section.

Recall that Spartacus was "famous for his spear"; his spear as impressive as his memory.

The forty-seven Ronin also come to mind.

XXV. The smallest seed can grow to split the greatest of stones. Patience—and a little watering—is the key.

XXVI. Patience and persistence . . . These challenge Fate and entertain the Gods.

XXVII. The face of my enemy is ever before me . . . His head on my pole the best of reminders!

This could almost qualify as humor on Spartacus's part if not for the fact that Crixus's Celts, like many ancient peoples, were (in)famous for taking the heads of their enemies. Ancient Scythians drank from skull-cups made from fallen foes.

XXVIII. Do not become over-fat feasting on patience. Rather, patience is a meal to be savored . . . **Quickly!**

We are reminded that revenge is a meal best *eaten* cold.

There is a time for patience, and a time to act. *Blessed* is the man who knows the difference and a *blessing* is the enemy who doesn't!

> *"A life of reaction is a life of slavery, intellectually and spiritually. One must fight for a life of action not reaction."*
> —Rita Mae Brown

WALLS

XXIX. Walls over-thick lock some inside just as surely as they lock others out.

In other words, a good knife cuts both ways.

XXX. Come nightfall, the Master locks tight his gate. There he remains trapped with his fear till dawn, while we are free to move with the night.

In the East they speak of "The Five Weaknesses" (Jp. *Gojo-goyoku*), five universal emotional outlooks that dominate our day: Fear, Lust, Anger, Greed, and Sympathy.[75]

---

75. Known in the West by the mnemonic "The Five Warning F.L.A.G.S."

While we freely use more than one and even all these emotions during any given day, at any given moment one of these five emotions dominates. Most important, one of these five emotional outlooks dominates us on a consistent basis, helping form our core *persons*, around which the other four emotions orbit.

For example, some people seem to be angry at the world—all the time, while others take a more sympathetic view of life. Still others are greedy and lust-filled.

In keeping with the whole "yin-yang balance" paradigm of Eastern thought in general, all five of these core motivators possess both positive and negative aspects. For example, "fear" is a bad thing when it paralyzes you, preventing you from helping yourself and others. Yet fear is a good thing when it prevents you from doing stupid things that might endanger yourself and others.

Likewise, each of us has capabilities, aspirations, and resources that— when properly focused—work to our benefit. Left underdeveloped and unfocused, or when manipulated by a wily opponent, those same "walls" that defend us suddenly become our prison.

XXXI. Every guard placed on the wall is one less guard at the gate.

Sun Tzu pointed out that when your enemies have to prepare *everywhere* then they are strong *nowhere*, i.e., their forces are spread too thin to defend your breach effectively.

Upon being told by his partners-in-crime that he should "lie low" for a while since the FBI had all the fat banks staked out, expecting a visit from the infamous Dillinger gang, John Dillinger just smirked. "They have to be at *all* the banks . . . I only have to show up at *one!*"

XXXII. One slave at the gate is worth a hundred soldiers on the wall.

During his march across Rome, Hannibal took several cities after they were betrayed from within, the city gates flung wide by slaves on the inside. Spartacus likewise took the walled city of Thurii after the gates were opened for him by slave sympathizers.

This same ploy played out in the 410 A.D. sacking of Rome itself after Gothic slaves killed the soldiers guarding the Salarian Gate, opening it from the inside for the besieging army of Alaric, King of the Goths.

XXXIII. Just as **murmillo** *and* **thraex**[76] *fighting in the sand*[77] *must not be swayed by the fawnings and fartings of the mob,*[78] *so too those besieging a city's walls cannot allow themselves to be swayed by those wailing within those walls.*

Whether Spartacus is referring to those casting catcalls or those lamenting the city's eventual fall, praying for mercy, isn't known for certain. The adage stands sound in either case.

XXXIV. A man shouting from atop a besieged city wall is only in danger of falling.

Sooner or later, you have to put your money where your mouth is. Put up or shut up.

You can only bluff so much—so far—in life before, sooner or later, somebody's gonna call your one-bluff-too-many.

In the words of that great philosopher Kenny Rogers: "You got to know when to *fold 'em*."

A *great* burglar never breaks into any place he hasn't already mapped at least *two* exits from.

Ever notice how *everything* keeps coming back to Sun Tzu? "Know yourself" being Job One.

You have to do regular assessments of your capabilities and resources—*realistic* assessments.

The minute you let your mouth (bravado) write a check your ass(ets) can't cover . . . then bankruptcy is gonna be the least of your problems.

Getting an opponent to become overconfident, thereby overextending himself, takes you *more than* 50 percent of the way to winning.

A shouting (i.e., bragging, "smack-talkin'") enemy is a good thing: (1) He's literally wasting his breath—nothing better than an opponent who's out of breath!, and (2) so long as he keeps yelling, you'll know where he is at all times.

---

76. The two main types of Roman gladiators, the former larger, more heavyweight (e.g., Spartacus), the latter lighter, usually with less armor.

77. i.e., in the arena.

78. The cheering crowd.

XXXV. A wall is not solid for its single stones, rather for the mortar binding those stones together.

It could be argued that Romans had *many* reasons for fighting Spartacus (e.g., pride, fear, hatred, greed, ambition), while Spartacus's people had only one: *freedom*, the "mortar" holding them together.

XXXVI. Rich men shape their stones before building their homes.
The poor man builds his home with the stones of the field.

On the one hand, this saying reflects the truth of Spartacus's cause: he literally built an army, not from trained Legionnaires but, rather, from the "stones" of the field, often simple slaves willing to take up kitchen knives and farm implements and march beside him.

Of course, in the way of wry humor, we could see Spartacus's reference to "rich men" as being a slight at "Crassus the Rich's" expense.

XXXVII. A patient commander builds his walls with stone.
An impatient commander builds his walls with the bodies of his own soldiers.

While Spartacus's point here is obvious—Don't sacrifice your soldiers needlessly—purely for historical purposes, it's worth noting that, during the Battle of Thermopyle (480 B.C.) the defending "300 Spartans" piled up the dead bodies of invading Persians, most notably the bodies of the Persians' elite "Immortals," as a makeshift bulwark. And, recall that Spartacus stands accused by some of deliberately herding Roman POWs forward and into Crassus's spike-filled trenches in order to create a passage for his own fighters.

Of course, that's not the same as using your own men as cannon fodder.

WORDS

XXXVIII. Words rule the world. So rule your words.

In all times and climes, orators, masters of the spoken word, have been prized . . . and persecuted.

In our modern day of mass media, of 1,000 visual images that can be "beamed" into our heads in less than a minute, it's important to remember just how important the ability to rouse men with your words was in Spartacus's time, in Classical times, when not only were the masses—especially slaves—illiterate but, even if you could scribble down your thoughts, before the advent of the printing press a couple thousand years later, there was no way to get your writings out to people on a mass basis.

Indeed, in Spartacus's day, *words* ruled.

XXXIX. The dagger lies silent until stirred by words of anger.

Spartacus knew that men are moved by emotion, that men are not so easily moved by trying to *dissuade* them from their dominant emotion, quite the contrary: It's easier to move men by *feeding* them even more of their favorite emotion.

In other words, when confronting a greedy man, don't try to convince him of the merits of being generous—of "doing the right thing." Instead, *feed* his greed by convincing him he can acquire *even more* by following your lead.

XXXX. A man in a sinking boat must decide whether to row all the faster, else swim for that far shore. He can scarce wait for word to be shouted to him from afar.

Shouts made in Rome can scarce be heard in Messina.[79]

Sun Tzu (and every commander since!) railed against a king trying to run a battlefield while sitting on a throne a hundred miles away.

Ever since WWII there's been speculation as to how much more Hitler's generals could have accomplished had not *der Führer* insisted upon commanding the battlefield from a bunker in Berlin.

This "commanding-from-afar" has been somewhat negated by modern instantaneous "real-time" communication. Unfortunately "commanding from afar" still occurs today in the form of (1) saddling the boots on the ground with too much "political correctness" and (2) someone sitting safely in D.C. second-guessing what *they* would have done "better" when the bullets started flying in Kabul.

Words don't win wars.

XXXXI. Sword and spear wound. Words, even more so.

---

79. The southernmost point of Italy.

*"Why are the words that take us to war always so much louder
than the words that finally bring us home?"*
—C. B. Black

XXXXII. Words lie easier than they speak truth.

Words spoken today, easily turn to other words tomorrow.

Words written today, unrolled tomorrow, still speak the same truth.

*The spoken word is free to roam. The written word, trapped forever on
the scroll.*

Vlad Tepes disagrees with Spartacus about the value of the *written* word.
Thus his Certainty V: "Treaties signed in ink are too soon re-written in
blood." See also Vlad's VI, VII, and VIII "Certainties" on the power of the
spoken word.

XXXXIII. Oaths, like stones, roll more easily downhill.

So too truth.

*Better the lie pushed uphill than a sacred oath left to roll untended
downhill.*

Truth untended flows downhill like the lie.

*Lies, however well-tended, can never be truth . . . Though many might
wish it so and even more believe it so.*

THE HUNGRY MAN

XXXXIV. A belly empty of food is the same as a belly filled by a sword.

Both render a man useless.

Recall Hannibal's admonition that "a wise general must fill his head
before he fills his belly. A wise general must fill the belly of his army before
he fills their hand."[80]

*XXXXV. A man with food, but lacking a sword, can easily pick up a
rock to defend himself.*

*A man with a sword, but lacking food, can scarce lift either sword or
rock.*

Priorities. Don't place the cart before the horse.

---

80. Truth XXII.

The Germans lost at the Battle of the Bulge not because of what the Allies had, rather from what they, the Germans, didn't have, namely: petrol to keep their vastly superior tanks rolling.

An army indeed runs on its belly . . . and a tank's belly needs enough petrol the same way a bow needs enough arrows.

It matters little if a commander knows what he *wants* if he is ignorant of what his soldiers *need*. This is simple physical logistics, without which a campaign is doomed before it begins.

Interpreted philosophically, mentally, recall the sixties hippie-rallying call: "Free your mind and your ass will follow!"

XXXXVI. The man who cannot feed his own belly can scarce cut the belly of another.

An argument in favor of scorched earth policy if ever there was one. Sherman's March to the Sea, Hannibal's XXXth and XXXVIth Truth, seemingly at odds with his Truth XXXVIII: "Waste is worse than war. Never burn a field that may one day feed your sons."

XXXXVII. A hungry man is dangerous to others. A starving man is dangerous only to himself . . . For having allowed himself to fall that far.

The difference between "staying hungry" and "being hungry" is that the former makes you the *hunter* while the latter makes you the *hunted*.

XXXXVIII. A slave without sandals seldom runs away. A slave without food . . . Never!

IL. Better to die by iron than by starvation.

STRATEGY

L. If you threaten a man's home with fire, he will rush from the battlefield to put out that blaze.

Yet if that same man receives word while on the battlefield that his home has already fallen to flame, then that man will plant his feet all the firmer on that battlefield.

Accomplished interrogators (okay, *torturers*) know not to "damage the goods" too quickly during the course of an "intensive interview," i.e., not to permanently scar or otherwise maim the person being questioned *too* horribly lest that person give up all hope and become unresponsive, perhaps even begin longing for death.[81]

The *scent* of the meat is what baits the trap. The *promise* of the meat is what draws them to the trap. Meat in the mouth is what springs the trap!

LI. When a rich man's stores are threatened by fire, he races to the nearest stream for water.

Lie in wait for him there.

A predictable enemy is a godsend. An enemy you can *make* even more predictable . . . means we'll all be eating at *his* house tonight!

LII. Running away is the first of wisdoms. Turning suddenly, the first of strategies.

Compare this with Hannibal's "Drunken man" (Truth XXXI).

LIII. We flee, our enemy pursues until finally we permit him to draw near us.

Already rested, we turn on him as he arrives.

Still trying to catch his breath, we snatch that final breath from him!

LIV. You have nothing to fear from a running slave . . . unless he is running towards *you!*

LV. We choose to run . . . and our enemy pursues us. In this way we choose when our enemy moves. We choose when we will turn and fight.

We turn and fight where we choose, whenever it pleases us to do so, when it displeases our enemy all the more!

LVI. Whoever controls the arena decides life or death.

Whoever chooses the battlefield, chooses the place of his victory.

LVII. All we were free to choose in the arena was how well we died. Now we can choose how well our *enemy dies!*

Before relieving himself, our enemy must seek permission from his Masters in Rome, far removed from the battlefield . . . farther still from his bowels!

---

81. See *Theatre of Hell: Dr. Lung's Complete Guide to Torture* (Loompanics Unlimited, 2003), and "The Art of In-*Terror*-gation" in Lung and Prowant's *Mind Assassins* (Citadel Press, 2010).

LVIII. Brothers! We have battled the lions of Libya and bested the bulls of Gaul.[82] *What is there in the barking of a few Roman dogs to frighten us?*

LIX. Seize the bush and soon the birds will have to come to you for their berries.

Seize or otherwise threaten something your enemy values and he will be forced to respond. In this way, smaller "harassing" units tie up much larger forces. Guerrilla Warfare 101.

LX. A single Consul's head stuck up on a pole, collecting flies, will teach the Senate[83] *more than all the scrolls collecting dust in Alexandria.*[84]

In other words, never underestimate the value of *propaganda*.

One death to save a hundred, a thousand, six million? Sounds like more than a fair deal:

> One arrow aimed directly at your adversary's leadership can achieve what a barrage of arrows cannot. (Kaihan Krippendorff, *Hide a Dagger Behind a Smile*)

LXI. A rock is only a rock . . . until it strikes your head!

To the sharp eye a sharpened stick can do the work of the sharpest dagger.

Here Spartacus argues against "object fixedness," that tendency of the human mind to see only singular uses for objects . . . *and people*.

Down through history, oppressed populations, denied weapons by the powers-that-be, have resorted to adapting everyday objects as defensive and offensive weapons. Perhaps the best-documented example of this is how, after the sixteenth-century Japanese invaders of Okinawa confiscated all swords and other weapons from the indigenous population, crafty Okinawans turned their everyday objects into many of today's well-known martial arts weapons. The walking staff became the fighting *bo*; fish-skewers became *sai* fighting-prongs; simple chains became the dreaded *manriki* fighting-chain (weighted at each end for better striking); the simple farmer's sickle became razor-sharp *kama*; while an everyday rice-beating tool became the famed *nunchakus*.

---

82. i.e., in the arena.
83. i.e.,, rulers of Rome.
84. Reportedly the largest library in the ancient world.

Recall how Spartacus and his fellow gladiators made good use of "Environmental Weapons," including kitchen knives and cooking skewers, when making good their escape from the slave pens at Capua.

But, more than anything, Spartacus is telling us not to judge a book (or scroll, as the case may be) by its cover.

Recognizing potential is the same as putting a down payment on success.

LXII. We can fight the sword or we can fight the man swinging that sword. Which one breaks more easily?

LXIII. Break your enemy's sword, and he will soon purchase another. Break his courage, and what merchant sells that keenest of blades?

LXIV. Though I am no physician, I clearly see that our enemy has too much blood in his body. Look how even now his face flushes red in anger. Let us cure him of his excess!

Recall that as far back as the fifth century B.C., Sicilian philosopher Empedocles (490–430 B.C.) theorized that the four basic elements making up all creation—Earth, Air, Fire, and Water—had their physical/emotional correspondences within the human body as Phlegm, Blood, Choler (aka Yellow Bile), and Black Bile, known as "The Four Humors."[85] An imbalance (deficit or overabundance) *in any one of these* leads to all manner of disease and defect.

On the one hand, Spartacus is making a joke at the Romans' expense. On the other hand, he is pointing out that prodding your enemy into acting out of anger is *your first step*—and *his last step!*—in the direction of victory.

LXV. As the tiny seed hides the great tree, as the slave hides his freedom within his heart, so too the wise commander guards his strategy.

To command, and ultimately to conquer, first, I must know more about my enemy than he knows about himself. Second, I must know more about myself than my enemy knows about me. Finally, I must know more about myself today than I knew yesterday, but less about myself than I will discover tomorrow.

It has been said that a commander can celebrate a victory with his men, but not the confusion of sifting through contradictory intelligence, balancing potential gain against inevitable loss, and, ultimately, making decisions that

---

85. For a complete discussion of "The Four Humors," how they can be manipulated for cure or ill, see Dr. Lung's *Mind Control* (Citadel Press, 2006).

come with death attached—all the things a commander must first do in order to secure a victory worth celebrating.

LXVI. Sow confusion to reap certainty.

For the man obsessed with order, chaos is the enemy. For all others—the prisoner obsessed with escape, the criminal obsessed with ill-gotten gain, the guerrilla in search of victory—*chaos = opportunity*.

Where chaos doesn't exist naturally, it becomes necessary for the prisoner, the criminal, the guerrilla to *create* it.

Reacting to unexpected, perhaps sudden, chaos tests your ability to keep a cool head and to adapt.

Creating chaos in order to profit from it, by then being the one offering a "timely" solution to that chaos, is the perfect way for the ambitious (and unscrupulous) to gain the upper hand. It's called "C.H.A.O.S. Theory" as in "Create Hassles (Hardships, Hurdles, etc.) And (then) Offer Solutions."[86]

As Hermann Hesse assures us, "Chaos demands to be recognized and experienced before letting itself be converted to a new order."

So embrace the chaos. Own the chaos!

And remember, it's only "chaos" if you don't see it coming. And the one way to be certain you *always* see the chaos coming is by making sure *you* are always the one *starting* the chaos!

> *"There is no life without pain, just as there is no art without submitting to chaos."*
> —**Rita Mae Brown**

LXVII. It was not the goring tusks nor the stamping feet of his great beasts[87] that made Rome fear Hannibal so. It was the mighty heart of that great beast beating in Hannibal's breast that troubled their sleep!

Reputation often spills less blood.

Most people only play games they *know* they can win. A well-played PR campaign, in this case standing for "propaganda and *ruthlessness*," can have your opponent throwing in the towel before you ever step in the ring.

---

86. For a complete "how-to" course on creating chaos for fun and profit, see "Arts of C.H.A.O.S." in Lung and Prowant's *Mind Assassins* (Citadel Press, 2010).

87. i.e., elephants.

Remember Sun Tzu's Golden Rule: The best battles are those we don't have to fight. Better the fire extinguisher than the fire department.

LXVIII. Shine your blade daily with your enemy's blood and it will never rust.
And neither will *you*!

LXIX. No ancient scroll with words of wisdom written therein can serve us on the battlefield . . . Unless we stuff that scroll down our enemy's throat!
Crude, but true. A little more in-depth interpretation? Appreciation is easy, application is not.

Playing chess—no matter how good you get at pushing around those little plastic pieces—won't make you the next General Patton. Only reluctantly sending your men to bleed, bleeding yourself, and successfully draining the blood from your enemy time and time again can make you *appreciate* how hard it is to *apply* what men like Sun Tzu, and Hannibal, and Patton themselves learned the hard way.

LXX. The hate a man holds in his heart is always more dangerous than the sword he holds in his hand.
What a man holds in his heart guides what he holds in his hand.
Heart and hand must be of one accord, just as shield and spear must be of one accord.
Superior firepower—while preferable—is no guarantee of victory.

Courage has often overcome the club. Determination can be honed sharper than the sharpest dagger. The bullet is nothing without the brain to point it in the right direction.

Concentration of force(s), focus, rapid deployment, these three have always been—and will always remain—the key to victory—from the battlefield, to the boardroom, to the bedroom.

LXXI. Curved or straight,[88] the blade cuts the same.
Master or slave, it is all the same to the blade.

---

88. i.e., *sica* or *gladius,* two main types of gladiator swords. The word *gladiator* comes from the latter.

LXXII. Stubborn sticks bundled together become unbreakable. Thus we will not waste vigor trying to break what is unbreakable.

Instead, we will cut the gay ribbon that holds those sticks together.

The symbol of Rome was the *fasces*, a bundle of wooden rods bound together with a cord, often around a protruding axe.

Spartacus is obviously making reference to the strength and *apparent* unity of the Romans. Like Hannibal, Spartacus went to lengths to convince whole towns to come over to the greater cause by defeating Rome by exploiting already obvious cracks in the veneer of Roman-imposed "unity" on the Italian peninsula.

LXXIII The stronger and straighter our spear, the more sons we leave this world.

Obviously, the stronger (more disciplined) and straighter (more focused) we are, the better our chances of success. Ergo, the better the chances of *our* DNA living on and your enemy's DNA ending up DOA.

In a similar vein, however, Spartacus may be casting a bit of ribald humor our way, reminding us in a roundabout way that he was "famous for his spear!"

LXXIX. As a bee steals the color from many different flowers, so too the wise commander molds his strategy.

It cannot be too oft emphasized that *predictability* = *death*.

A good leader doesn't change things whimsically, willy-nilly, just for the sake of causing confusion. Rather, we pick and choose *varying* tactics and techniques that (1) keep our enemy guessing, and (2) already have a *proven track record* of success.

The men trusting you for both their succor and their success are not lab rats.

LXXX. When hunting the hare, the wolf can make many mistakes.

When hunted by the spearman, the wolf can scarce afford a single mistake.

The "wolf" is, of course, Rome, its two semi-mythical founders, Romulus and Remus, having themselves been saved and suckled by a she-wolf. Three guesses who "the spearman" is. . . .

LXXXI. The long light at Pharos[89] could draw in the mightiest of ships from leagues around.

So too, a single man can light the way for many.

LXXXII. You can scarce hope to defeat a commander whose men fear him more than they fear you.

But he can likewise scarce hope to beat a commander whose men love him more than they love life itself.

This echoes (pre-shadows?) Machiavelli's "Is it better for a prince to be loved or feared?" quandary.

This may also be a specific reference to Crassus in his hated (feared) role as "Crassus the Decimator," slaughtering one-in-ten of his own men as a means of imposing discipline—which he obviously equated with fear.

In the end, Machiavelli decided that being loved, while preferable, wasn't something a prince could depend on. Fear, well-applied and well-eyed, was much more constant and dependable.

If men fought for Crassus out of fear and fought with Spartacus out of love, then, in the end, *fear* proved the more powerful player, at least in this particular scenario.

Of course, those who truly *love* you will never stab you in the back. The same cannot be said of those who truly *fear* you. . . .

LXXXIII. Cutting the head from the snake is best.

Next best: Breaking the snake's spine . . . And even the most venomous of serpents is **all spine!**

An antidote for every poison, a cure for every ill. Every man has a strength that may be useful to you. Every enemy has a weakness that may be even more useful to you!

LXXXIV. What is more prized by the victor? A palm branch,[90] a sword of wood,[91] or his next breath?

Which will men fight the hardest for?

Like his hero Hannibal, Spartacus commanded respect from the repre-

---

89. The famed lighthouse on an island (formerly a peninsula) in Alexandria in northern Egypt was one of the "Seven Wonders of the Ancient World."

90. Traditionally given to a victorious gladiator.

91. i.e., a *rudi*, a wooden sword given to a freed champion gladiator.

sentatives of many different nationalities making up his slave "army." Many of these were men who'd already fought beside him (some perhaps *against* him!) in the arena. Others had joined him during the break-out from Capua. Still others—countrymen—may have known him from even before they were brought to Rome in chains. Yet even those joining the party late, would have soon recognized the Thracian's courage and determination, watching him not only order his followers into battle but, more often than not, bravely place himself at the fore of any charge against the enemy.

Admittedly, as with Hannibal's own largely mercenary force, the men (and women) under Spartacus's command fought for a variety of reasons: most for freedom, some for revenge, with none of them being above pocketing whatever booty came their way.

But, whatever their individual reasons for hitching their collective horses to Spartacus's war-cart, all were in agreement—unified—as to, and by, the Thracian's charisma and courage.

Hermann Hesse once observed that "Some people regard themselves as perfect, but only because they demand little of themselves."

Spartacus wasn't perfect, nor did he ever—so far as we know—lay claim to being so. What he was, was the perfect man for the times, and for the bloody job at hand. And those who followed him all recognized this. They fought for what he *represented*.[92]

LXXXV. The tree is an easy target for the cast spear. Not so easy the man hidden behind that tree.

From Minutemen to Maoists, guerrillas all know the "Boxer's Drill": Stick-and-move, stick-and-move!

LXXXVI. Where your enemy sees the limb of a tree, you must see a spearhead hardened by fire.[93]

Where your enemy sees only darkness, you must see a stolen cloak with which to wrap yourself.[94]

---

92. Review "Hannibal's Six Movers of Men," page 000.

93. This harkens back to saying LXI, "A rock is only a rock. . . ."

94. We are reminded of saying XXX. For a practical "How-to" course on "wrapping yourself in the night" (and protecting yourself from enemies who do!) read: Dr. Lung's *Knights of Darkness: Secrets of the World's Deadliest Night-Fighters* (Citadel Press, 2004).

Where the enemy sees only a shepherd boy, I see a savior!

A hundred years after Spartacus, anyone from that new "cult" known as "Christians" would have gotten a kick out of the Thracian's praise for a "shepherd boy as savior." The truth of the matter is Spartacus employed slaves as spies[95] as often as possible. As any good commander knows to do, Spartacus augmented his *innate* intelligence with *gathered* intelligence, twin sides of the same blade.

The best known of Spartacus's spies was the young slave Publipor (literally meaning "Publius's boy," a possible reference to the boy having once been owned by a Roman named Publius). Reportedly Publipor helped Spartacus and his men find hidden paths through the treacherous mountains near Varinius. Keep in mind that other spies had overpowered the guard to open the gates of Thurii to Spartacus's advance.

The value of *slaves* as spies cannot be underestimated, especially since Romans—like all slave masters—would have made a bad habit of ignoring their lowly servants in social situations, speaking freely (imprudently) around them. A perfect example of ignoring the "Little People" at your own peril!

LXXXVII. A single slave girl sent to fetch water at the stream sees more in a single morning than a Consul sees all year.

Roman Consuls placed in administrative positions commanding Legions were traditionally given a commission of one year. Exceptions and extensions were granted reluctantly (for fear of one Consul gaining too much loyalty with the army, tempting him to seize power, as Caesar would one day do).

LXXXVIII. In the morning, the sun shines on this side of the mountain. At mid-day, the sun graces both slopes of the mountain equally.

Not even the "great" Spartacus can halt the movement of the sun across the sky!

Yet, the wiseman, patiently plotting the sun's path, manages always to stay in the shade.

---

95. See Vlad Tepes's take on spies, his "Certainty LIX, "I can scarce abide spies. . . ." in Section IV of this book.

In the biblical book of Joshua, warlord of Israel, the sun stands still in the sky, enabling the Israelites to overcome the Amorites.[96]

Whether or not Spartacus, obviously a well-traveled if not a well-educated man, may have heard this tale, or tales similar, we have no way of verifying. However, beyond the obvious: Spartacus breaking the news to his followers that he *isn't* their "messiah," that if they want freedom they're going to have to fight for it tooth-and-nail, this saying also contains practical lessons for the would-be guerrilla to "plot the sun's path" (i.e., that by studying the habits of both earth and their fellow man, they can always be at the advantage—"stay in the shade" or, in today's parlance, remain "off the grid").

LXXXIX. Best: The enemy does not know the direction of my march.
Next best: My enemy does not cypher my destination.
Better still: An enemy pulled in two directions!

The only thing more important to a commander—to *anyone* for that matter!—than innate and gathered intelligence is *guarded* intelligence. Guard your own intelligence—both kinds!—while denying your enemy the same. All else is guessing.

XC. The door[97] that opens wide for you must not remain open for your enemy.
Let the open door beckon to your enemy . . . before it slams shut in his face as he rushes to enter!

Dangle the carrot, pulling it back at the last instant, just as your enemy jumps for it.

XCI. Should I fill my sack with silver or with the head of my enemy?
Both are precious to me.
One buys me pleasure. The other gains as glory . . . and a good night's sleep.

XCII. Swords and spearheads are made from the same iron as the slave's shackles.

---

96. See Joshua 10.
97. i.e., *cochles*.

According to Barry Strauss, in *The Spartacus War*,[98] Spartacus and his men actually melted down their slave irons to make weapons.[99]

FEAR AND BLOOD

XCIII. My assurance of victory does not come from the sharpness of my sword, nor from the strength of the hand that grips that sword, nor even from the focused eye that aims my hand.

My assurance of victory comes from knowing my own fear . . . and knowing my enemy's fear.

> *"If you know the enemy and know yourself, in a hundred battles you need not fear defeat. If you know yourself but not your enemy, for every victory gained will come one defeat. If you know neither your enemy nor yourself, you will be defeated in every battle."*
> —Sun Tzu, *The Art of War*

XCIV. A man owns his thoughts, truly naught else. Not ever. Or at least not for long.

This verse could be the motto for the Black Science Institute!

XCV. My greatest proof that The Gods do not know my every thought is that they allow me to draw another breath!

And if The Gods themselves cannot cipher my next thought, what hope does my enemy have of doing so?

XCVI. As you wonder, so do most men wonder.

As you dream, so do most men dream.

As you fear, so do most men fear.

And as you bleed, so do all men bleed![100]

Spartacus is telling his followers (and us) that no matter how seemingly invincible our enemy, his thought patterns can be discerned, his dreams dis-

---

98. Simon & Schuster, 2009.

99. Joel 3:10 says, "Beat your plowshares into swords, and your pruning hooks into spears. Let the weak say, 'I am a warrior.'"

100. Review Hannibal's Truth LXIX.

covered, his fears exploited. He bleeds as we bleed. . . . Our job is to make sure he bleeds *first!*

XCVII. Two men tremble at the coming fight: One trembles from fear, the other trembles from the fury within him.

And while our tremblings spring from separate thoughts, together, we may hasten their departure.

Rise, brothers! We rid ourselves of our fear by giving it to our enemy!

Those untrained in the martial arts, when confronted with a stressful situation, often mistake their body's reaction (e.g., sweating, "butterflies in the stomach," shaking limbs) to be signs of *fear* when, in reality, these are signals from your body that it is ready for either "fight" or "flight" or both.

These "tremblings" come from the adrenaline flooding directly into our bloodstream. Like the tension created by drawing a bow, so too "tension" increases in the body *until* our "arrow" is released in *a burst of power* that helps us survive the threat—whether by fleeing (always an option when faced with superior numbers and/or superior firepower) or else, trapped, we fight back with a surge of energy that both surprises and overwhelms our enemy.

Any *good* martial arts training will concentrate on teaching students to (1) recognize and then (2) release this *natural* "tension," in the same way an archer learns to hold his drawn bow steady before finally releasing it to the bull's-eye.

XCVIII. Let us polish our swords, and spearpoints, and shields well, that our enemy may see his fear reflected there!

IC. Better by far to color our name with blood than with fear. For the former can more easily be washed clean when this day's harsh work is done.

Spartacus would have appreciated Shakespeare's "A coward dies a thousand deaths, the brave man, only one."

C. Fix your mind thus: In the battle to come, there is only one man within the enemy ranks to whom The Gods have entrusted the task of slaying you. Determine to fight your way through to him! For The Gods have, with equal measure, marked you as his slayer in turn.

Regard all others, it matters naught they be legion, as but high marsh weeds barring your path to him. . . . Cut them down!

Focus, determination, pushing all thoughts of failure aside, eyes ever on the prize. Full victory is full effort!

As previously mentioned, at the Battle of Oliveto Citra, Spartacus dedicated both himself and his elite "bodyguard" to hacking their way through the Roman line with the express mission of taking Crassus's head. How apropos then if these were the very words—perhaps his final words—the Thracian used to inspire his men. . . .

CI. Let us not flee from our fear. Rather, let us herd our fear before us!

CII. If our enemy would drink blood this day . . . then let it be his own!

DEATH

CIII. The voices of the dead can teach us much, both from their ancient scrolls and from their whispers left riding on the wind . . . But only if we are keen to listen to them in advance of meeting them face-to-face!

CIV. None can choose the manner of his birth. Yet every man can have some say in the manner of his death.

CV. Death looks much different when sitting in the high seats[101] than it does standing on the blood-thirsty sand . . . Yet Death is still Death, regarding the gladiator and the mob alike.

Compare this with Spartacus's verse LXXXI.

CVI. When slave and Master go seeking Death, both find him waiting at the same crossroad.

CVII. Just as the footprint the gladiator leaves behind in the sand is not the man who stepped there, so too what sword and spear spill upon the ground is not the man.

THE GODS

CVIII. Not the wisest of men in old Athens could fully anticipate the will of The Gods . . . Else we would be Greeks this day!

---

101. i.e., seats in the arena.

CIX. As the ground drinks freely from the torn waterskin, so too The Gods drink deeply the spilt **genius**[102] *of the dying man.*

Guard your **genius** *well, for The Gods are a thirsty lot!*

Compare this with Hannibal's Truth XLVIII.

CX. We can scarce hope to please other men by our living.

Mayhaps we can at least amuse The Gods by our dying.

CXI. The gladiator[103] *must close his mind to the fickle roarings of the* *mob*[104] *. . . Perhaps as well to the fartings of The Gods!*

No better insight into the fickle psychology of those attending the Roman gladiatorial games (and perhaps the Roman Gods as well!) has been given than by Saint Augustine of Hippo[105] (354–430 A.D.), early Christian Church patriarch and all-around philosopher, as he lamented the cautionary tale of how his young protégé Alypius was first physically dragged into, and then seduced/brainwashed by watching, the gladiator games by a group of his pagan "friends." At first, in protest, Alypius refused to even open his eyes, until:

> In the course of the fight a man fell and there was a great roar from the vast crowd of spectators which struck [Alypius's] ears. He was overcome by curiosity and opened his eyes, perfectly prepared to treat whatever he might see with scorn. He saw the blood and he gulped down savagery. Far from turning away, he fixed his eyes on it. Without knowing what was happening, he drank in madness, he was delighted with the contest, drunk with the lust of blood. He was no longer the man who had come there, but was one of the mob. He was a true companion of those who had brought him. There is little more to be said. He looked, he shouted, he raved. He took away with him madness which would goad him to come back again and again. And he would not only

---

102. Back in Spartacus's day, "genius" meant "life force."

103. i.e., *murillo*.

104. i.e., arena audience.

105. Present-day Algeria.

come with those who first got him there, but would drag others with him.[106]

CXII. If a God allows his people to die, can he not then simply call up more people from the dust, else he carves them anew from the trees?[107]

But if a people allow their God to die, then will not those people themselves follow soon after?

CXIII. The Gods do not bleed. Thus, we bleed for them.

MISCELLANEOUS WISDOM

CXIV. Bleed only where you are cut.
The world hates a complainer.

CXV. A woman's touch warms the heart . . . and inflames all else!
A little known fact is that women also fought in the gladiatorial games. While most often placed in semi-comedic roles (e.g., chasing around midgets with wooden swords), there were some true "gladiatrix," some of whom may have later found their way into the ranks of Spartacus's army.

Then again, Spartacus may have been remarking on his curious liaison with the "Thracian Woman," his witch-priestess-lover-muse.

CXVI. The wind in my face only strengthens my step.[108]
The wind at my back, that is the favor of The Gods.
How quickly both can turn.

CVII. Better the grape turned to wine, given to the drunk, who stumbles and is crushed beneath the chariot wheel, than that the sweetness of the grape should wither on the vine, untested, untasted.

For the same wine that further blinds the drunken fool can likewise calm the troubled mind of the wiseman.

---

106. cf. Matthews, 2004:118.

107. Many northern European peoples, including Medieval Norse (Vikings), believed the Gods made the first man and woman from an ash and an elm. Perhaps Crixus and the other Celts (and Germans?) in Spartacus's army likewise held this belief.

108. Compare with Hannibal's Truth VI, "I give thanks for my enemy . . ."

The chariot that today carries along the drunken Master, may tomorrow spirit away the sober slave.

Why should the grape and the chariot wheel and the wiseman suffer the stumbling of fools?

Part III
Yorimoto's Thirteen Powers of the Steel Shogun

"Do not bother asking me how I gained my power . . .
Lament instead, how I took yours!"
—Duke Falthor Metalstorm

Introduction

TO A GREAT EXTENT the history of Japan up to—and still including—much of the twentieth century—and beyond?—is the story of *Samurai* cunning and craft and cut-throatery.

Even in the modern day the Samurai *Bushido*[109] ethic has continued to influence, mold, and motivate the minds and manners—fancies, finances, and possible felonies!—of Japanese businessmen,[110] Japanese artists like the world-renowned Yukio Mishima,[111] even Japanese *Yakuza* gangsters.[112]

Of course, the Western stereotype of the Samurai will undoubtedly remain the stern-faced warrior fiercely flashing three feet of lethal steel, stoic, steadfast, regardless of the odds arrayed against him.

This "steel" image indeed stands up to scrutiny. But there was/is so much more . . . depth beneath any such superficial rendering of Samurai as mere bloodthirsty thug.

Of course, history has truthfully recorded that, unfortunately, many

---

109. Literally, "The Way (*d_*) of the Warrior (*bushi*)".

110. For more on how modern Japanese still use *Bushido,* see "Three Diamond's Way" in Dr. Lung's *Mind Control* (Citadel Press, 2006).

111. Famed Japanese author, actor, and Samurai militia leader who committed ritual *seppuku* suicide in 1970.

112. For a complete examination of the Yakuza "Mafia" of Japan, their methods of mind manipulation and—when need be—murder, see "8-9-3" in Dr. Lung's *Mind Penetration* (Citadel Press, 2007).

Samurai *were* little better than murderous thugs—venting their will and wantoness at whim on the *heimin* common folk.

But beyond that three-foot length of lethal *katana* steel resides a measureless reservoir of intelligent insight, Machiavellian machinations, and strategies simultaneously subtle and unfathomable: the necessary "silk" component needed to complement—to *balance*—the "steel," diplomacy designed to diffuse deadly contest, negotiation that negates the need for further bloodshed, perhaps even a drip of subtle nightshade accomplishing the work of the more crude (and *traceable!*) dagger?

Accomplished Samurai were expected to embrace both the sword and the writer's stylus, *bu* and *bun*, ideally to be not only a blood-letter but a man of letters as well.

Ideally.

And, as with most of man's high ideals: Of those aware a mark to shoot for even exists, fewer still are found with the requisite wonder, will, and wherewithal to take focused aim, let alone approach that bull's-eye.

Down through Japanese history those Samurai who successfully and, in rare instance, brilliantly—as in the instance of Miyamoto Musashi—succeeded in grasping sword in one hand, inkwell in the other, are highly praised, the telling strokes of both their sword and brush strenuously studied to this day.

One such Samurai was Yoritomo-no-Minamoto, the first *Shogun* of Japan.

Many men (some might argue, effectively *any* man) can affect history, either by his inaction—refusing to step forward, to do the right thing at the right time—or else via his actions, either commendable or damnable, or both.

Yoritomo has been accused of—and, by a preponderance of the historical evidence—been found guilty of actions, both commendable and damnable. But seldom has he been accused of *in*-action, either through his discipline—and *survival* instinct!—to (1) play the shrinking violet, (2) keep a low profile, (3) collect allies, and (4) bide his time, before gaining the upper hand over his enemies, reads like a Machiavellian *how-to* manual on how a prince cannot only outlast, outthink, and ultimately return from obscurity to revenge himself on those who sent him into exile in the first place.

A little background:

The Samurai class of Japan can be traced back to a specialized cadre of eighth-century knights from well-to-do Japanese families. Known as *Kodei* ("Stalwart Youth"), these warriors distinguished themselves from the mainly spear-wielding foot soldiers of the time by taking up the sword as their weapon of preference. Eventually the sword—literally the long and the short of it!—would become these knights' symbol of distinctive rank.

Clans of these Samurai families were formed together under clan leaders known as *Daimyo*.

Inevitably, after defeating their real "barbarian" enemies, the *Daimyo* entertained themselves by manufacturing imagined trespasses for warring with one another.

By the eleventh century, the various *Daimyo*-led clans had aligned themselves behind the two most powerful families, the *Taira* (aka *Heike*) and the *Minamoto* (aka the *Genji*).

Starting out as underdogs, between 1051 and 1087, the Minamoto fought a series of campaigns, consolidating their power. For example, between 1051 and 1062, a period known as "The Nine Years War," the Minamoto succeeded in eliminating the powerful Abe clan from the north of Honshu. *Daimyo* Minamoto Yoshiie followed this up by destroying the rival Kiyowara clan also in north Honshu during "The Three Years War" (1083–1087).

It bears mentioning that Yoshiie, master archer and direct ancestor of Yoritomo, would later, under Yoritomo's rule, be officially canonized in the *Shinto*[113] religion as *Hachiman Taro*, literally "the eldest son of Hachiman," Hachiman being the Shinto God of War and commandeered-patron of the Minamoto.

A showdown between the Taira and the Minamoto, effectively a Japanese civil war, was inevitable, given what the Taira saw as increasingly insatiable Minamoto hegemony, as evidenced by the latter's "suppression" of the Abe and Kiyowara clans—adding these resources, men, and material to their own growing influence.

By the eleventh century, the great Samurai families had become *de facto* power brokers, with the various factions often promoting their particular claimant for the Imperial throne, albeit always with at least some tenuous legacy or link to legitimacy. For example, the fourteen families comprising the

---

113. "Official" animistic ancestor-worship religion of ancient Japan.

Minamoto traced their lineage back through two Emperors: Saga (786–842) and Seywa (850–880).

For their part, the Taira boasted the Emperor Kammu (737–806) as their ancestor.

Not surprising then that controversy over Imperial succession should prove the firebrand for setting off this Taira-Minamoto powderkeg.

As both clans jockeyed to seat their candidate for Emperor, other feudal lords and families were forced to choose sides. Like we said, *civil war!*

Officially, this Japanese civil war became known as "The Hagen War" (1156–1158). Its conclusion: the destruction of most Minamoto leaders by master strategist Taira Kiyomori (1118–1181).

By 1158, Daimyo Taira Kiyomori had crushed the Minamoto and had seized total control of the civilian government in then-capital Kyoto. He quickly settled the Emperor-succession argument by placing his *two-year-old* nephew, Antoku, on the throne. Of course, good ol' Uncle Kiyomori would be glad to "look after things" until little Antoku reached maturity. . . .

Taira Kiyomori's victory over the Minamoto ushered in the "Rokuhara Period" of Japanese history, 1156 through 1185, when the Taira ruled with near-absolute power.

But for all his necessary (?) savagery on the battlefield, coupled with his savvy political skullduggery for making friends (and marking potential enemies) at court, Kiyomori made *two* mistakes that would prove ultimately fatal to the Taira.

First, early in his campaigning, Kiyomori made the mistake of alienating the influential—and conspiracy-prone—Buddhist temple monastery at Nara[114] as well as destroying the militant temples (*ji*) at Todai-ji and Kofuku-ji.

This would not be the last time both ambitious and aggravated Samurai leaders targeted militant religious enclaves. In the mid-1500s Shogun Oda Nobunago and his two generals, Hideoshi Toyotomi and Ieyasu Tokugawa (both later his successors), launched pogroms to wipe out rebellious Buddhist "cults." Still later, after assuming supreme power, Ieyasu's Tokugawa clan

---

114. Right, kinda like that *Shaolin* monastery in China where they spent more time practicing martial arts than they did meditation. See "The Rise and Fall of Shaolin" in Dr. Lung's *Mind Penetration* (Citadel, 2007).

would crush the growing power of Japanese Christian cultists at the siege of Shamabara in 1638.[115]

But, at the time, Daimyo Taira Kiyomori had no idea his suppression of these Buddhist enclaves would come back to bite him on the ass.

Kiyomori's second mistake—and it was a *doozy!*—was in leaving some of the sons of the Minamoto alive.

In his 1531 *Discourses*, Machiavelli praised the practicality of the Roman admonition to "Kill the sons of Brutus!" i.e., when destroying a dangerous enemy, be certain you destroy his sons as well, lest those sons grow up seeking vengeance. To put it in modern parlance: A three-legged dog still bites!

In other words, had Daimyo Taira Kiyomori taken the time to completely finish off the Minamoto bloodline, Japanese history in general—and the fortunes and fate of the Taira clan in particular—would have taken a completely different course.

When it became obvious by 1158 that the Minamoto cause was lost, Yoritomo's younger half brother Yoshitsune was spirited away to safety in anticipation of what all knew would be the inevitable hunting down and slaughter of the Minamoto in the wake of a Taira victory.

Indeed, as predicted, slaughter followed the Taira victory but, by then, Yoshitsune (to Kiyomori's dubious credit, high on the hit man's list) had been securely hidden away in a monastery friendly to the Minamoto cause.

Lore has it that many of the militant warrior-monks from temples destroyed by the Taira (in addition to many displaced Minamoto Samurai refugees forced to become *Ronin*[116] went on to found many of the Shinobi "Ninja" clans who held sway in Central Japan in the Middle Ages.

Simply put, Yoshitsune (who would live on in legend as Japan's answer to Robin Hood and William Wallace) survived by hiding out with, and mastering the skills of, the dreaded and despised *Ninja*!

FYI: With the reassertion of Minamoto influence, Yoshitsune is credited with founding a martial arts school specializing in teaching Minamoto forces Ninja fighting tactics—technically forbidden to Samurai under the

---

115. See Dr. Lung's *The Sinister Mind* (Citadel Books, 2011).

116. A Samurai warrior unattached to a particular family, living somewhere between a mercenary and an outlaw, a gun—or sword, if you will—for hire. The most (in)famous of these being Miyamoto Musashi.

strict "Look 'em in the eye while you're sending 'em to hell" *Bushido* ethic.[117]

When the time came for the Minamoto to rise again, young Yoshitsune would be ready.

Fortunately, so far as the long-term prospects of the Minamoto cause was concerned, Yoritomo also survived the Taira-sponsored genocide, but did so employing a completely different strategy than his "Hide in the hills till the time is right" half brother.

Young Yoritomo survived—and prospered—by throwing his lot in with the Hojo family, ironically, themselves vassals of the Taira clan.

It is telling that even in their time the Hojo were usually referred to as "the *clever* Hojo"[118] or qualified—or cursed!—with some such similar adjective praising them—and warning others!—of the Hojo's deserved reputation for both diplomacy and duplicity in equal measure.

It was universally acknowledged—and *feared!*—that the Hojo were the undisputed masters of "the wet finger." Behind this somewhat humorous saying lies a more sinister reality.

In Japan "the *shoji* have eyes" has been a common caution against unguarded speech since the founding of the Imperial court.

Shoji are those sliding doors found in traditional Japanese homes, opaque paper "walls" on wooden frames.

A master intriguer was thus "a wet finger" since all that was required to literally see through one of these walls was to wet one's finger and poke an eyehole through the paper-thin veneer in order to spy on those on the other side.

In all times and climes, *intelligence is power*, and intelligence—both the innate kind we're born with, as well as the strategic and tactical intelligence we successfully spy out—often spells the difference between victory and defeat, life and death:

> As often as the future fate of Japan was decided on fields of
> bloody battle, with a shimmering stroke of samurai sword (or
> perhaps a ninja knife in the back!), just as often lives were lost

117. See *The Nine Halls of Death* by Dr. Haha Lung and Eric Tucker (Citadel Press, 2007).

118. See *Secrets of the Samurai: The Martial Arts of Feudal Japan* by Oscar Ratti and Adela Westbrook (Tuttle Publishing, 1973).

and an empire won through intrigue within the imperial palace itself, where the rich and powerful samurai clans vied for the ear of the emperor—all the while plotting to replace him with one of their own. (*Mental Domination*, 2009)

Exactly *why* the Taira allowed the Hojo to safeguard and educate young Yoritomo has been the cause of much speculation.

Some argue the Hojo convinced the Taira that young Yoritomo might make a useful hostage, helpful in convincing stubborn Minamoto loyalists to lay down their arms.

Others venture that the Hojo "called in their markers" with the Taira, in order to save the boy. But, if so, this explanation beggars the question, why?

That the Hojo were ambitious in their own right is common knowledge. For those who would be successful, being *patient*, planning for the long haul, goes hand-in-hand with any realistic ambition.

In historical hindsight, and in light of Yoritomo's later rise to power, it's not a far stretch to surmise the Hojo were hedging their bets for the long run. Consider: (1) If the Taira remained in power, it was in the Hojo's best interest to continue in the Taira's good graces, remaining "useful" to the Taira.

And/or (2), if by some whim of fortune—and just the right combination of education and egging on—young Yoritomo grew to fan his own embers of ambition and smoldering hatred for the Taira into a flame hot enough to not only consume his enemies, but also hot enough for the Hojo to be able to roast a few of their own marshmallows when no one was looking. . . . Well, then, their investment in the boy would more than pay for itself.

In which case, the boy—having grown to manhood under their watchful eye and wily tutelage—would, upon coming into his own, undoubtedly be grateful to the "helpful" Hojo. . . .

And that's exactly how it played out.

Yoritomo learned his lessons well: Honing his innate intelligence while gathering intelligence on his enemy, all the while forming alliances—the enemy of my enemy being my friend.

It took fifteen years of patience and plotting but, by the mid-1180s, the Minamoto and their allies (both overt and, in the case of the Hojo, covert) had grown strong enough to launch a series of devastating attacks against Taira assets and allies, culminating in the major battles at Ichinotani in '84,

Yashima a year later, and the telling battle of Dan-No-Ura in 1185, which effectively sealed the fate of the Taira—the cherry on top of this Samurai slaughter sundae being the suicide of trapped Taira Emperor Antoku.

By the time it was safe enough for the cherry blossoms to emerge in the spring, Yoritomo was already *de facto* ruler of Japan, ushering in the Kamakura Period of Japanese history.

Assuming the title of *Seii Tai-Shogun*,[119] good to his word, Yoritomo was quick to reward those who had first schooled him in "The Thirteen Paths to Power." Thus, immediately upon gaining power, Yoritomo gave his Hojo *patrons* their due.

Rewarded "munificently" by Yoritomo, the Hojo proved to be "exceptional statesmen" during the tumultuous Kamakura Period, e.g., helping crush a revolt of the nobility in 1221; revamping how Emperors were selected; even uniting contentious clans against the Mongol invasions of 1274 and 1281. They are even credited with promoting the Zen school of Buddhism, which soon became synonymous with the Bushido warrior ethic (Ratti and Westbrook, 1973).

As quick as he had been to reward his friends and allies, Yoritomo was quicker still to deal with anyone and everyone who had dared stand in his way.

And, just to be on the safe—Sons of Brutus—side, he began systematically killing off anyone he thought might pose a future problem to his rule.

Topping Yoritomo's pragmatic hit list was his popular half brother, Yoshitsune.

Strangely, Yoritomo's killing of his half brother has garnered him more condemnation than his wiping out entire family lines—the Sons of Brutus, again—and cutting bloody swathes through provinces and territories resistant to his novel "One Man/One Rule" concept.

Thus, despite his great accomplishments, Yoritomo has often been condemned by more "genteel" historians, those incapable of understanding that certain times demand certain hands. Harsh times, harsh hands. Indeed, Yoritomo has often been mentioned in the same breath as Stalin.

---

119. A combination of *Seii-shi,* literally "He who fights against barbarians" and *Taisho,* "General-in-Chief" of the Emperor's army.

To his dubious credit, a testament to his having fully grasped the "Sons of Brutus" concept,[120] like Stalin, Yoritomo outlived his enemies.

Ironically the warlord who succeeded in ultimately bridling and breaking the wild stallion that was Japan before his determined—and harsh—hand seized the reins, finished out his remarkable life by mundanely dying from a fall from his horse.

Following his death in 1199, the power of the Minamoto fell into the hands of the Hojo. This is perhaps apropos seeing as how the Hojo had been so instrumental in shepherding the Minamoto back into power in the first place. The Hojo would rule quite well over Japan for the next two centuries, until 1334, when Imperial power was restored to the Emperor.

Worthy of noting is the efforts and effect of Yoritomo's "astute, crafty, resourceful and heroic"[121] wife, the Lady Masa, a candidate for the Black Lotus[122] if ever there was one, accordingly:

> During her husband's lifetime she wielded immense influence and after his death she virtually ruled the empire. This seems to be the only recorded instance in the history of Japan when the supreme power was wielded by a woman who was neither Empress nor Empress-dowager. Nominally, of course, Lady Masa did not rule, but her power and influence were very real. (Gerald Mere)[123]

As you will come to understand in a moment, the operative word when speaking of Lady Masa is "influence," as it is when speaking of her husband.

---

120. The closest Japanese rendering might be *Masakatsu!*, literally, "Whatever it takes!" to get the job done right the first time.

121. Ratti and Westbrook, 1974.

122. For more on this pan-Asian all-female secret society see: "Secrets of the Black Lotus" in Lung and Prowant's *Mental Dominance* (Citadel Press, 2009) and in Dr. Lung's *The Sinister Mind* (Citadel Press, 2011).

123. Gerald Mere, "Japanese Women, Ancient and Modern" in *Transactions and Proceedings of the Japanese Society,* Vol. 18–19, London, 1920–1922.

THE THIRTEEN PATHS TO POWER

While moralists never tire of belittling Yoritomo's accomplishments by claiming he "indiscriminately" slaughtered his way to power, nothing could be further from the truth. . . .

Yoritomo's "slaughters," when demanded of him, were most *discriminate*! More the surgeon's scalpel than the psycho's axe.

So while Yoritomo was not above making swift and sanguine examples of any who stood in his way, the deeper truth is that, following the example (and counsel) of his Hojo mentors, Yoritomo used diplomacy just as often as he did decapitation, wrapping his terrible swift steel in more seductive silk whenever and wherever possible, prudent, and profitable.

Early on, young Yoritomo learned that the easiest, truest path to both conquest and total control, over both individuals and empire, depended on one's ability to exert *influence*.

The exercise of "influence"—substituting one's own will for that of others—was hardly a unique concept. By Yoritomo's day ancient principles and ploys of manipulation and military success codified by such masters as Kautilya, "The Indian Machiavelli,"[124] and Chinese strategists the T'ai Kung[125] and the great Sun Tzu[126] were already well known in Japan.

No surprise then that, by the time they had taken young Yoritomo under their corvine wing, Hojo strategists, in their notoriously efficient manner, had already "distilled" the dark elixir of exerting influence into an even more intoxicating tonic guaranteed to stagger and swoon even the most stubborn of opponents.

The *first* equation in the manipulation math the Hojo taught Yoritomo is also the *last* of power principles:

INFLUENCE = POWER

---

124. See "Kings, Kautilya, and Kipling" in Lung and Prowant's *Mental Dominance* (Citadel, 2009).

125. See "The Six Secrets of T'ai Kung Kung-fu" in Lung and Prowant's *Mind Assassins* (Citadel Press, 2010).

126. See "Sun Tzu Storms the Gate!" in Lung and Prowant's *Mind Warrior* (Citadel Press, 2010).

The Hojo divided their "Thirteen Paths to Power" into "The Twelve Cuts" (*nuki tauke*)[127] and "The Final Cut" (*kiri tsuke*).

As much of their intrigues, espionage and out-and-out conspiracies often took place, or at least took root, while they were forced to at least feign civility at the courts of suspicious Daimyo and/or when visiting the Imperial Court, where displays of undisguised dislike and disrespect, let alone displaying open hostility or revelation of hidden allegiances, could literally prove fatal.[128] In response to such restrictions (and if only for the common sense of not wanting an eavesdropping enemy to become privy to their conspiracies), the Hojo mastered the art of euphemism, innuendo, and "side-talk," their overt speech conveying covert messages.

One such way the Hojo communicated surreptitiously was by making reference to the popular Chinese game of *Mah Jongg*, based on similar games played in China since before 500 B.C.

In Mah Jongg, players hold thirteen domino-like tiles, undoubtedly the inspiration for the Hojo organizing their "Paths to Power" along thirteen routes/sections.

An underlying sinister note to the Hojo use of "13": In the West, the number "13" is considered unlucky while, in the East, the number "4" is avoided as equally unlucky. This is because the word for "4" is *shi*, which in turn is a homonym for "death" to both Chinese and Japanese. Curiously, so far as the Hojo's thirteen paths to power are concerned, "13" breaks down in numerology (still a potent belief in the East) to "1 + 3" As in 1 + 3 = 4. This is a subtle way for the Hojo to remind themselves (and students like Yoritomo) that these thirteen paths, correctly navigated, indeed lead to power for self and doom for your enemy.

Incorrectly applied, inattention to detail dooms oneself.

---

127. This and the following term are also used in *Iaido,* the Samurai art of drawing the sword. See "Iaido: Secrets of the 'Fast Draw'" in Lung and Prowant's *Mind Warrior* (Citadel Press, 2010).

128. As in the much-heralded case of Lord Asano of "Forty-seven Ronin" fame being ordered to commit *seppuku* after allowing himself to be goaded by a rival into drawing his sword in anger while on Imperial grounds—a capital offense. For the complete tale, see Lung and Prowant's *Black Science* (Paladin Press, 2001) and their *Mind Manipulation* (Citadel Press, 2002).

FYI: This same "*shi*" syllable is found in the Japanese word for warrior, *bushi*, where *shi* (death) is paired with *bu* (sword).

YORITOMO'S "TWELVE CUTS"

Influence equaling power, following the Hojo school of thought, Yoritomo employed the twelve[129] "Paths" (or, as he preferred "Cuts") to gaining influence (as in *total control!*) over others. They are detailed in the chapters that follow.

The Power of Psychic Forces

"Psychic Forces" is a synonym for mental ability and agility. This includes (1) our powers of perception, (2) concentration, and (3) decision-making.

Yoritomo believed (based on his firsthand observations) that we all have an innate need for what he called "the perpetual pursuit of the highest," a desire to strive to be the best we can be, to experience and express ourselves fully. Says Dangennes:

> The struggle for life becomes more and more arduous, and the power of our hidden faculties should expand in accordance with ever-growing necessities.

In other words, if not born with the innate ability to adapt (and we're all born with at least a smidgin of this evolutionary deal-breaker!), then we had better go out of our way to *develop* the ability to adapt.

Learn to think on your feet if you want to *stay* on your feet!

Several hundred years after Yoritomo's time, on the other side of the world, philosophical bad boy Friedrich Nietzsche (1844–1900) called this same innate evolutionary urge to adapt to—and *influence*—the world around us the "Will to Power."

According to Nietzsche, failing to live up to this potential, either because of our own indolence or else by cause of deliberate interference from our

---

129. In the interest of continuity and brevity, we follow the same ordering of these twelve "Cuts" as rendered into English via Yoritomo translator and interpreter B. Dangennes in 1916. See *How to Exert Influence* by Taisho Yoritomo. Trans. B. Dangennes (Kessinger Publications, 1916).

adversaries, creates that vague smoldering of dissatisfaction within us that an alert and incendiary adversary can all too easily fan into more destructive flames of self-doubt, self-loathing, and defeatism.

Of course, if you're already smart enough to pay attention, then you're probably also smart enough to take steps to, if not increase, then at least safeguard what Yoritomo describes as "the power of our hidden faculties," those abilities of a trained mind he calls "Psychic Forces."

Yoritomo's "Psychic Forces" has little to do with what we think of today as "ESP." Instead, his ideal is the full development (and often *ruthless* unleashing!) of our mental ("psychic") abilities ("forces").

Ergo, the first step on the "path" to personal power (vouchsafed by our growing power over others), thus the first step to increasing our overall influence—if only in order to better protect ourselves—is to make full use of our mental abilities.

It's a myth—and an oft-used *excuse!*—that "the average human being only uses 10 percent of his brain."

The fact of the matter is that the average person only uses his brain 10 percent *effectively*.

The cure to this is obvious: *Refuse to be average!*

And, thanks to Yoritomo (by way of the Hojo), we have a clear curriculum for increasing (or, at the very least, safeguarding) our innate mental processes by:

1. Increasing Our Power of Perception. This means paying closer attention to life around us. To what is seen, and to what (and whom) may be going out of their way not to be seen.

Keep in mind that *we can't trust our own perceptions*.[130]

On the positive side, our enemy can't trust *his* perceptions either. . . . Making it all the easier for us to go out of our way to lead him even further astray (once we learn to patch up the defects and deficits in our own faulty perceptions). Or, as Shihan Peter Gilbert tells his Shotokan students when they complain about Anatomy being part of their required studies: "The more you know about how human beings are put together. . . . The easier it is to take them apart!"

2. Increasing Our Power of Concentration. Simply paying closer atten-

---

130. See "Understanding the Mind" in Lung and Prowant's *Mind Manipulation* (Citadel Press, 2002).

tion (easier said than done!) helps here, as does learning to meditate[131] and. . . .

3. *Increasing Your Ability to Make Decisions.* We should qualify that as the goal being to make *good* decisions. (More on how to do this in the next chapter.)

The Power of Persuasion

Exerting influence by using the power of persuasion requires our subtly bringing ourselves more into sync with another person in order to "nudge" them in the direction and into the deeds we desire. We do this in four main ways:

1. *Establishing Trust.* Human beings establish trust by banishing suspicion. If you give people no reason to think you're "up to something," they probably won't think you're up to something.

Loyal readers of Dr. Lung know "There's no such thing as *altruism*. Everybody gets paid." So, when approaching another person with the goal of persuading them to see (and do) things your way, first tell them *what's in it for them* . . . and then, *what's in it for you*. (Of course, you can always *lie!*)

People are *by nature* suspicious of other people—strangers in particular—offering to do something for them "out of the kindness of their heart."

That doesn't mean that there aren't true "Good Samaritans" in the world, there are. But even these do-gooders "get paid" (if only with warm feelings that they "did the right thing" and/or that their particular God loves them).

Therefore, when approaching a target, uh . . . mark, uh . . . *fellow human being* with a proposition, rather than promise how you're going to make *them* all kinds of money out of the kindness of your heart, instead, you'll have a better chance of their saying "yes" if you come with the approach, "I know a way we can *both* profit. . . ." This also implies you will be sharing half of any *risk* involved in the mutual venture, giving you and your prospective "partner" something in common. "Something in common" = *bonding*, and we don't "bond" with people we're suspicious of.

---

131. For a complete course on everything you'll need to know about how to meditate, see "Jing Gong Senses Training" in Dr. Lung's *Mind Penetration* (Citadel Press, 2007).

2. Learning to Listen. First up, this means learning to listen not only to what others are saying but also to what they're *not* saying—30 percent conscious/70 percent unconscious! What they're *not* saying may be more important than what they are saying.[132]

Second, we need to learn to *listen to ourselves* more, to that "gut feeling" that "something's just not kosher. . . ."

Your "gut" (that funny "butterflies" feeling in the pit of your stomach, those hairs standing up at the nape of your neck) evolved millenia before your always-second-guessing, oh-so-politically correct "higher reasoning" frontal cortex part of your brain.

What they don't tell you is that "higher reasoning" is synonymous with *slower* reasoning. Slower reasoning is never the first hog to the trough.

3. Don't Browbeat. Learn to win gracefully. On the great playing field of life, there's a fifteen-yard penalty for too much end-zone shenanigans.

Okinawan Karate saint Gichin Funakoshi warned, "Slay, but never humiliate." Likewise, Sun Tzu warned we should always leave an enemy a way out, that backing an enemy into a corner only makes them double their resistance.

Just as important: Recognizing when the other person is ready to give in.

4. At Least Pretend to Sympathize. While we in the West hold "sympathy" to be one of the more nobler virtues (thought synonymous to "caring and compassion"), people in the East (just as caring and compassionate as their Western counterparts) also accept that "sympathy" can have its dark side.

Thus, in the East, "sympathy" is listed as one of the "Five Weaknesses," derived from the Chinese *wu-hsing* (Earth, Air, Fire, Water, and Void, the five original "elements" composing all things. In Japanese, *Gojo-goyoku*).

In English we call these "the Five Warnings F.L.A.G.S.," composed of Fear, Lust, Anger, Greed and, finally, *Sympathy*.

Sympathy, in the negative, makes us drop our guard when we see an old lady drop her purse, hear a baby or puppy crying somewhere in the darkened park, or see a stranger stranded by the side of the road. Not that all of these examples can't be valid "humanitarian" reasons for risking life-and-limb (as opposed to dialing 911 and waiting for *the professionals* to arrive . . .).

---

132. See "Shadow Language" in Lung and Prowant's *Mind Manipulation* (Citadel Press, 2001).

Keep in mind that these scenes can also be set up by those possessing a little less "Samaritan" sentiment than yourself. . . .

Of course, convincingly *pretending* to share your target's concerns, hopes, and fears is the perfect way to bond with them. Misery really *does* love company. It's human nature to like people who are like us, even if the only thing they share in common is suffering.

THE POWER OF YOUR EYES

"Few persons escape the influence of the human eye. If its look is imperious, it subjugates; if it is tender, it moves; if it is sad it penetrates the heart with melancholy."
—Dangennes

From that stern look of reproach from parents and teachers that we're taught to cringe from as children, to those alluring, wallet-sucking looks cast by that babe sitting across the bar from you, to the hypnotic, will-sapping gaze of Rasputin and his reincarnation Charlie Manson, it's no secret eyes hold the power to scold, seduce, stupify.

But just because "it's no secret" doesn't mean most people are *consciously* aware of the effect others' eyes have on them, nor the potential their own *practiced* gaze can have over others.

In *Mind Manipulation* (Citadel Press, 2002), we learned the importance of making eye contact for effective communication, as well as taking the time to learn how to read another person's eyes in order to tell when they're lying through their teeth. Crash course in liar-spotting: Looking to the left usually indicates true remembering, while repeated glances to the right are often a tip-off a person is being less than truthful.[133]

Yoritomo takes this *defensive* study of the eyes to the next—*offensive*—level, teaching us how to extend our influence over others by deliberately developing the ability to better communicate (i.e., influence and *control!*) with our eyes. We do this by allowing our emotions—sincere or fake—to freely,

---

133. See also "Who Lies . . . and How to Catch Them Doing It!" in Lung and Prowant's *Mind Warrior* (Citadel Press, 2010) and also Dr. Lung's *The Truth about Lying* (Publication pending for 2011).

deliberately, and with direction, flow from our eyes. This means not only investing the time to develop a forceful, dominating stare (guaranteed to stop someone dead in their tracks!), it also means mastering those sincere and sympathetic (compassionate and caring) looks that are the key to unlocking the heart of another.

Stop to consider for a moment what all a person's eyes can tell us about them . . . or *them* about *us*:

- Eyes downcast tell people you're subservient . . . and no threat.
- Eyes demurely turned aside tells a person you're modest . . . and maybe just a little shy. (Seduction Guy Tip: Gals love it when you do the "shy guy" routine.)
- Eyes wide means you're very interested in both the other person and in what they're saying. (Throw a smile in for good measure.)
- A wink with a broad smile can hasten friendship.
- A wink with a petite (and moist) smile can open the door to passion.
- Locking eyes with another person before then glancing side-to-side quickly can cause, at the least curiosity, *in extremis* fear and paranoia. (One of the simplest of distraction techniques: Suddenly look right/exit stage left!)

Thus, with a single *practiced* glance we can show approval that promotes bonding, incite passion, or sow confusion and paranoia.

Human beings have a natural "mirroring response" that, at its most basic, makes us smile when we see someone else smile, while inducing us to (unconsciously) also adopt a sad or fearful visage in response. (To prove this to yourself, you need only observe other people while they're watching a heart-warming movie scene—they're faces mirroring those of the smiling actors on the screen.

In the same way, we can affect others by deliberately adapting our eyes to fit the emotion we are trying to get the other person to "share."

Conversely, we can "dominate" and cow another person via our fierce gaze. The "trick"[134] to staring someone down is not to look directly into

---

134. "Tricks" well-mastered are called "techniques." "Techniques" half-learned are merely "tricks."

their eyes but, rather, to fix your gaze directly *between* their eyes. Since the other person's eyes might blink or else dart around rabbit-like (distracting you in turn), by fixing your eyes *between* their eyes, your own gaze will not waver and, soon, their gaze will falter altogether.

THE POWER OF WORDS AND SPEECH

"If you're scared *to ask,*
you'll probably be terrified *by the answer."*
—C. B. Black

Yoritomo advised us to keep it short and sweet, warning that "too great wealth of words is hostile to conviction," and that:

> The word is the most direct manifestation of thought; hence it is one of the most important agents of Influence when it clothes itself with precision and clearness, indispensable in cooperating in creating conviction in the minds of one's hearer.

Yoritomo was well ahead of his time in understanding the value of concise, targeted propaganda. And he practically pioneered the idea of countering "Short-Attention-Span Syndrome" with a well-crafted sound bite. According to Yoritomo:

> Those that know how to present their thought in a few phrases, in a way that impresses itself on their listeners, may easily become leaders of the masses.

Yoritomo's method for creating simple and effective messages stresses five main points:

1. Think deeply on what you want to say beforehand.
2. Transform your thoughts into images.
3. Transform your thoughts into images by using incisive words that . . .
4. Draw mental pictures you can easily . . .
5. Implant in the minds of others using "the form of lights and shades" (i.e., openness when appropriate, subterfuge when necessary—don't lie unless you *have* to.)

Yoritomo's "Rules of Speech" should likewise be practiced:

1. Speak with conciseness.
2. Speak with clearness.
3. Speak with moderation. Less is more. Never invest five-dollar words in a fifty-cent conversation.
4. Speak with discretion. Warns Yoritomo: "From indiscretion to lying the step is short. . . ."

Yoritomo was also ahead of his time in that he figured out about those "mirror" neurons we all have in our head, neurons that make us unconsciously mimic others' facial expressions and body language and, as previously mentioned, can also cause us to unconsciously "share" others' emotions.

Yoritomo intuitively understood such "mirroring," advising that, rather than remain victim to such "mirroring," we recognize it and, whenever possible, turn it to our advantage:

> Speech is the distributor of the thoughts that surround us, of which the reiterated suggestions, after impregnating certain groups of cells in our brain, travel by affinity to haunt the same group of brain-cells in other auditors.

In other words, rather than us being *unconsciously* influenced (and *controlled?*) by others' "mental telepathy" (in the all-too-real physiological fact of neuron "mirroring"), it behooves us to study to develop our own ability to *consciously* project intentional "mirroring" on our part, influencing others without their being aware of it.

THE POWER OF YOUR EXAMPLE

*"Our most frequent associations are never indifferent to our
mentality, and we always submit, voluntarily or unconsciously,
to the ascendancy of those that surround us, unless we have
sufficient influence over their minds to compel them to submit
themselves to us."*
—Yoritomo

This sounds an awful lot like what we in the West call "peer pressure,"
the influence others—cohorts and coconspirators—have over us.

We'd like to think this is something we grow out of once we survive
puberty but, the fact is, we're influenced by others all our lives—from the
slang we speak to the clothes we wear to the politicians we pick. So few of
us are self-starters.

And those who go out of their way to protest how *they* are *never* influenced by others—these would be the same people claiming that hypnosis,
con games, and cult lures *never* work on them—are, like Lady Hamlet,
betrayed by their own loud protest:

*"Those who claim they're not interested in what others think of
them . . . already know **exactly** what others think of them!"*
—C. B. Black

The only sure way to insure you don't fall victim to such "peer pressure"
is to make sure *you* are the peer putting the pressure out there.

"Peer pressure" being just another name for "influence," and our having
already been taught by Yoritomo that "Influence = Power," we can now
harken to the advice—or is it warning?—from J. Paul Getty (1892–1976)
that "No psychological weapon is more potent than example." In other
words, you're not only known by the company you keep, you're also *influenced*
by them.

We influence those around us. They, in turn, influence us, sometimes
forming a positive protective network, one that strengthens our position in
life, stimulates our imagination, and ultimately challenges our abilities—
making us better people, making us stronger in the long run.

Conversely, our associations can also be negative, as we find ourselves trapped in toxic relationships, surrounded by emotional vampires and what Chuck Norris has dubbed "shadow warriors,"[135] people in our circle who siphon off our life energy, draining our life's blood while simultaneously ravaging our resources.

It's been said, "You can't teach what you don't know, you can't lead where you don't go!" Sure you can. High school phys-ed coaches are routinely called in to pinch-hit for sick algebra teachers, and political leaders no longer fight beside the soldiers they so callously send to die in senseless wars.

Come crunch-time, you "fake it till you can make it" . . . or at least until you can make it out the door.

Would you really be surprised to learn that, in *most* situations, *most* people have no clue what the hell they're doing? That's why *most* people are so relieved when some "take charge guy" (or gal) steps up to the plate who does *seem* to know what he or she is doing—someone willing to take the *responsibility* off them, i.e., the weight of making decisions they probably won't get the credit for if they're successful, and will *definitely* have to take the blame for when things go horribly wrong!

No surprise (again) that a lot of women (and probably quite a few men) are looking for this type of guy.

We lead by example. We teach by example. And, whether we're consciously aware of it, we are influenced by the example of others. Call it "awe" or idol worship—*it is* (mixed in with a little envy). We learn from the example of others, consciously or unconsciously imitating those examples.

Nothing inspires the faint of heart so much as seeing the example of a lone hero standing his ground against impossible odds. In fiction: Gary Cooper in *High Noon* (1952). In fact, that lone protestor defiantly blocking the path of Chinese army tanks sent to crush the pro-democracy demonstration in Tiananmen Square in 1989.

Mastering the art of speaking confidently (paired with the right body language needed to "sell" your confident demeanor), will instantly make you a person whose "example" others want to follow.

Standing up to "take charge" during a crisis (whether the office copier needs fixing, or helping coordinate rescue efforts during a *real* emergency)

---

135. See *The Secret Power Within: Zen Solutions to Real Problems* by Chuck Norris (Little, Brown and Company, NY, 1998).

will (1) influence people to look up to your example and (2) inspire them to do likewise by *following* your example.

Of course, were you of a more diabolical bent, you might have been the one who set up the "crisis" in the first place, just so you could arrive in the nick of time to play "hero." It's called "C.H.A.O.S. Theory" as in "Create Hassles (Hardships, Hurdles, etc.) And (then) Offer Solutions."[136]

> *"Ability and achievement are bona fides no one dares question, no matter how unconventional the man who presents them."*
> —J. Paul Getty[137]

THE POWER OF YOUR PSYCHIC INFLUENCES

So far as Yoritomo is concerned, "psychic influences" is best defined as "the art of substituting for the want of resolution in others our own will, which they obey blindly, sometimes unconsciously, ever glad to feel themselves guided and directed by a moral power which they cannot elicit themselves."[138]

Yoritomo himself is quick to point out that this overpowering "Psychic" (i.e., mental) influence is not some magical ESP-like force, nor is it outright hypnotism—though, as a student of the Black Science, you'll quickly spot elements of hypnosis technique in Yoritomo's description.[139]

Yoritomo goes on to describe *psychic influence* as "an intensity of determination" that surges outward from us like a wave, washing over and inundating the will of others. Says Yoritomo:

It is not necessary to have, as many pretend, recourse in magic in order to become past masters in the art of influencing our fellows; what is needed above all is to keep ourselves constantly in a condition of will-power sufficient to

---

136. See "How to Create C.H.A.O.S." in Lung and Prowant's *Mind Warrior* (Citadel Press, 2010).

137. See "Getty's Five" in Dr. Haha Lung's *Mind Control* (Citadel Press, 2006).

138. B. Dangennes, in Yoritomo, 1916.

139. See section on "Hypnosis" in Lung and Prowant's *Black Science* (Paladin Press, 2001) and their *Mind Manipulation* (Citadel Press, 2002). See also *666 Devilish Secrets of Hypnosis* by C. B. Black (Publication pending).

impose our commands on minds capable only of obedience. Intensity of determination, when it reaches a certain point, possesses a dazzling influence which few ordinary mortals can resist, for it envelops them before they are aware of it and thus before they have dreamt of endeavoring to withdraw themselves from it.

What Yoritomo phrases as "will-power" and then "intensity of determination" boils down to our ability to (1) focus and (2) make others focus on what you want them to focus on.

As even the cheapest, most cheesiest of "Hypnotism 101" manuals emphasizes, the basis for all hypnosis is getting your subject to *focus* their attention pin-point on both the sound of your voice and/or on the visual constant you present them (e.g., metronome, swinging pendulum, revolving "hypno-disk," etc.). As any accomplished hypnotist will tell you, getting people to "focus" is the hard part, "putting them under" (once you get them to focus), much easier.

Focus is transferable. This is, to a great extent, what Yoritomo refers to as "psychic influences." In other words, and this harkens back to "Increasing Your Influence by Your Example," people "pick up on," they "tune in" to our emotions *and to our focus*.

When we appear focused—projecting calm and confidence in general, all our attention trained to a specific task in particular—others cannot but find their own attention drawn, first to us and then, with perhaps just a little coaxing, toward the object of our attention. This response in others to our projected focus is triggered by those "mirror neurons" we discussed earlier.

Simple, huh? Increase your own powers of focus.

The secret to developing your powers of *mental* focus, counterintuitively, begins on the *physical* level.

You may recall that young Yoritomo's patrons, the Hojo, are credited with introducing the Zen (Ch. *Chan*) school of Buddhism to Japan where, in short order, it was embraced by, and soon became synonymous with, the Samurai warrior class.

Zen took root in the life-or-death world of the Samurai because, at its most basic practice, it helped the Samurai to *focus*—the ability to focus being *the* consummate warrior skill.

Schools of Zen vary in their philosophical estimations of how quickly a

Zen student might achieve "enlightenment" (some arguing for instantaneous enlightenment, others insisting a student must spend years in deep and dedicated meditation to achieve the next level of understanding).[140]

What Zen schools all agree on is the basic methodology of Zen meditation, more correctly *Zazen* "sitting meditation."

First, you sit, your body said to resemble that of a mountain. In fact, the Chinese term for the Indian import *dhyana* ("meditation") is *Chan* (often spelled *Shan* in the West), *shan* also meaning "mountain."

Then you *breathe*, in and out, concentrating only on your breathing. When your attention drifts, you gently pull it back.

As you breathe in your initial breath, mentally visualize the letter *Z*, the letter we often associate with relaxing and, ultimately, going to sleep (i.e., "Catch some Z's").

Having breathed in a full *Z* breath, feeling it fill your lungs all the way down to your stomach, now gently push the breath out of your lungs while visualizing the letter *E* for "exhale."

Having firmly (but not forcefully) emptied your lungs, breathe in a second breath, in your mind seeing the letter *N* (think "in").

When exhaling this breath, mentally count "1."

Repeat this process as long as you meditate to a "Z-E-N-1," repeating the process, finishing with "Z-E-N-2, 3, 4" in turn. Completing your fourth cycle, begin again at "Z-E-N-1."

You can use this Z-E-N meditation the next time you feel anxious, or even angry, to help "center" yourself.

Also, before attempting to "influence" someone to see things *your* way, first take the time to take a deep *Z* breath, exhaling (*E*) slowly as you smile, looking the other person in the eyes (actually, *between* their eyes, remember?), as you slowly but firmly say, "I *need* you to do X *because* you're the only one who can do X."

Speaking (1) slowly and (2) firmly and (3) as quietly as possible so long as the person targeted can still hear you, all make the person *focus* on you. This kind of "trailing off," lowering your voice almost to a whisper, will make them unconsciously lean in closer to you, adding an air of conspiracy-bonding to your talk.

---

140. See: *The Samurai and the Sacred* by Stephen Turnbull (Osprey Publishing, 2006).

THE POWER OF MAKING EFFECTIVE DECISIONS

We admire people who can make expedient, effective decisions.

And we like it when others see us as someone capable of making expedient, effective decisions. Being around someone capable of making expedient, effective decisions makes us feel safe.

Quiet as it's kept, people like being around movers and shakers who can make expedient, effective decisions *for them* because it removes responsibility (i.e., blame) *from them.*

As much as people, especially Westerners, like to talk big about being "self-starters" and "stepping up" to "do the right thing" and take responsibility, the truth is most people will gladly give up their share of the praise for a job well-done in return for not having to lose sleep worrying about their being caught liable when things go wrong.

We talk a lot about how "it's better to have loved and lost than never to have loved at all" and "it's not whether you win or lose, it's how you play the game" but, deep down, we *do* care whether we win or lose. (Winners get praised while losers get "You couldn't have tried just a little harder?" glances.) That's why, given a choice, most people only play games they know they can win.

Schmooze Hint: When you invite a targeted person (e.g., potential client, prospective love interest) to your playdate, make sure you pick a game they either shine at or else a game you can *convincingly* lose at!

And that's also why, rather than face rejection (again!), most of us opt for "never to have loved" rather than risk having our heart broken (again!).

Sorry fact bottom line: *Most people aren't that good at making decisions.*

Schools today teach regurgitation, not problem-solving.

Not surprising, people being pretty much the same no matter where you look in time or clime, that people were much the same in Yoritomo's time. He observes:

> The majority of the irresolute love to deceive themselves by delusions which their imaginations create, and thus become only too often the architects of their own misfortune.

Right, we're our own worst enemy.

Born stupid, we don't have to remain that way. Bored stupid by society, we need not succumb, at least not permanently.

According to Yoritomo, we can teach ourselves to make better decisions, thereby increasing our influence over others:

> You can instruct yourself in this art [of decision making], so difficult and nevertheless so important, for the influence which he who is accustomed to wise and prompt decisions exerts over others is always considerable.

Yoritomo gives us slight considerations—*requisites*, if you will—that, once in place, help us increase our influence:

Practice Reflection and Concentration. Your Z-E-N meditation will help you with this. Having completed your meditation, when possible, take time to "reflect" (in the military we call this "debriefing"), going over in your mind any recurring thoughts or ideas that may have kept "intruding" on your mediation (alerting you to areas of stress and/or concern). Now concentrate (i.e., give some deliberate attention to) dealing with these areas of concern.

Practice Presence of Mind. Another word for "awareness," presence of mind means taking care of the little things before they become big things—Sun Tzu in a nutshell! Deal with today's problems, better still, the concern of the moment or, as sixties Zen hipsters preferred: "Be here now!" You'll find yourself pleasantly surprised that, having expediently and effectively dealt with the problem of the moment, that you often have "leftover energy" you can "bank" for dealing with future (unforeseen) problems.

Practice Exercising Your Will. This doesn't refer to "willpower" (often just a synonym for "stubbornness"). This "will" is the will of Nietzsche's "Will to Power," that inner reserve of drive and determination we're all born with, that some of us succeed in safeguarding despite society's dogged determination to exorcize this "Will" demon from us.

Your *Will* looks to the next moment, looks to tomorrow, looks far into the future and locks itself on to what it sees there like a pit bull on a pork chop! And, despite all the weathering blows and Will-withering comments and criticisms along the way, despite scorn and scourge—or perhaps because of them!—despite failures from the past resurrected to derail us, in spite of all present protestations and predictions of disasters to come, our Will still refuses to be tempted or torn loose from that future that only its blood-bruised eye alone can see!

Determination is halfway to destiny.[141]

Maintain Energy. Begged, borrowed, or stolen, Will finds the energy to make the hard decisions, expediently and effectively, be that "energy" in the form of functional philosophy, finances, or—best still—*friends* who share the journey with you.

Practice Impartiality. This entails the ability (innate or acquired) to observe truthfully—minus any person "mind-filters foisted upon us by Mama, Drama, or Trauma." Give each man his due . . . after you pay yourself first.

Develop a Desire for Justice. Taoists, Buddhists, even the followers of Confucius, all believed in "balance," that there is a natural "balance" or harmony to the Universe and that it is only man who is so often out-of-balance, so often in need of techniques (e.g., meditation, feng shui, acupuncture, etc.) designed to help "realign" him.

Religions of the West also seek to re-establish what they see as the original Edenic pre-eating of the forbidden fruit "status quo."

And there is the earthly "An eye for an eye" legalistic attempt to balance/redress a wrong committed against one's person.

According to the Gestalt school of psychology, desire for "balance" is one of the natural states of healthy psychological equilibrium.

Of course, helping "restore balance to the universe" has been used by more than one person as a euphemism for bloody revenge. That whole "eye for an eye" thing again.

One man's "revenge" is another man's "justice." And what does blindfolded (or is that *hoodwinked?*) Justice personified, standing on that pedestal outside every court in the land hold in her hand? A balance.

Practice Forethought. Man is so good at hindsight, so good at looking over his shoulder—second-guessin' not only his own decisions, but the decisions of his fellows as well.

To the indolent and the uninitiated, your use of foresight and forethought will seem like you possess some sixth sense—ESP.

"Foresight" doesn't mean you have ESP, it simply means you see the possibilities—and a path to those possibilities—*before* your enemy does. Awareness, attention to detail, chance favors the prepared mind.

---

141. A Charles and Carolyn Shumway contribution, by way of Leanin' Tree, Boulder.

"Forethought" is what carries you *between* your perception and those possibilities. To others, this will, indeed, appear magical.

At this point Yoritomo warns us not to get too cocky:

> We should not confound forethought with the art of divination, although, in the eyes of the vulgar, it sometimes takes on the appearance of it.

Japanese *Ninja* were not above encouraging their enemies to believe they possessed special powers, freely employing *Kyonin-No-Jutsu*, playing on the superstitions of others.

Of course, *you* would never be tempted, or at least never give in to the inevitable temptation to play on the gullibility of others in order to feather your own nest, would you? It's been done many times before:

> He who would influence others should above all things know how to influence himself in order to acquire the faculty of self-concentration which will allow of his reaching the highest degree of discernment. Many soothsayers have owed their influence over the multitude only to that spirit of concentrations that passed for prophecies. It is wrong and delusive to give credence to magic which is trickery, but we bear within us a power equal that of the sorcerers whose deeds are related; this is the magic of the influence which the prudent and self-possessed man always exercises over his fellows.
> (E. B. Condillac)

So merely by our attention to making expedient and effective decisions, others may imagine—and fear!—we have some unnatural power they themselves lack.

Fortunately, as Yoritomo maintains, expedient and effective decision-making can be learned or, already possessing a modicum of decision-making ability, we can always hone that most useful of scalpels to an ever even-finer edge.

Problem Solving 101

"Decision-making" is synonymous with "problem-solving." Sounds simple, except for the too oft-documented fact that—don't be shocked— *most people aren't that good at problem-solving.* Insert *gasp!*

Your problem-solving/decision-making has—or should have—four distinct stages:

Clearly define the problem. As simple as this sounds, most people never get past this initial stage. When you fail to pass beyond this initial stage, it's called "bitchin'."

The more initially specific you can be about a problem, the better your chances of ultimately finding a solution to that problem.

Often people ignore this process of clearly defining a problem because they lack the personal skill to do so (in which case, don't be afraid to ask/or hire someone more familiar/more expert with this type of problem that you are).

When looking over your problem, whenever possible, *break your big problem down into a list of smaller, more manageable problems* (steps), solving each "smaller problem" as a way of making the "big" problem less intimidating.

Brainstorm your options. Write down every possible solution to your problem, no matter how seemingly far-fetched those options. This accomplishes two things:

First, writing something down, maybe even scribbling a doodle or two, engages *more* of your brain, putting different areas of your brain to work on the problem.

Second, initially entertaining *all* possible solutions, no matter how "crazy" and unlikely, helps stimulate your imagination. In a group brainstorming session, entertaining "far-fetched" and "out there" ideas can sometimes elicit laughter, lightening mood and increasing the group's overall relaxation—relaxation in and of itself being conducive to brainstorming.

Prioritize your most realistic options. Cut your written-down brainstormed ideas by half, keeping only those *six* options with the most likelihood of success. . . . Now, cut them in half again, arranging the *three options* you have left in order of "most doable."

"Most doable" takes into consideration every bit of *reality*[142] you can cram in. This includes such factors as (1) your presently available resources, (2) personnel, and (3) energy you can *realistically* apply to implementing your option plans.

Implement your first best option. Just do it!

---

142. As opposed to "really-like-it-to-be."

Adjust and adapt. Tweak and fine-tune your solution as need be to keep it viable and moving (at the speed you've already calculated) in the direction of ultimately solving the problem.

If necessary, be prepared to move on to your second option, and then your third, keeping those elements of options one and two that were the most viable and the most likely to augment option three.

Be prepared to repeat the process. Failure, when it occurs, is almost always the result of a "glitch" at step one—not having clearly defined the problem, which, in turn, inevitably poisons your next step: prioritizing. This would be the "planting" stage.

Else, failure occurs at the "harvesting" stage, with a failure of implementation. This can result from something as simple as required material not arriving when and where needed, or from faulty personnel—wrong person in the wrong place at the wrong time.

When things go south, when the fecal matter collides with the oscillating rotor in the worst possible way . . . *suck it up*. Accept responsibility. Retreat. Reorganize. Redeploy.

Don't waste time playing "The Blame Game."

Account for unforeseen material problems—it's called "logistics." Note any inadequacies and idiosyncrasies of personnel that might be responsible.

There is much disagreement on when—and how—to punish indolent, indecisive, insubordinate, or just "in-the-way" workers.

One school of thought advises openly punishing one person as an *example* to others. Hence the ancient Chinese adage: "Kill one to control ten thousand."

In the West this was the idea behind what in Middle Ages Europe was known as "The Theatre of Hell"—the gruesome public torture and execution of criminals. The obvious idea being that if Little Johnny sees his brother Billy get his behind paddled, then Johnny will think twice about doing the same thing.

Sure, works sometimes.

However, in group problem-solving, publicly dressing-down an employee *will* terrorize most of your other employees. Unfortunately, depending on the justification and/or severity of your punishment, it could have the opposite effect: paralyzing and preventing your remaining employees from calling attention to themselves (by offering new ideas) out of fear of failing and suffering similar punishment.

The other school of thought says that punishment should be delayed during the course of an operation, until the successful completion of that operation—when rewards *and punishments* are normally doled out.

Of course, when following this latter course, it's still possible (and advisable) to *subtly* shift (some call it "give a promotion to") the offender to responsibilities where they can do the least amount of harm to the project.

Your decision.

THE POWER OF EXHIBITING AMBITION

"It is by believing steadfastly that we shall attain the highest power, that we shall acquire the qualities that make a man almost more than a man, since they allow him to govern and subdue those by whom he is surrounded."
—Yoritomo

Nowadays, "ambition" is a dirty word. But back in Yoritomo's day, a man was known—and often *feared!*—for his ambition:

> It is not given to all to possess in themselves the aggressive spirit necessary to command the influences which must emanate from our brain in order to result in forming the convictions of others.

Yeah, nowadays, if you're *caught* trying to better yourself, of being a "real go-getter," you'll just as likely be accused of being "ambitious," implying you somehow "think you're better" than the next guy (or gal); "ambitious" more and more becoming synonymous with being racist, sexist, or otherwise chauvinistic.

The retort to this kind of thinking begins with an "F" and ends with a "you" . . . Right, "Forget *them*, remember *you!*"

You can't be good to anyone else unless you first take the time to improve your own lot in life.

Two stupid people standing together do not somehow increase the overall IQ in the room. Just the opposite. One stupid apple can corrupt the whole barrel.

And, if you're one of those people somehow "offended" by our use of the word "stupid" . . . well, maybe that's 'cause it's hitting a little too close to home!

By first strengthening yourself, you naturally put yourself in a better position to help those you care about, to influence not only your own life, but the lives of those around you.

Yoritomo gives two examples of how personal ambition is a good thing, of how it helps increase our influence:

First, ambition shows we have courage and boldness, making us an example to be held up to others, inspiring courage in others.

Second, ambition is the cure for poverty. Says Yoritomo:

> Poverty is only allowable if it is voluntary, that is to say, if it is the result of a decision which prefers that condition to another more brilliant but less independent . . . Nevertheless, riches are the key to many marvels and they are above all the key of many influences.

In other words, *rich* good . . . *poverty* bad.

Riches give us the power to help others, as well as a means of exciting interest and influencing the multitude. Thus Yoritomo points out the obvious:

> The poor man exercises little influence over the multitude.

While running after riches in and of itself is not an exalted ideal, being rich has several benefits beyond just being the concrete evidence of our ability to make decisions, solve problems, map out a campaign—be it military or monetary—and sojourn that campaign through to success.

The righteous man may influence us through his words and actions to be righteous ourselves. Likewise the bull of a man would influence us to kiss his ass, his riches being just another carrot *and stick* he can hold over the heads of those less fortunate.

Riches in and of themselves are far from evil. Remember: It is the *want* of money that's the "root of all evil," not any particular portrait of George Washington.

"Money can't buy happiness". . . . Oh really? Tell that to the hungry kid who just got fed. Tell it to yourself when you're rich enough to fly in that cancer specialist to save your mother, your wife, your child. . . .

Of course "ambition" and "being rich" are not necessarily synonymous.

Hitler was ambitious, but hardly concerned with amassing great wealth. (In his case, it *literally* came with the "territory"!) Other political leaders of equal or aspiring bent likewise seem more concerned with amassing power rather than actually accumulating wealth.

In this sense then, "ambition" can be likened to "drive," more similar to Nietzsche's "Will to Power" than to opening a savings account.

In this regard, Yoritomo tells us that true ambition should be:

- *Without false modesty*
- *Without unworthy means*
- *Without intrigue*
- *Without illusion*

According to Yoritomo, these four are the flaws in character that a wily enemy can spy out and exploit.

"Without false modesty" means being justifiably proud of one's accomplishments, hence feeling no "shame" (i.e., having no hesitation) in freely employing those assets and accomplishments we've rightfully acquired.

"Without unworthy means" refers to our having acquired our wealth and wherewithal through honorable means . . . an "ideal" in any age. One that goes hand-in-hand with having acquired our wealth and exercised our ambition "without intrigue."

There's a reason they're called "ideals." Just remember that, while you're taking the high ground, shooting for lofty ideals, your enemy may be satisfied with taking potshots at your privates!

It's a tried-and-true observation that "the winners write the history books." So, if you don't ever want anyone to write something bad about you . . . make sure *you* are the one left to tell the tale when the smoke clears.

Being "without illusion" refers not only to doing things "above board," dealing honestly with folks when possible, "without illusions" also refers, most importantly, to holding no false illusions yourself.

At the risk of being redundant, that's *false* illusions, again: seeing things in *reality* versus seeing them as we'd *really-like-them-to-be*.

As to the inevitable detractors, backbiters and out-and-out "haters" you'll collect along the way the more you follow your ambition, Yoritomo gives us this advice for how an ambitious and successful man keeps his head above the murky waters of envy and conspiracy:

He lifts his eyes too high to recognize the vulgar herd of the envious who swarm around his feet, he is content to spurn them with the tip of his shoe; unless, overmuch beset or tormented by their incessant attacks, he crushes them under foot, as we do with an importune insect, which we try at first to drive away and which we destroy, without ill feeling, simply to rid ourselves of its repeated and irritating stings.

Yoritomo came from the "No guilt" school.

Having invested your time and effort into mastering this "Art of Influence," you must never feel guilty when you find you can so easily—effortlessly—exercise this power over others.

Should the alert tiger feel guilty for snatching the distracted monkey who, distracted, imprudently strays from the safety of its tree?

Should an honorable ditch-digger sweating all week to provide for his family feel guilty when he picks up his paycheck?

Should the graduate student feel guilty when he is finally handed his scroll and key?

Yoritomo dismisses any such "weakening" thoughts of guilt.

Having gotten yours the hard way, entertain few qualms about *keeping* all you've won "the hard way."

Yoritomo tells it this way:

As for those in whose minds we substitute our own will for that which they tend to manifest, they are generally dull or frankly vicious souls, who combine with their natural defects a kind of moral weakness, which renders them accessible to outside influence.

THE POWER OF PERSEVERANCE

"For perseverance is the mother of many gifts; from her is born circumspection which clasps hands with application and patience."
—Yoritomo

"Perseverance" is synonym to "patience and persistence," antonym to "pest."

Being "patient" shows off your discipline. Being persistent pays off. Being a pest just pisses people off.

When people come to recognize you as someone who perseveres until the job gets done (and done right the first time), people see you as a dependable leader they'll gladly follow down any rocky road.

When we exhibit the patience to stay the course, we inspire that most precious of commodities, *respect*, allowing us to exercise more influence than our "half-assin'" competition.

We persevere by simply going forward, over obstacles, around obstacles, else undermining our way past obstacles, using any and all means at our disposal to accomplish our goal.

In Yoritomo's world, this was called *Masakatsu!*[143] literally, "by any means necessary."

Dangennes[144] defines "perseverence" as "the slow but sure ascent toward a goal that assumes a more definite shape the nearer we approach it." The operative words to note here being: "slow" (patient); "sure" (steady); "ascent" (implying higher or nobler aspirations); "a goal" (if you don't know where you're headed, how do you know how much gas to put in the tank?); and the promise that our approach to success will "assume a more definite shape" the closer we get to our goal. In other words, if you find your goal always *receding* from you, you're doing something wrong.

Dangennes' succinct synopsis as to the part perseverance plays in increasing our overall influence in life is an echo of Yoritomo's own words:

> Every work is made up of a chain of acts more or less infinitesimal; the perfection of each of them contributes to the whole . . . everybody can aim at conquering fortune by a series of continual and rational efforts . . . The man who would spring up thirty cubits at a single leap would spend his life in ridiculous attempts, but if he wishes steadily to mount the steps that lead him to that height, he will attain it, sooner or later, according to the dexterity, the agility, and the perseverance which he displays.

---

143. Always written in English with capital M, completed with a !.
144. In Yoritomo, 1916:128.

In layman's terms: A clearly defined goal, broken down into a series of manageable "sub-goals," the accomplishment of each leads smoothly into the next, until success, first a vague shadow, becomes ever-clearer each persistent step we grow near.

Men will marvel at your perseverance, your every word and action holding influence over them.

THE POWER OF INCREASING YOUR CONCENTRATION

"If we reflect well on it, we shall see that most of our troubles can be set down in carelessness. . . . Without concentration, no success is possible."
—Yoritomo

Concentration is synonymous with *mindfulness,* antonym to "Huh?"

Concentration is the next-to-last step on the wise Buddha's "Eight-Fold Path" to enlightenment.[145]

In Buddhism in general, concentration (sometimes written as "mindfulness") manifests physically in the practice of meditation. Meditation is at the core of most schools of Buddhism, particularly the Zen branch that came to be favored by the Samurai, in great part due to the efforts of Yoritomo's guardians, the Hojo.

Zen emphasis on developing one's powers of concentration fits perfectly—sword to scabbard—with the Samurai way of life, where the already thin line between life and death must be trodden daily.

Even when "only" training in the *dojo,* the last lapse in a Samurai's concentration could result in serious injury, let alone the cost of a lapse in concentration on the unforgiving battlefield.

Concentration is the key to exercising your influence—i.e., *winning!*—in *all* areas of contest and conflict, be it the bloody battlefield, the equally treacherous boardroom, even the unforgiving bedroom!

Consequently, those who do not take time—*make* time!—to develop their powers of concentration, those who allow their concentration to waver,

---

145. Right Views; Right Desires; Right Speech; Right Conduct; Right Livelihood; Right Endeavors; Right Concentration (aka Mindfulness); Right Meditation.

and those whose concentration *we can purposely and successfully break,* are already lost.

Not surprising, Yoritomo had little patience with, and little good to say about, anyone lacking in this most fundamental of skills:

> [They] can only with difficulty concentrate themselves on a task that requires a little application; they are the slaves of the instability of their impressions; beginnings, however arduous, always find them full of enthusiasm, but this fervor soon grows cold, and if success does not present itself immediately they will hasten to give up their project and devote themselves to another which will soon have a like ending.

In other words, they talk a good game at the start, but don't have either the muscle nor the mental fortitude to stay the course.

You *don't* want this kind of person working for you. You don't even want this kind of person anywhere *around* you, distracting *you* with their distractions.

On the other hand, these are *exactly* the kind of workers, advisors, and lieutenants you hope are in your enemy's camp.

Zen practitioners use a variety of methods to increase—and hone—their own powers of concentration. Even those Zen practitioners not actively involved in martial arts training still require the full use of their powers of concentration in such arts and skills as the *chado* (tea ceremony) and such benign arts as flower arrangement (*ikebana*) and *bonsai.*

The most basic tools for improving your overall concentration, indeed, leading to even *deeper* levels of concentration . . . approaching the "mystical," is the *Zazen* Z-E-N meditation you've already learned.

Other such methods of meditation and other concentration-improving exercises include Chinese methods collectively known as *Zizhi-dai* ("The Art of Control")[146] and the Japanese art of *Nin Riki.* [147]

In purely military terms, "concentration" refers to collecting men and

---

146. See "Zizhi-dao: The Art of Control" in Lung and Prowant's *Mental Dominance* (Citadel Press, 2009).

147. See "Nin Riki Mind Power" in Lung and Prowant's *Mind Assassins* (Citadel Press, 2010).

material, hopefully at the right place and time, in time to prevent your enemy from doing the same.

Concentrating your superior forces at a place where the enemy is weakest is, of course, the epitome of outwitting your enemy.

In the same way, "concentration" in the Yoritomo sense means to gather together all your mental resources, rallying them (as you would your troops) toward the campaign (problem) you have chosen.

Games such as chess, *go*, and *mahjongg* have traditionally been applauded as helping improve concentration. And, nowadays, we're told doing crossword puzzles and *sudoku* may help stave off Alzheimer's, and we're all for that (those of us who can still *remember* to be for that!). Indeed, anything that helps improve (or safeguard) your powers of concentration should be at the top of your "to-do" list . . . every day.

Ironically, the mere fact of concentrating on concentrating can improve your powers of concentration.

Focus = concentration. Concentration *internalized* = confidence. Concentration *externalized* = increased awareness and increased influence.

Others notice our increased alertness, they marvel at our powers of concentration and they either flock to our cause, else they stay out of our way for fear of having to match their paltry powers of concentration against our *obvious* ability to bring our considerable powers of concentration to the fore . . . and *aimed* right at them.

Thus, through concentration, we *influence* others to either bond with us, binding their fortune to ours, else we warn them to stay behind us, leaving the field wide-open before us!

> **"One should never risk one's whole fortune unless supported by one's
> entire forces."**
> —Machiavelli, *Discourses*

THE POWER OF INCREASING YOUR CONFIDENCE

"My assurance of victory does not come from the point of my sword,
nor from the hand that grips that sword, nor the eye that aims my
hand . . . My confidence in victory comes from knowing my own fear
and knowing my enemy's fear."
—*The War Scroll of Spartacus*

There's a TV commercial going around of late that states the obvious that "Confidence is sexy!" True. Confidence wins people over, and not just in the bedroom. That's why Dangennes calls confidence "the mother of conversion." In other words, if people believe *we believe* in what we're saying, they will naturally be attracted to both our message and to us personally.

Our show of confidence can thus inspire others, either through their corresponding confidence (belief) in themselves, or else the confidence we instill (plant) in them by assuring (convincing) them they can succeed as well.

However, the prerequisite to instilling confidence in others is having some confidence of our own in the first place. Says Dangennes: "In order to implant [confidence] in the heart of others, it is necessary to possess it—this splendid confidence in ourselves which works wonders."

Possessing true confidence in ourselves, we've no need to strut around *acting* confident. Like Forrest Gump's stupidity, "Confidence is as confidence does."

But what if we don't possess confidence naturally? And, even if we possess confidence in one area of expertise, what if we then lack confidence when forced to campaign outside our "comfort zone"?

How do we acquire confidence—and confidence in abundance, enough to vouchsafe us through any challenge?

We gain confidence simply by trying. Experience is what you get when you don't get what you wanted.

Just by trying, even if not ultimately succeeding, you can still congratulate yourself for having mustered up the courage to initially throw yourself headlong into the unknown.

Failure at least leaves us with scars, and scars are only thicker skin.

To adapt Yoritomo's example when speaking on *ambition*: You try to jump high . . . you fall short. You try again.

Provided you've *realistically* factored in all pertinent variables—divesting yourself of all distracting and discouraging superstition and wishful thinking—sooner or later, exercising not only muscles but discipline and due diligence as well, *you will succeed.*

And you need not wait for full success to reap the benefits of your "budding" confidence: Each step mastered, no matter how long, winding, and rocky the road, is one step closer to the goal. Thus the ancient Taoist adage: "The journey of a thousand miles begins with a single step."

The accomplishing of each step, builds our confidence for the next step. This is *real* confidence, confidence vouchsafed by blood, not by bravado browbeat and bludgeoned into us.

Strengthen both your arm *and your confidence* by finding a *true* accomplishment you can pat yourself on the back for every day.

Nietzsche said, "Do the thing and you have the power!"

Or, in today's parlance: "Stop talkin' smack and start takin' up the slack!"

> *"Step by step walk the thousand-mile road. . . . Study strategy over the years and achieve the spirit of the warrior. Today is victory over yourself of yesterday; tomorrow is your victory over lesser man."*
> —**Miyamoto Musashi**

POWER THROUGH SYMPATHY

"Sympathy" in Yoritomo's philosophy isn't the same "sympathy" we use today as a synonym for "pity." Rather, Yoritomo's "sympathy" refers to "being in sync" with others. Simpatico.

Having established sympathy, we can then exercise this newfound *influence* to practice what Dangennes calls "beneficent suggestions."

Having established rapport with another person, we can now use this kind of "sympathy" to see things the way other people see them and, more importantly, to get people to see things *our way.*

We get people to see things *our way* by at least pretending to see things *their way,* by agreeing-without-really-agreeing: "Sure, Bob, we're on the same page. We see eye-to-eye. We are *here.*" (Two fingers gesture your eyes to Bob's eyes.)

When people *believe* we feel the same way they do, both emotionally and when it comes to other issues, when they feel we are "in sympathy" with them, they trust us and gravitate toward us, they open up to us . . . all of which gives us power over them. That's one kind of "sympathy."

The other kind of sympathy begins by our noticing the "little things" about others and ends with their believing we can actually read their minds.

In a somewhat self-serving (mis)use of those "mirror neurons" we talked about, we first *deliberately* mirror ("mimic," if you will) the other person's actions, emotions, and even voice and word inflection. By purposely bringing ourselves into sync with the other person, they relax and accept us into their lives. Having successfully penetrated their world, we can now slowly, surreptitiously, begin to "tweak" our words and actions, imperceptibly drawing them over to *our* way of thinking.

This is how cults suck seemingly smart, educated, people in . . . inch-by-inch.[148]

Depending on your patience, your willingness to literally take things slow-and-steady, you can win over 99 percent of the people *all the time.*[149] And it all begins with "sympathy," what most people think of as the most *passive* of emotions.

In Asia, "sympathy" is considered one of the five main *weaknesses* human beings are susceptible to, along with Fear, Lust, Anger, and Greed—together making up "The Five Warning F.L.A.G.S."

Ninja and other ne'er-do-wells often use sympathy ploys (e.g., the "old lady" who drops her purse, the stranger stalled beside the road, that sound of a baby crying in the woods) to trap the unsuspecting and the "sympathetic."

---

148. See "The Cult Craft" in Lung and Prowant's *Mind Manipulation* (Citadel Press, 2002).
149. See "The Art of Seduction" in Dr. Lung's *Mind Control* (Citadel Press, 2006).

POWER THROUGH DECEPTION:
THE THIRTEENTH SECRET OF POWER

*"The basic point is that deceit is your most valuable asset in
war . . . If you think about it, you will find that the majority of
important military successes have come about as a result of trickery.
It follows then that if you are to take on the office of commander,
you should ask the gods to allow you to count the ability to deceive
among your qualifications, and should also work on it yourself."*[150]
—**Xenophon (430–355 B.C.)**

Whoever said "Honesty is the best policy" . . . obviously wasn't a con
man, cult leader, politician, or would-be dictator!

Deceit has always been a prized commodity. "Commodity" coming from
the Latin *commoditas*, meaning "convenient." And that's just what "deceit"
usually is: the *convenient* path—tread by many, tempting to all.

For some, deceit remains the course of last resort. For others, deceit is
a way of life, especially in wartime:

Warfare is deception. (The prophet Muhammad)

After exhausting all other twelve avenues for increasing one's "influence" over others, or simply when deceit and deception were the most expe-
ditious and effective path, the wily Hojo fully accepted the value of deceit.
This lesson they taught to their young guest Yoritomo.

Often referred to as *kiri tauke*, literally "The Final Cut" (named for a *coup
de grace* that removes all an opponent's pieces—often including his head!—
from play), by the sixteenth century in Japan, this "Thirteenth Path to
Power" came to be thought of under the catch-all term *Hyori*.

Hyori translates to "hidden, not being seen," but is more often more
descriptively called "double dealing."

With a flair for Zen-like contradiction (often employed to "shock" the
Zen student into greater awareness), sixteenth-century sword master Yugu
Munenori (1571–1646)[151] defined Hyori as "obtaining truth through decep-
tion."

---

150. See Hannibal's Truth L: "Trust in The Gods...but always carry a spare sail."
151. See "Munenori's War to the Mind" in Lung and Prowant's *Mind Assassins* (Citadel
Press, 2010).

Sounds a little like Orwellian *1984* double-speak. Indeed, at one time Munenori was chief of the much-feared Tokugawa regime[152] *Tokko* secret police.

At its most fundamental, Hyori depends on the use of *kyoku* ("deception") techniques to lure your opponent in by feigning weakness—basic Sun Tzu.

We can surmise that the Hojo clan, operating in a "deficit" power position, kept their own secret counsel, literally kowtowing and making themselves indispensable, first to the ruling Taira, and then to the Minamoto once Yoritomo assumed power.

Hyori goes hand-in-hand with *Masakatsu!*, accomplishing your goal "by any means necessary."

Ruthless? At times. Yet Yoritomo (for all his "ruthlessness") would be the first to caution us against ruthlessness for ruthlessness's sake.

Savagery has its place at times—not just to punish the one, but to "convince" the many of your "sincerity."

Likewise, deceit for deceit's sake, while immediately satisfying, in the long run *undermines your credibility*. And this is counterproductive to your increasing your overall influence by (1) increasing your powers of persuasion, (2) gaining power through your words and speech, (3) influencing others via your example, and (4) gaining power through exhibiting sympathy for others.

That is, if we *get caught* using deceit and deception!

The viability of Hyori technique was proved brilliantly in sixteenth-century Japan when a commoner—not a Samurai!—named Hideyoshi Toyotomi (a former "Ninja" nonetheless!) ruthlessly used Hyori to seize control and rule all Japan, declaring himself *Taiko*, "Supreme Ruler."

By Toyotomi's time, Hyori had been refined into eight techniques, modeled after actual sword-fighting moves.

Kasha (aka *Korinbo*) means "flower wheel" in English and comes from the most basic of Sun Tzu directives of feigning movement in one direction in order to open your way in the opposite direction:

> When near appear far away. When far away, make it appear your forces are nearby.

---

152. The Tokugawa came to power in 1598, ruling Japan for the next 250 years.

YORITOMO'S POWER OF INFLUENCE

"If the ancient Chinese thought tongues were shafts in people's mouths, wars of words must have been frightful."
—Kanji Kanji by The East, 1972

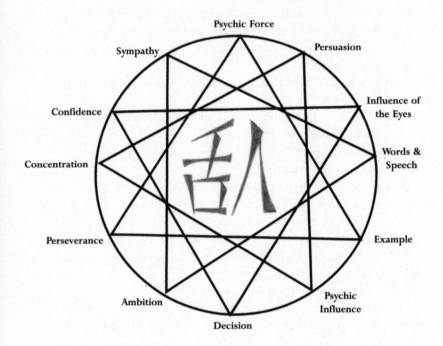

In *Kasha* swordplay, you offer your opponent your left side, before immediately striking in from your right side.

In *Kasha* "mind-play" you might pretend to fear or be subservient to an enemy (as the Hojo did) until better able to maneuver yourself into a more advantageous position of power from which to strike. Or, you might distract your enemy with a false offer of peace.

As already mentioned, not everyone believes "honesty is the best policy" . . . at least not all the time.

HYORI "DOUBLE-DEALING"

Japanese Name	Also Known As	English Translation	Physical Sword Strategy	Mind Assassin's Strategy
Kasha	Korinbo	"Flower Wheel"	Offer your left side, strike right.	Distract them with a false peace offering. Pretend to fear him.
Akemi	Fugenbo	"Open body"	Bait him in, draw him in.	Make him your friend, make friends with his friends.
Zentai	Tarobo	"Waiting fully"	Wait patiently, strike forward suddenly.	Make him paranoid. Make him prepare everywhere so he is strong nowhere (Sun Tzu).
Tebiki	Eiibo	"Entrap"	Fake sudden withdrawal, draw him into an ambush.	Pretend to listen, pretend friendship (or weakness) to draw him into ambush (à la *The Cask of the Amontillado*)
Ranken	Shu tokubo	"Wild sword"	Appear to strike blindly, fake a first deliberately ineffective attack, before launching real attack.	Make him overconfident, make him underestimate you (same ploy as "drunken style" kung-fu).
Jo	Nigusoku	"Two weapons"	Fighting two opponents simultaneously, keep one foe in the other's path.	Divide and conquer by playing one foe off against the other. "Get a dog to eat a dog." The enemy of my enemy is my friend.
Ha	Uchimondo	"Development"	Use a two-pronged attack, distracting with initial strike before making your coup de grace (similar to *Ranken*).	Divert his attention and energies away from your true target. Make him waste valuable resources.
Kyu	Futarikake	"Final cut/ coup de grace"	Fighting two opponents simultaneously, push one into the other (similar to *Nigusoku*).	Drive a wedge of suspicion between allies. (à la *Othello*)

For example, Islam permits both "lies of commission" (*tagiyya*) as well as "lies of omission" (*kitman*) for both (1) personal survival and (2) in order to "promote the interests of Islam in general."[153]

The prophet Muhammad himself set the standard early on when making a truce (*hudna*) with his numerically superior enemy, the Quaraysh. To win over the Quaraysh (or at least get them to drop their guard!), Muhammad agreed to elevate the Quaraysh's three favorite goddesses to the same status as his god, "Allah." Muhammad even went so far as including verses *praising* these three goddesses in early versions of his holy book, the *Koran*. But no sooner had he gotten the upper hand over the Quaraysh than he quickly edited these "Satanic Verses" out of his final version of the Koran.

FYI: This is not something Muslims like to talk about, even to this day. In fact, daring to write about these "Satanic Verses" in his novel of the same name earned British author Salman Rushdie (himself a Muslim) a *fatwa* death sentence from Iran's Ayatollah Khomeini in 1989—a death *fatwa* that still stands to this day.

Historically notable is Muhammad's 628 "peace treaty" between his *nascent* Muslim cult and the pagan Huddaibiya tribe, a treaty he also broke as soon as he gained the upper hand:

> Since then, "Huddaibiya" has been taken to mean a temporary peace or tactical agreement, intended to be swept aside when ever expedient. (Kenneth R. Timmerman, *Preachers of Hate*, 2002)

In 1802, the Islamic holy city of Mecca fell to the militant *Wahhabis* sect of Islam who tricked their way into the city under a flag of truce. Immediately upon entering the city, the Wahhabis began burning, looting, and killing every man, woman, and child in the city (Swartz, 2002:77).

Wahhabis . . . the sect Osama bin Laden belonged to, by the way.

Akemi (aka *Fugenbo*) means "open body" in English and includes any and all tactics and techniques designed to draw your opponent in, to make him overextend himself and his resources.

The easiest, tried-and-true way to draw someone in is to feign friendship with them.

---

153. See *The Two Faces of Islam* by Stephen Swartz (Doubleday/NY, 2002). See also *The Politically Incorrect Guide to Islam* by Robert Spencer (Regnery Publishing, 2005).

In swordplay, an Akemi tactic pretends to cower away from an opponent, only to catch him with a devastating counterstrike when he "comes in for the kill." At its most basic, we see here the guerrilla's ploy of "running" from a superior force, only to draw that pursuing force into an ambush.

Zentai (aka *Tarobo*) translates into English as "waiting fully" or "waiting patiently." As the phrase implies, we wait patiently for the ideal time to strike the telling blow.

In swordplay this means fighting a defensive match, alert for the least weakness in our opponent's attack. . . . *There!* As he raises his sword overhead, his rib cage and heart are exposed! Or, as Sun Tzu advises: Concentrate on first making yourself invulnerable, while awaiting the moment of your foe's vulnerability.

Or, to put it another way, Chance favors the prepared mind.

In mind-play, *Zentai* both instills paranoia in your enemy and/or nurtures his existing fear(s) until that fear either becomes paralysis—freezing up your enemy's mind and resources—or else a paranoic rage that leads him to rash—ultimately disastrous—actions . . . with you *encouraging* him all the way!

Paranoid, he will be forced to prepare for attack *everywhere*. And, as Sun Tzu warns, having to prepare *everywhere*, we find ourselves strong *nowhere*.

Tebiki (aka *Eiibo*) means "entrapment" in English. This is the strategy Hannibal used to defeat the Romans at the battle of Cannae in 216 B.C., first putting up fierce resistance to the Roman advance before purposely allowing the center of his defensive line to "collapse," drawing the unsuspecting and imprudent Romans too far in, allowing Hannibal's flanks to then encircle the extended Roman lines.

In *Tebiki* mind-play, you initially resist your opponent before then, suddenly, "packing it in," making him falsely believe you have withdrawn from the fight, from the bidding, etc. Emboldened by your "retreat," your incautious foe now rushes in to fill the void, only to overextend his resources, leaving him nothing in reserve with which to stave off your counterattack.

In mind-play, you again feign friendship in order to be taken into your target's confidence, using your friendship and "trusted" counsel to draw him to his doom.

Ranken (aka *Shu tokubo*) literally means "the wild sword." Employing this strategy the Hyori swordsman *appears* to hack helter-skelter at his opponent. This seemingly uncoordinated attack at first confuses and then emboldens your enemy, making him overconfident.

Dismissing your "wild" inaccurate swinging, your opponent rushes in . . . only to be met by your firm and fierce—and for him: *fatal!*—combination of bone-shattering defense blended with (literally) heart-stopping offense!

This is the same idea behind "Drunken Monkey"–style kung-fu. Credited to famed Chinese poet Li Po, in this form of kung-fu the actually sober and adept practitioner pretends to be staggering drunk in order to get his opponent to underestimate him and drop his guard.

Sheathing your actual sword in favor of employing your (no less deadly!) *mind-sword*, use Ranken technique to make your enemy overconfident, by making him underestimate you. This is the ploy future Roman emperor Claudius used to outwit those who would have had him killed as a youth, had he not exaggerated his infirmities (a limp and a stutter) to the point where they no longer thought him a viable candidate for the throne.[154]

Jo (aka *Nigusoku*) means "two weapons." In swordplay this refers to fighting two opponents simultaneously, the proven technique being keeping the first opponent in the path of the second opponent—a proven technique in such unarmed fighting arts as *karate-jitsu* and *Aikido*.

Notable here is sixteenth-century Japanese *Kensei* ("Sword Saint") Miyamoto Musashi's *Nito-ryu* ("Two Swords School"), which, as the name reveals, specialized in fighting with two full-sized *katana* swords, one in each hand.[155]

Of course, Samurai, as well as other Japanese warrior cadre such as the *Ninja* and *Yamabushi*,[156] all knew the value of both mastering the art of fending off more than one enemy at a time, often by being able to effectively wield two weapons simultaneously. Best example: A Samurai who could use his *katana* long sword and *wakizashi* short sword simultaneously.

When it comes to *Jo* mind-play, "divide and conquer" was the operative

---

154. Best rendered in Grave's fictional I, Claudius.

155. For more on the life, lore, and unmatched martial prowess and mental mastery of Musashi see: "Cutting at the Edges" in Lung and Prowant's *Mind Manipulation* (Citadel Press, 2002); "No-Sword, No-Mind" in *Mind Control* (Citadel Press, 2006); "Musashi Crosses at the Ford" in *Mind Penetration* (Citadel Press, 2007); "Musashi: No-Sword, No-Mind" in *Mental Dominance* (Citadel Press, 2009); "The Musashi Method" in *Mind Assassins* (Citadel Press, 2010); and "Musashi: Taste the Wind, Ride the Wave" in *Mind Warrior* (Citadel Press, 2010).

156. Literally "mountain warriors," priests and religious vagabonds who spent more time practicing sword and spear technique than they did studying religious scripture.

phrase: Sowing paranoia and ambition between two allies, as well as taking every opportunity to encourage one of your enemies to jump on another of your enemies.

Known as "Get a dog to eat a dog," this ploy is a win-win for you: When two of your enemies clash, even if they fight to a draw, *both are weakened*, making it easier for you to attack and overcome either—or both.

Even when one of your enemies wins flat-out, doing you the favor of obliterating another of your enemies, the victor is still weakened, his energy and enthusiasm for battle drained, his resources depleted. They call this a "Pyrrhic victory," after King Pyrrhus of Epirus (319–272 B.C.) who won a major victory over the Romans at Asculim in 279 B.C., but at such an expenditure of his men and material that he never again posed a threat to Rome.

Thus "The enemy of my enemy is my friend" . . . even if—*especially* if—he doesn't know he's doing me a favor!

Jo harkens back to the ancient Chinese adage that it is best to "Kill with a borrowed knife."[157]

Ha (aka *Uchimondo*) means "to deploy correctly."

Ha is also, in many ways, similar to *Ranken* in that both strategies aim at first confusing and distracting an enemy, before suddenly striking with an unexpected counterattack.

In swordplay, *Ha* tactics rely on a two-pronged attack, distracting your opponent by making him respond to your initial strike, thereby inadvertently opening himself up to your telling strike.

In *Ha* mind-play, you divert your opponent/competitor's attention away from your true target.

This is the first of a magician's blinds: your right hand points in the direction you want your audience to look while your left hand is busy making objects "appear" and "disappear into thin air"!

Forcing your opponent to respond to your feint makes him (1) overextend himself (2) in the wrong direction while (3) needlessly expending valuable resources. While your enemy's busy chasing ghosts, you should be busy chasing victory!

In ancient China this most basic of distraction tactics was called "*Sheng tung chi hsi,*" simply translated, "Clamor east, attack west!"

---

157. See *Hide a Dagger behind a Smile* by Keihan Krippendorff (Adams Media, 2008).

Kyu (aka *Futarikake*) is the *coup de grace*, helping you finish off two opponents simultaneously.

Similar to, and going hand-in-hand with, *Jo-Nigusoku*, *Kyu* finishes the work of driving a wedge between two former allies.

In swordplay, as with a *Jo* tactic, you force one opponent into the path of a second opponent, in effect using the first opponent as a shield (or buffer) against the second attacker. We see this behavior instinctively in trapped criminals who think nothing of putting a knife to a hostage's throat in order to negotiate their escape.

We see this same despicable ploy used on a larger scale during wartime when whole villages are used as "human shields" against potential enemy bombing.

In mind-play, this *Kyu* strategy can be used to shield you from one enemy's *immediate* notice by "sacrificing" a second enemy, in effect pushing one enemy to the forefront of another enemy's attention—i.e., *paranoia*! War-by-proxy, with your "proxy" kept just as much in the dark as your enemy!

The wily Hojo, lacking sufficient soldiers and resources to seize power themselves, in effect trapped between the mighty warring forces of the Taira and the Minamoto, chose to back the winning side—the Taira—while still protecting (and nurturing) their Minamoto ace-in-the-hole, young Yoritomo—toward the day when the Minamoto would once again make a play for power.

Fast-forward to the twentieth century and we see Russian "country bumpkin" Josef Stalin being grossly underestimated by the citified "intelligentsia" of the Bolshevik Party, many of whom ultimately felt and fell to Stalin's *kyu-futarikake* machinations.

We also see this in Stalin's *only* rival, Adolf Hitler. Hitler, underestimated by so many, ultimately rose to power in Germany as a "compromise candidate," meant to stifle parliamentary in-fighting.

The Hojo would be proud, Yoritomo, pleased.

> **"In wartime, truth is so precious it should always be attended by a bodyguard of lies."**
> **—Churchill to Stalin, 1951**

RECAP: THE THIRTEEN PATHS TO POWER

    I. Gain power by increasing your psychic forces.

   II. Gain power by increasing your power of persuasion.

  III. Gain power by increasing the power of your eyes.

  IV. Gain power through your words and speech.

    V. Gain power by your example.

  VI. Gain power by increasing your psychic influences.

 VII. Gain power by making effective decisions.

VIII. Gain power by exhibiting ambition.

  IX. Gain power through perseverance.

   X. Gain power by increasing your concentration.

  XI. Gain power by increasing your confidence.

 XII. Gain power through sympathy.

XIII. Gain power through deception.

Part IV
Blood Tells:
The Dark
Art of War
The Seventy-two
Certainties of Dracula

"Vlad is portrayed as a fierce and brave leader who was skilled in psychological warfare, but lacked a good PR guy."
—Jayne Clark[158]

---

158. See "In the Shadow of Dracula" by Jayne Clark, *USA Today,* October 29, 2010, 5D.

Introduction

"As with many great and ruthless leaders, it's hard to separate the man from the myth from the monster. . . . Still we are left only to ponder the same question that lesser men always ask at the passing of greater men: Was he a product of his times—seizing opportunity where he found it? Or was he instead the driving architect of those times—clearing the chaff from a too-long neglected field, planting the seditious seeds of a bold new crop, and then patiently waiting— unafraid!—till time to harvest the whirlwind!

"Inevitably, all that we're left with in the wake of the passing of any great man is that man's philosophy—hopefully the actual philosophy that drove the man to greatness and then vouchsafed his claim to same—as opposed to some tepid, watered-down idealization of that man's thoughts, adulterated and amended in later times to fit the self-serving needs of those that, had they lived in his day, would not have been fit to ride beside him yet, in our day, ride on his name."
—**Lung and Prowant, 2010**

THE NAME "Dracula" is forever etched onto the pages of popular fiction, having become synonymous with "sinister" and "bloodthirsty." Today no student of history—nor student of all things sinister—would dare protest both those appellations being fit to the historical Dracula. That is, if by "sinister" we mean "craft and cunning," and by "bloodthirsty" we are referring to his near-demon-like lust to see the "Trespassers will be shot!" postings at the borders to his lands freshly painted in the blood of his foes, their entrails substituting for brushes!

Christian Crusader–knight Vlad Tepes (pronounced "Tepish") was dubbed "Dracula"—literally "Son of the Dragon"—in honor of his father, Vlad Dracul, "Dracul" meaning both "dragon" and "devil" in Rumanian.

Like his father before him, founder of the Vatican-sanctioned Draconist Order of the Dragon (fl. 1387), Vlad "The Impaler" (as he would later come to be called) spent most of his life defiantly warring against both invading Muslims and against equally treacherous Christian kings and would-be princes seeking to wrest and weasel Wallachia from his fire—and often ferocious!—grasp.

As astute observer—and, by default, manipulator—of the human condition, if Dracula was not a "born survivor," then he was at least a man who learned his lessons well, both from the constant internecine fighting in the unforgiving Machiavellian politics of the Western "Christian" courts of Europe, as well as ancient Asian lessons of mind-manipulation and manslaughter from his harrowing time as a juvenile hostage—and *student*— of his lifelong Eastern enemy: Islam.

Ruler of the much-fought-over territory of Wallachia (south of the better-known Transylvania, in what is today Rumania), in Dracula's time Wallachia was the frontline in the battle of Eastern European states against encroaching Islam.

During the course of his life (1431–1476), Dracula would sit on the throne of his beloved country three times: in 1448, from 1456 to 1462, and for a final time, before being assassinated, literally stabbed in the back during a battle in 1476.

As with *all* great leaders of his day, Dracula was a mix of both the benevolent and the brutal, fully cognizant of the fact that "Treaties signed in ink are too soon rewritten in blood."

By all accounts a man more accustomed to ruling from horseback than from a throne, even his enemies—both Muslim and Christian—record his bravery in battle, while grudgingly admitting to his craft and cunning, not only in his successful use of subterfuge and guerrilla tactics against much larger forces in the field, but also his adroitness in wielding those same techniques in the just-as-deadly royal courts of the time.

That he slew his enemies with a certain élan is not in dispute.

Terror is ever a teacher that demands our full attention.

And while we may never fully know the truth of the multitude of murders—and the occasional massacre—he is said to have relished in committing, it can be said with straight face (if not with clear conscience) that no man died a "useless" death under Vlad the Impaler's reign—their lingering screams acting as both encouragement and warning to future violators that, while in Wallachia, one must hang on Dracula's every word . . . or, most assuredly, they would hang by his single word!

Thus, not all historians have judged Vlad Dracula so harshly:

> Dracula was probably not insane—in the sense in which an Ivan the Terrible was. Most of his crimes had a certain rational purpose. Through his "terror tactics" he saved the Wallachian nation from Turkish conquest in 1462. . . . Failing to rally the powers of Europe in defense of the borderlands of European civilization, he was compelled, given the slender means placed at his disposal by a nation in arms, to carry out this task himself as a member of the Dragon Order . . . making use of a mixture of truly extraordinary tactics, unusually well suited to the terrain of his country, he was able to repel an army three times the size of his own and inflict upon Mehmed the Conqueror one of the greatest humiliations of the latter's lifetime. (Florescu and McNally, *Dracula: Prince of Many Faces*)

Ultimately Dracula's German enemies succeeded in mastering the printing press ahead of the rest of Europe and, after printing up a few Gutenburg Bibles, they immediately went to work vilifying their longtime, much feared foe Vlad Dracula by publishing incendiary propaganda tracts—wildly and widely popular—that later influenced Bram Stoker's crafting of his fictional vampire "Count Dracula." Thus, as with all things Fate, a single step left (sinister) rather than right and today, rather than being the all-time favorite bugaboo of horror fans worldwide, Dracula would today instead take his rightful place in the history books as not only one of the world's great military strategists, but, more specifically, as the warrior-prince heralded as having bravely and cunningly "held the line," preventing Medieval Islam from over-running first Eastern Europe, then the rest of Europe, and perhaps the world.

Isn't it time we literally "Give the Devil his due?"

CERTAINTIES OF THE FIST

I. An open hand, far from comforting, is an uncertainty. Today it grips my hand in friendship, tomorrow it grasps at my purse and raises a sword against me. Give me the certainty and honesty of the fist!

In other words, better the devil you know than the devil you don't. The more you know—for certain—about the intentions of your enemy, the more certain your strategy to counter him. Conversely, convincing an enemy of the "certainty" that you plan to dodge left when your intention is to dodge right, is the most basic, most necessary of thought and action. Sun Tzu: "When near, appear far. . . ."

II. Keep the faith . . . but fill the fist!

Or, as accomplished sailor and master warlord Hannibal the Conqueror (247–183 B.C.) put it: "Trust in The Gods . . . but always carry a spare sail."

III. Thoughts are not required of action, but action is required for greatness.

Basic Nietzsche: If your philosophy of life doesn't lead you to action . . . well, then it's not much of a philosophy. This bold call to "put up or shut up" when it comes to putting your money where your philosophical mouth is led one biographer to declare that "before Nietzsche philosophy was just philosophy, but after Nietzsche, philosophy became dangerous!"

IV. On one shore of the river they praise my name. On the far shore, they despise those self-same syllables. Fear is the only constant on both shores!

Dracula isn't only speaking here literally of the mighty Danube River separating his Wallachian properties from lands conquered by the Muslim Turks, he is also figuratively condemning the mercurial loyalties of his time.

Harkening to Machiavelli's "Is it better for a prince to be loved or feared?"—FYI: Machiavelli came down in favor of "feared"—Dracula is of the opinion that fear of the fist—i.e., swift and overwhelmingly *dis*proportionate violence in response to trespass—was the only constant for ensuring both one's personal safety as well as the viability and inviolate nature of one's realm. Recall Xenophon (c. 360 B.C.): "Fear is apparently a formidable ally for a guard."[159]

CERTAINTIES OF WORDS

V. Treaties signed in ink are too soon rewritten in blood.

For six years during their youth, Christian princes Vlad Tepes and his brother Radu lived among their Muslim enemies as hostages following their father Dracul's subjugation by the Turkish Sultan. Vlad was around twelve years old when this ordeal began and his brother seven. By all accounts their experiences while in captivity differed greatly.

According to Florescu and McNally (1989), "Because of their differences of character, temperament, and physique, the two brothers developed for each other an intense hatred, which was exacerbated by the associated differences in treatment they received." That is, perhaps due to his younger, more impressionable age at the onset of their captivity, Radu—by all accounts a "pretty" youth—reveled in the attention shown him by both the women and the men in the Sultan's court, eventually "embracing" his captors, literally becoming the Sultan's minion (male lover).

The older Vlad, on the other hand, remained defiant, even while learning his lessons well, observing the wiles and ways of his captors. The most important lesson the future ruler of Wallachia would learn from his Muslim jailers was their Prophet Muhammad's declaration that "War is deception!" a credo he himself exemplified:

> Numerous examples are found in the life of Muhammad himself where he freely used lying and other forms of deceit: from his promising safe passage for defeated enemies, only to slaughter or else sell them into slavery later; to his entering into treaties with his enemies, pretending kinship (even to the point of inserting convenient verses into his Koran, e.g., The Satanic Verses) to placate his enemies, before then unexpectedly staging 9/11-like attacks on them. Muhammad even

---

159. See also "The Art of A.W.E." in Dr. Lung's *Mind Penetration* (Citadel, 2007).

killed diplomats and other peacemakers whose safety he had vouchsafed. (Joshua Only, *Wormwood: The Terrible Truth about Islam*[160])

As a result of his Muslim studies, even at so young an age, Dracula already realized that no treaty entered into with his Muslim enemies could ever be binding. And while there is ample evidence that, as an adult, Dracula himself remained a man of his word, the same cannot always be said for his fellow "Christian" princes with whom he'd be forced to deal later in life.

VI. Words always cost more than silence.

VII. Warm words make us drunk. Fortunately, cold words can sober us just as quickly.

VIII. I do not fear the grumbling of the people . . . I fear their silence.

Men openly *scream* in rage, but they *plot* in secret. Don't fear the noise, fear the silence.

IX. It is said that one day the lion and the lamb will eat grass together, side-by-side. Bah! That will only serve to fatten the lamb and thin the lion.

Things were much different in Dracula's time, so much so it's sometimes hard for those of us living in these modern, oh so more "enlightened" times (where we're not only dedicated to the proposition that "all men are created equal," but we're also more than willing and able to use the politically correct baseball bat to beat down any of our fellow man who dares exhibits anything even approaching incentive, innovation, or invention— holler out to Ayn Rand!) to recall that, in Dracula's day, royal hierarchy and feudal authority was still the rule of the day. As such, Dracula was born into the position in life he was expected to occupy all his life. But with rule comes responsibility. Not only were Dracula's subjects expected to serve his House, their ruler in turn was expected to watch over them, watching out for their best interests. With this IXth "certainty" Dracula is not so much challenging the biblical ideal of "Peace on Earth" as he is stating an earthly reality of his time. Egalitarian social revolution having not yet reared its hydra head, Drac-

---

160. (Bookstand Publishing, 2009). See also Idn Warraq, *Why I Am Not a Muslim* (Prometheus Books, 2003).

ula knew the common folk (lambs) were not meant to sit at the same table as the lion (the Royalty).

Likewise, in Vlad's *experience*, the Muslim could never be trusted to sup with the Christian.

X. The day may indeed come when the lion and the lamb lay down together . . . but no treaty can insure both will rise back up!

Cynic? Or realist.

XI. All alliances spring from either weakness or duplicity. When the cat and the rat hunt the cheese together, the rat practices wishful thinking while the cat practices patience.

In praise of patience, especially when dealing from a deficit position:

> Victory will be achieved with patience. (Osama bin Laden, February 2003)

CERTAINTIES OF NATURE

XII. The nature of man is to seek rest, food, and fornication. Offer these to your foe in abundance. Deny them to your sons.

Or, as Chinese strategist Chen Hao so bluntly phrased it:

> Entice an enemy with young boys and maidens to distract him, offer jade and fine silk to draw out his greed.

Hannibal, on the other hand, in the VIth of his (in)famous "Ninety-nine Truths," gives thanks to the enemy who denies him rest:

> A warrior is known by his enemies, even as a fat man is known by his appetites, a lean man by his fears. I give thanks for my enemy. Were it not for my enemy I would sleep past dawn, I would eat too much, I would become loud and over-proud, and both my arm and eye would grow lax. My enemy determines when I rise, when and where I sleep tonight, what I eat and when, and whether I will ever see my home again. I thank my enemy for making me strong and look forward to repaying him in kind!

As with the father, or at least, as with Hannibal's father, so with the sons.

XIV. One ally still abed does me more harm than a thousand enemy already on the march.

What's that old saying about "Better a true enemy than a false friend"? Better a dependable—better yet, predictable!—enemy, than an ally who leaves you in the lurch. Better the devil you know than the devil you don't.

XV. If a man can truly be likened to a tree—from firm roots and strong limbs can come abundant fruit . . . better still to be the axe!

This "certainty" is believed to stem from a philosophical discussion between the Wallachian ruler and a long-winded priest who, while waxing metaphoric, made the mistake of boring Vlad with praise of some rival princely lineage or the other that Dracula held in scant regard. Dracula's subsequent succinct—and, given Dracula's growing reputation for shortness of patience and increasing reach of blade—reserved response, "Better to be the axe!" was undoubtedly meant to encourage the holy man toward brevity, with the Prince of Wallachia literally giving them him a chance to save his—last!—breath.

XVI. The tree is felled by the axe, 'tis true. But what good the steel of the axe blade without the stout axe handle—traitorous limb of that self-same tree?

As mentioned above, in a literal case of sleeping with the enemy, Dracula's younger brother, Radu, betrayed him to their Muslim enemy. See also Certainty LXV.

XVII. The simplest of tree can grow fruit for a man and his family to live. Even when old and broken that self-same tree can still provide wood with which a man can warm his bones and cook his food. Ah, but the same tree that feeds and warms a man also gives him the bow and the arrow and the handle for seating the dumb axe-head that know no difference twixt the trunk of a tree and the neck of the man himself. Always remember that each and every branch in your enemy's garden, though today heavy-laden with fruit, can tomorrow all too quickly, all too easily, become the stake he drives deep into your heart.

The Allies are often criticized for the World War II fire-bombing of Tokyo that left over 100,000 Japanese, overwhelmingly civilians, killed. What many historical revisionists fail to realize is that a great deal of the manufacturing for the Japanese war effort was carried on, not in the targeted large factories, but also in "cottage industries" in average Tokyo homes near those factories. The decision to fire-bomb Tokyo with newly created napalm, with the intention of igniting a conflagration designed to devastate Tokyo, was, therefore, not only a well-thought-out military operation with a clear-cut military objective, but also a blistering success.

Just because *you* buy your son a bicycle for his twelfth birthday, don't be surprised if your enemy buys his son a Kalashnikov.

We living in such "comfortable" times, believing ourselves safe, so far from the frontlines, often forget that "forgive and forget" only works if our enemy likewise believes in forgiving and forgetting.

Machiavelli repeatedly championed the ancient Roman ideal of finishing the job by killing "the Sons of Brutus" (i.e., sons who will one day grow up and grow strong enough to seek vengeance for their fathers' defeat). Machiavelli reminds us that Hannibal launched the Second Punic War against the Romans partially in revenge for his father's defeat in the First Punic War.

In Japan, many are the Samurai tales of underdogs whose clans are beaten down, only to rise again to gain their vengeance: Yoritomo Minamoto, who as a young man survived the slaughter of his clan to become Japan's first Shogun,[161] and "The Forty-seven Ronin," who willingly suffered humiliation before eventually gaining the upper hand and their revenge.

How many of us don't love a "good" movie where the wronged man, defeated, humiliated, and perhaps left for dead at the onset, recovers and ultimately returns to get his revenge—or "justice" if you prefer.

For some the idea of defeated underdogs biding their time, licking their wounds till the time for vengeance presents itself, is only the stuff of Hollywood's next big action flick . . . But for others, such dreams—all too often passed from generation to generation—becomes the motivation for strapping on a suicide-vest.

Thus Hannibal's ruthlessness, if not forgivable, is at least understandable:

---

161. See "Yoritomo's Art of Influence" in Dr. Haha Lung's *Mind Control* (Citadel, 2006).

"Do not make war on women and children," they cry. Why not? Without his woman's arms to comfort him, his ears filled with the hungry cries of his children, I have twice discomfited my enemy! (Truth XXXVII)

and

Mercy is the most costly of conceits . . . as if life and death were truly yours to give! The power of life and death is but on loan from The Gods. Use both wisely. (Truth XLVI)

XVIII. Even the most bent and twisted of trees can fuel my fire, shelter me from high winds and from arrow.

No man is useless. Likewise, there is no situation—no matter how seemingly dire—that an alert and patient man cannot turn to his advantage. History is full to overflowing with examples of this. Thank God fools don't read history!

XIX. Today's small seed, tomorrow's great wood barring my way.

Basic Sun Tzu: Deal with the little problems before they become big problems. Deal with the little man before he becomes too big for his britches.

XX. Crush a man's ambition and his actions will never beggar your attention. Crush a man's dreams and his wakening will never disturb your sleep.

Thought is the prerequisite and precursor to action. Stifle his thoughts before fully formed, strangle his thoughts before fully up to speed, and you will never be troubled by your enemy's action. Near a repeat of the preceding "certainty."

XXI. Now a smile, now a frown—how easily a face flutters. Not so easy the heart—which is why we keep it behind shutters.

Hide your heart, hide your thoughts, thus we guard our present actions in order to realize our future goals.

XXII. A man's telling of his dreams often tells you more about the teller than about the telling.

Or, as wise and observant Hannibal pointed out, "A fool begins by telling you what he knows and ends by telling you what he doesn't know" (*Hannibal's Black Art of War*, Truth XX).

CERTAINTIES OF HOW TO MOVE MEN

XXIII. To move mountains, to move castle walls, both can easily be accomplished by engines. Ah, but to move the hearts of men. . . . That can only be done by other men!

Glass half-full: Dracula is applauding the fact that a man's heart can be moved by the travail of his fellows.

Glass half-empty: How easily our fellows are moved by the right word whispered at just the right time in the wrong ear. Black Science.

XXIV. To move men is as simple as holding bread in one hand and a bludgeon in the other.

Yin-yang. Push-pull. Attraction or repulsion. All men are moved by one or the other, vice versa, depending on all-too-changeable time and clime.

All people either react to the "carrot" or the "stick," bribes or threats.[162]

XXV. Though men may speak different tongues, two things reflect all faces equally—the shine of silver and the flash of steel.

There's something everybody needs—or wants. There's something everyone is afraid of.

All men have their price. For some, it may be a high-minded goal like "ending world hunger." Show them how to accomplish this and you'll have them eating out of your hand in no time.

For others, those with more sinister agendas, feed their greed, show them the secret back door leading into the Halls of Power, and they will forever be in your debt . . . especially if you get it all on video!

XXVI. Men are moved as much by signs as they are by swords.

By "signs" Dracula means omens, superstitions, as well as all those clan,

---

162. See "The Five Types of Power" in Dr. Lung's *Mind Control: The Ancient Art of Psychological Warfare* (Citadel, 2006).

cultural, racial, religious, and national symbols people everywhere seem in such a hurry to die for. Sure, it's always nice to have a suicide-bomber or two at your beck-and-call (if only for intimidation purposes when heading to the negotiation table), but convincing such "symbol-driven" people to *live* for you is a whole lot more profitable, power cult–wise and otherwise.

XXVII. What a man loves, defines him. What a man hates, refines him. Both, in turn, confine him.

This reminds us of Hannibal Barca's IVth Truth: "What a man loves, what he hates, what he needs, what he desires: These are the four pillars that support his house."

In both instances, both master strategists are telling us these are the vulnerabilities by which a man can be attacked, i.e., his loved ones can be targeted by the ruthless, his hatreds can be inflamed by the manipulative. Either "attack" can succeed in draining his resources, making him even more vulnerable to attack. This is part and parcel of Miyamoto Musashi's "Cutting at the Edges" ploy (i.e., when unable to overcome an opponent through direct action, "bleed" and weaken him by attacking his extremities).[163]

XXVIII. Men have memories as short as the hangman's rope is long. Guard your memories well, that your memories may well guard you.[164]

This "certainty" of Dracula's isn't, as might first appear, some milquetoast call to "forgive and forget," rather it invokes the time-honored strategy known as "rocking your enemy to sleep," i.e., a forgetful enemy is a God-send, and the Devil take any enemy too soon to forgive!

Part-and-parcel for the sinister is to appear nonthreatening, so that a target person never sees your arrow hurtling at them, so an enemy is made to believe you have been dissuaded from your path of revenge or conquest or both.

Thus, through your words and actions (or lack of overtly threatening actions), you convince your enemy to relax, assured that you've finally reformed from your felonious ambitions, assuaging his suspicions, minimizing his bad memories of you, patiently, soothingly rocking him to sleep the

---

163. See "The Musashi Method" in *Mind Assassins* by Lung and Prowant (Citadel, 2010).
164. See The War Scroll of Spartacus, saying XXII. Did Vlad study Spartacus?

way you would an innocent babe until, all too late, he realizes that's *not a pacifier* in your hand!

XXIX. "Better a rope over-tight than one too slack!" cries the horse-man, the hangman, and the king.

Always use the right tool for the job. See Dracula's Certainty XXXVI. Also "Hitch the right horse to the right cart."[165]

XXX. When the highest receive timely reward, and the lowest receive punishment both swift and just, then right and wrong never contend.

All great commanders, from Sun Tzu to Ssu-Ma, Hannibal to Patton, all knew the importance of swift rewards and even swifter punishment when it comes to controlling minds and inspiring hearts.

For the sinister strategist, the purposeful doling out of *dis*proportionate reward—especially when clearly not merited—can be used to engender distrust between former allies and to cast suspicion upon the recipient of such undeserved rewards, promotion, and praise.

XXXI. A little man with a big knife is still but a little man . . . but it's still a big knife!

Glass half-empty: Tyson's Buster Douglas. Never underestimate your enemy.

Glass half-full: Hope your enemy underestimates you, and go out of your way to help him do so. Classic guerrilla strategy. Classic Sun Tzu.

XXXII. Nature knows what we need. . . . so often different from what we desire.

"Nature, if consulted, gives us the means to the end," assures painter Paul Cézanne, acknowledging that Mama Nature not only knows best but also provides aplenty for her children. Granted, they're often too stupid and ungrateful to fully appreciate it, misinterpreting "desires" for "needs." So warns Hannibal:

---

165. See "The Slyness of Ssu-Ma" in Lung and Prowant's *Mind Warrior* (Citadel Press, 2010).

Distinguish between gain and loss. Nothing you can hold in your hand can ever truly be held for long. Distinguish between need and desire. I desire many things. I need few. My enemy can entice me with both of these—drawing me here, sending me running there. All I truly need beats within my breast. All I desire can all too easily fall into my enemy's coarse hand. The more a man possesses, the more easily he can be possessed.

XXXIII. Single steps, correct or sinister, lay the stones that pave our way through life.

In this instance, Dracula's use of "correct or sinister" can be interpreted literally as both right steps and left (sinister) steps, as well as their figurative—moral—meaning of right and wrong. As in all things in life, a decided step one way instead of the other and we find ourselves either attending our coronation or else being late for our own funeral.

This brings to mind the time "Vlad the Impaler" purposely tested two monks visiting his castle by showing them a courtyard filled to overflowing with the crucified and impaled bodies of his enemies. Rightly sensing a trap, the first monk showed no sign of the horror he undoubtedly felt, wisely replying, "Lord Tepes, you are appointed by God to punish evildoers and are obviously doing a fine job of it!" But the second monk, unable to stifle his chagrin, openly condemned the ruler of Wallachia, "From where I stand, you have placed your immortal soul in peril by committing such atrocities!"

"That is how it appears from where you *stand?*" Dracula rubbed his chin. "Perhaps you would see things more clearly if you were *sitting?*"

So adept, so practiced, were Dracula's executioners that the second monk remained alive long after he had been hoisted high aloft via the impaling pole thrust up into his body via his anus!

XXXIV. To bar the door against the wolf is prudent. Yet how much better to strike the wolf when he is still a fair distance. Better still, secure your lands in such a way that the wolf does not think to trespass.

Chance favors the prepared mind. Reputation spills less blood.

XXXV. Followers end a question with a question mark. Leaders end a question with an answer.

XXXVI. Men are not tools. . . . They're **weapons!**

Recall Certainty XXIX? In other words:

> As much as we might admire those who dedicated (and in many cases literally gave) their lives to complete non-violence—the Gandhis and Martin Luther King, Jrs., of the world—there are situations where a shovel cannot do the work of the hammer. (Dr. Haha Lung, *Mind Fist*)

CERTAINTIES OF STRATEGY

XXXVII. A man moves heaven with his prayers, earth with his will, and his enemies with his cunning.

XXXVIII. War is, at best, controlled chaos. The more we can control that chaos the better we war!

Though he may have called it by a different name in Rumanian, Dracula obviously subscribed to the strategy of C.H.A.O.S.—"Create Hassles (Hardships, Hurdles, etc.) And (then) Offer Solutions" (the ones you've possessed all along), the tried-and-true technique of placing obstacles (real and imagined) in your enemy's path (in order to entice him to join with your cause), letting them stew in desperation for an anxious interval, before then—*voilà!*—coming up with the perfect solution to their dilemma. Thus, they become beholden to your "genius."[166]

XXXIX. Wars are won by winning battles. Battles are lost by worrying about winning the war.

How often has a great war hung on the outcome of a single battle? In any war there are the smaller battles and heroic skirmishes involving small groups of warriors that influence who survives to march down the many booby-trapped pathways and heavily patrolled and hotly contested highways, all of which inevitably lead to that final telling encounter: Zama, Waterloo, Stalingrad, Berlin, Armageddon.

Perhaps this is just another way of saying "the Devil is in the details," and Musashi's "Pay attention even to trifles."

---

166. See "Arts of C.H.A.O.S." in Lung and Prowant's *Mind Assassins: The Dark Arts of the Asian Masters* (Citadel, 2010).

Sadly, we all too often forget that the soldier in the field is as important—if not more so—than the generals in the command post.

Many are instances throughout history where some brave Roland singularly held the line, sacrificing himself and, by his example, inspiring his fellows to bravely step up to that firing line themselves—that line drawn in the sand—the 300 at Thermopylae, Crockett's Tennesseans at the Alamo, those first responders who fought back both the flames and the fear and those whose battle cry was "Let's roll!" on Nine-Eleven.

Thus both the general and the GI, the leaders and those who literally lay their lives on the line, both have their part to play, the correct fusing of their individual energies forming the synergy of success.

The wise commander must, by necessity, be privy to the "Big Picture." And while the commander may not always have leave to share the "Big Picture" with his troops, the wisest of commanders know that the "Big Picture" is painstakingly painted by the singular strokes of his troops . . . painted in sweat, and blood, and tears.

The words of Lao Tzu's *Tao te Ching* ring appropriate that "the Journey of a thousand miles begins with a single step." Likewise, "great" wars, under close scrutiny, can be seen constructed on "common" battles won by the uncommon valor of soldiers commanded by men of uncommon vision— who know both that you can lose the battle but still win the war, and yet you can never win a "big" war if you lose too many "little" battles.

XL. Attack your enemy's confusion. Doubling his confusion, you cut your own chances of losing by half.
See Dracula's Certainties L and LI for more of Vlad's "math."

XLI. Attack where the enemy is weak and loud with fear. Avoid where he is strong and quiet with cunning.
Recall Vlad's VIII Certainty, the understanding that conspiracy, cunning, and other things that can cut your throat while you sleep tend to grow in silence and secrecy.

The rattling of sabres never hurt anyone—except perhaps the would-be bully making the noise when someone finally calls his bluff.

This harkens back to one of the first mantras your mama ever taught you: "Sticks and stones may break my bones, but words can never harm me."

Men often hide their fear with loud, bold talk. We observe this behavior in novices, seldom in veterans. Even in ancient times, Masters of the rank of Sun Tzu and Cao Cao sent spies to carefully observe the enemy camp: a loud, clamoring camp often masking the fear felt by the soldiers. A quiet camp, on the other hand, meant that the enemy had already made his plans and that his men were ready for the coming battle—confidently enjoying their last night of relative peace before the death and destruction promised with the coming dawn.

Don't fear the noise, fear the silence.

XLII. My enemy knows the reach of my arm as well as he knows the reach of his own. Ah, but with a steel-eyed hawk perched atop my arm, how far now does my arm dare reach?

Dracula was well aware of the need for both intelligence and for counterintelligence, not only when fighting off Muslim invaders, but when dealing with the constant intrigue being mounted behind his back by his "Christian brethren."

Here we have the concept of conventional versus unconventional forces—large armies going toe-to-toe in the field versus guerrilla forces subtly employing tactics, terrain, and perhaps terror to their advantage against a vastly superior foe.

Ancient Chinese strategists called this "cheng and chi": "direct and indirect" tactics and technique, the seen and the subtle.

By "my arm" Vlad is speaking of traditional armed forces (which were impossible for his small kingdom to field). The analogy of "the hawk," however, was (as will become apparent in the following Certainties) Dracula's way of saying, "I may be just a small 'hawk,' but I am swift and my talons sharp!"

XLIII. Where the hawk cannot strike down the great bear, he can surely blind him with well-placed talon! Safely circling far above, the hawk then watches the great blind beast first stumble and then tumble from the unseen cliff!

No better metaphor can be found to so succinctly define guerrilla warfare—the type of fighting at which Dracula excelled.

XLIV. Attack the quail at your leisure. Do not waste time chasing after the hawk. . . . Else train the hawk to catch quail for you! If my hawk can but drive the quail down into the briar, then that thicket will do the rest of the job for me.

The enemy of my enemy is my friend. Those of common cause should find common bond. Often divided and disparate elements can be brought together to successfully combat a much larger, more powerful foe. This was Hannibal's intention in invading the Italian peninsula. Realizing his highly mobile army could never successfully lay prolonged siege to the city of Rome, his goal was to encourage Rome's disgruntled vassal states to join him. He came close to succeeding.

Thus the "hawk" perched atop Vlad's arm was not only his own unconventional—guerrilla—style of fighting, an especial advantage in terrain where large forces could not be brought to bear.

Vlad may also here be offering his unique fighting skills and services to more powerful kings (e.g., the Hungarian kings with which he was, for convenience sake, allied at times). His reference to "briar" and "thicket" is an adequate warning of much of the terrain his enemies often figuratively—and literally—found themselves trapped in when underestimating the Wallachian.

XLV. When two quail fight, only the hawk eats well that night.

It's always nice when two of your enemies (can be made to) weaken and, eventually finish each other off. Even in the case where one enemy comes out ahead, the "victor" is still weakened, their losses heavy, their men and material stretched to the breaking point, perhaps so much so as to make them now vulnerable to *your* attack.

Conversely, this echoes Benjamin Franklin's famous warning to bickering colonial representatives that, "We must all hang together or, most assuredly, we will all hang separately!" Similar fears helped keep the multi-ethnic, multi-religious, some say—"multi-*psychotic!*"—states of the former Yugoslavia together for as long as it did, at least until the demise of the ever-hungry Soviet bear.

XLVI. We prepare only for the storm we see coming. That is why my enemies are always soaked to the bone!

Vlad the wit. Still, wit born of wisdom, sired by his keen insight into the indolent and unobservant nature of his fellow man. (Don't worry. I'm sure people have changed since Dracula's time. . . .)

XLVII. My enemy begs me "play by rules familiar!" even as my unfamiliar vexes him sour. Therefore, to set him at ease to my coming, I dress my unfamiliar in trappings familiar, my sore disturbances in common sound and divers shape.

How often must it be said: Ignorant of the familiar, we fall to the unfamiliar. "Wolves in sheep's clothing" sound vaguely familiar?

Conversely, chasing after the unfamiliar, we so often trip over the familiar.

XLVIII. The taller man must reach down to strike the smaller man, but the smaller man is already poised to strike a telling blow to the taller man's vitals!

Another apt metaphor for guerrilla warfare.

Invading Dracula's lands in force, the Muslim Turks were nigh unstoppable. The Prince of Wallachia possessed neither the manpower nor the material necessary to meet the invader in pitched battle. Fortuitously, both the trying terrain itself, as well as Dracula's acumen for unconventional tactics, forced the larger invading force to divide up into ever-smaller units more susceptible to attack. Narrow defiles, treacherous—literally—slippery slopes, and marshlands all being the guerrilla's blessing and the big army's bane, from Sun Tzu (Chapter X) and the 300 Spartans, down to Francis Marion and Mao Tse-Tung.

Of course, Dracula's metaphor of the shorter man being "poised" to strike into what he euphemistically refers to as the taller's "vitals" brings to mind the defiant reply of World War II Major-General Terry MacAullife, his much-smaller force of the 101st Airborne surrounded and outnumbered by German forces besieging Bastogne. Asked to surrender, MacAulliffe sent this one word reply: "Nuts!"

XLIX. There is surrender and there is struggle, naught else but these. The latter at least holds out the possibility for glory. The former— unthinkable!

The proper response to travail is to prevail:

> We have nothing left in this world but what we can win with our swords. Timidity and cowardice are for men who can see safety at their backs—who can retreat without molestation

along some easy road and find refuge in the familiar fields of their native land; but they are not for you. You must be brave; for you there is no middle way between victory or death— put all hope of it from you, and either conquer, or, should fortune hesitate to favor you, meet death in battle rather than in flight! (Hannibal's address to his troops after they had just crossed the Alps and were facing the Romans for the first time in 203 B.C.)

L. Set your goal twice that of your enemy. Achieving merely half assures you victory. Failing to achieve at least half in attempting a goal twice that of your enemy, still assures you will be held in awe by all who oppose you.

While mathematics may not have been Vlad Tepes's strong suit, raining murder and mayhem down upon his enemies certainly was!

LI. Double the fear in your enemy's heart and you halve the chance he'll ever put a sword in his hand.

More Vlad math. And, unlike all that math they tried to teach you in high school, math you can actually use in real life.

LII. My first blow draws his attention. My second blow bloodies his nose! By my third blow my enemy is ready to listen to reason. Beyond three, and pain becomes his headstone

Pow! My sucker punch gets your attention. *Pow!* My follow-up punch makes you start leakin'. The ol' "one-two." Now that I've "gotten your attention" and amazed you with the fact that even a big, bad bully like you can bleed too, now maybe you'd like to start talking about how we can all get along better? Or about how you're going to "break me off a piece" every week just to make sure your favorite pet doesn't meet his demise in a highly improbable accident. *Capisce, paesan?*

Before any negotiation can begin, you have to (1) get the other side's attention, and (2) earn their respect.

Unexpected, swift, and telling pain is always a good attention-getter.

One tried-and-true technique of fringe political groups is for a "break-away faction" of the group to engage in heinous and high-profile acts of violence while a more moderate "political wing" of the same group calls for sit-down negotiations.

Whom would you rather deal with? A violent rogue faction "military arm" or a seemingly civilized "political wing" who, as an incentive to your coming to the negotiation table (i.e., recognizing their legitimacy), just "might" be able to talk that rogue faction into laying down their arms?

Terrorist groups today are still using this "good cop/bad cop" ploy, believed originated in the Middle Ages by Sinan, leader of the Syran branch of the Muslim killer Hashishin cult, known to Christian Crusaders as "The Order of Assassins."[167]

Of course, for those who refuse to listen to "reason," pain becomes a permanent condition—and legacy.

LIII. Value force only in proportion to its limitations.

While a "show of force" has its uses, the constant "threat" of force soon loses its terror. Likewise, the constant use of force can all too quickly inure a person, or a whole population, to pain and suffering. This saturation point to pain is often followed by bloody revolt.

There's a "stick" *and* a "carrot" for a reason.

Not every bullet fits every gun.

LIV. Nine men defend another—their ally. Such men do not fear dying as one. Ah, but let that ally they protect fall dead to the floor while safely in the midst of their circle and suddenly each fears he will die alone!

Dracula seems to be foreshadowing Nietzsche's railing against the collective power of "The Herd," bewailing the strength of the individual Ubermensch who makes his own way by exercising his "Will to Power."

Vlad would have probably gotten along just fine with Nietzsche.

This may also be Vlad's way of saying "Divide and conquer" and/or beware of whom you ally yourself with.

LV. The Great Architect[168] provided us two eyes in order that we might study twice what is before us . . . not look in two directions at once!

Practical application: Don't fight on two fronts. Ask Napoleon. Ask Hitler.

---

167. See Dr. Lung's *Assassin! Secrets of the Cult of the Assassins* (Paladin Press, 1997) and *Assassin!* (Citadel Press, 2004).

168. Alchemist and Freemasonry term for the mystical cosmic creative principle, i.e., God.

More philosophic: Don't split your loyalties. A man can't serve two masters . . . which is exactly what both Vlad and his father were called upon to do at times: not only appearing to "split" their loyalties by tipping their crown to both Christian and Muslim conquerors but also playing both sides against the middle when finding it impossible to steer clear of the internecine warring between the more-powerful "Christian" kingdoms surrounding him.

The choice of the term "Great Architect" is curious, perhaps revealing a more "mystical" side to the Prince of Wallachia.

LVI. When I look in the mirror, I see no reflection! Where I walk, no shadow hounds me! Were other men so fortunate.

A truly curious "Certainty" given the literary myth of later lore that "vampires" cast no shadow, nor can they see their own reflections in a mirror.

What Vlad is actually saying is that no man is his equal—if not in physical prowess, then in cunning. He may also be saying that no man is qualified to stand as his judge.

Many today do not realize the difference between "a threat" and "competition."

Whereas only those of equal skill can stand in "competition" to you, any other human being—be they possessed of mind sinister or, more likely, mind indolent—can be "a threat," an impediment to your plans, whether intentionally so (as in the case of the sinister-minded adversary) or simply because stupid people have a tendency to get in the way of their betters!

LVII. Give me steel tested by fire and men tested by ice and all I covet will soon be in my grasp.

A good steel blade is, of course, tempered by fire. Likewise Warriors.

By "men tested by ice" Dracula is using the same adjective and metaphor we do today when the ideal is to surround yourself with allies who have already proven themselves to remain calm and "cool" under pressure, and "cold as ice" when ruthlessness is required.

Sadly, such men are as rarely found as frostbite in hell. How did Hannibal put it:

> Test yourself with fire and ice, sand and sea, bile and blood,
> before your enemies do.

LVIII. Silver often succeeds where steel fails.

What cannot be obtained with the bludgeon and the blade can surely be obtained by the bribe.

This Certainty reflects the same sentiment (or is that "cynicism?") found in Certainty XXV.

While the idea of bribing someone might offend haughtier honors, which is more noble: to spend a hundred brave lives uselessly storming a gate from the outside, or spending a few coins getting that same gate opened from the inside?

LIX. I CAN SCARCE ABIDE SPIES . . . SAVE MY OWN! BUT, WHERE THE HORDE FAILS, THE HEMLOCK MAY YET SUCCEED.

Companion to the previous verse, here Vlad expresses the ambivalent feelings of many a noble man, wishing that spies were not necessary, knowing full well they are. In fact, Sun Tzu devotes an entire chapter, appropriately chapter 13, to the careful care and feeding of spies.

That those who lurk in shadows should also, on occasion, have cause to wield the dirk—or hemlock, as the case may be—in the service of their king, commander, cult leader, or whoever just happens to be paying their bills at the time, comes as no surprise. As with the breaching-an-enemy-gate analogy above, how many bullets and bombs—not to mention innocent lives—can be saved by a well-placed spike to the spine, a few droplets of snake-spit in the right cup?

Ironically, Dracula himself was betrayed by just such a spy-assassin.

LX. If today is not the day to win, then I left my pillow for naught!
Procrastination is hesitation with a bad case of the gout!

CERTAINTIES OF BLOOD

LXI. I entered this world awash in blood. Why should I expect to exit it any less soiled?

Evidently, Dracula was not big on apologies nor prone to making excuses. Rather, he was a man fit to his time, in a time when the respect given a ruler was in direct correlation to that ruler's capacity and willingness to spill blood swiftly and efficiently, if only as a prelude to calling others to the negotiating table. Certainty LII again.

LXII. A single drop of blood on a blade tells more a tale of truth than all the scrolls and scriptures of all the saints.

Actions ever speak louder than words. Don't tell me what you did, tell me how they made a movie-of-the-week about it.

LXIII. Blood paints the truest portraits.

Vlad the poet. Compare this with the LIVth of Hannibal's "Ninety-nine Truths":

> The nearer the blood, the more it burns. Blood always tells,
> but you may not like its tales.

LXIV. To drain a man of all his blood is to end him. To drain all he loves of lifeblood is to call him to task. Therefore, if a man's life proves worthless and petty, then perhaps his death might at least serve as instruction to others. Indeed, a hundred men may slip on a single drop of blood!

Nothing instructs others so much as swift and sudden and wholly unexpected misfortune befalling their friends and fellows. Thus the ancient Chinese adage: "Slay one to instruct ten thousand."

LXV. Turn your back on your blood and the world turns its back on you.

Positive spin: Vlad is admonishing us to be true to ourselves.

More probably meaning: Vlad's brother, Radu the Betrayer.

LXVI. I had scant say in my entering of this world. I fully intend to remedy that oversight upon taking my leave!

Though Nature gifts us with all the cunning we need to excel, in our liberal—and occasional libertine—use of that most excellent cunning history so often gripes and all too often does not always judge us kindly. What of it?

If we were looking for kindness being handed out, we would have done well to choose another world altogether!

Zen Masters have an ideal: "Seek passage without traces," passing through this world self-contained, seeking neither glory nor gratitude from their fellow man, nor even their fellows' recognition for a road well traveled. Ironically these monks are respected and revered worldwide for their disciplined ways and wisdom, Buddha and the begging bowl being enough for them.

For others of us, however, the path is not so serene, never so sure.

Instead of cooling our ardor and ambition, our "Will to Power" Nietzsche would say, instead of seeking "passage without traces," we are instead driven to "make a name for ourselves," challenge the road less traveled, drink the raven's blood, and spit in the eye of winter! Accepting that "There'll be time enough to rest when I'm dead!" we seize—whether the end prove wisely or woefully—the mantra of our success, satisfaction, perhaps even our salvation, those unrepentant words of Caesar: *"Veni, vedi, vice!"*[169]

Consider: They even make movies about those who try and *fail*. So long as you *try*.

CERTAINTIES OF DEATH

LXVII. Rest? Bah! That is only for women having only recently given birth. . . . And then only until the newly-born realizes its hunger. So too with a man's victories.

There truly is no rest for the wicked—or the *sinister*, if you prefer—or is there, nor should there be, rest for the truly driven and the ambitious.

Struggle is the first and final rule of Mother Nature—whether we fight on the cornfield to feed our families, on the battlefield to secure those families from being overrun, and in the equally treacherous boardroom, to vouchsafe our families' future prosperity.

If you can show me a species that has ever walked this earth who did not struggle each and every day to survive, then it's a good bet we will be standing in the "Endangered Species" wing of the Museum of Life!

While much is made of the dedication and determination of Hannibal the Conqueror, the man himself often openly praised the *enemies* from whom he learned, for example speaking in awe of the tireless drive of the intractable Roman foes, Marcus Claudius Marcellus:

> He neither permits us to rest when he has won, nor does he himself rest when he is overcome. It appears we will have to perpetually fight with him! When successful, his confidence, and when unsuccessful, his shame, both likewise urge him on to further enterprise![170]

---

169. "I came, I saw, I conquered!"
170. Quoted from *The Lives by Plutarch,* 100 A.D.

Basic Nietzsche. We must constantly push against our walls, or, most assuredly, those walls will begin to close in on us.

LXIX. For some, death is enemy. For others, welcome friend. Play the attentive host to both.

Again we hear the echoes of "Better a true enemy than a false friend" and "Keep your friends close, and your enemies closer."

It's always good to know what the opposition is thinking. Better still, when you can tell the opposition what to think.

LXX. A coffin is the best of beds, but death the worst of rests.

The tale is told of a certain prince who, whenever he led his forces to war, always carried in his train a coffin filled to overflowing with gold. When one day a visiting foreign diplomat ventured to ask the purpose of conveying something so bright and precious in a container so grim. The prince explained, "A constant reminder to myself that, as precious as is the gold now filling that coffin, one day I must fill it with something even more precious . . . *myself*!"

LXXI. Only the dead know rest . . . and sometimes not even then!

Prophecy on Vlad's part, given his postmortem vilification, growing more horrendous as the centuries passed, until the bold and noble warrior-prince of Wallachia ironically gained immortality as the fictional Dracula, Lord of the Damned.

LXXII. Thorns make us treasure the rose all the more.

If you can't be remembered for your fragrance, at least be remembered for your flagrance.

Dracula's final Certainty reminds us of the Samurai assertion that "death gives life its sweetness."

Part V
How to Start Your Own Cult and Secret Society

"Brute force is not enough to turn the masses into monsters baying for blood; this will only happen if they are won over, hearts, minds—and souls. . . . People are more easily persuaded by invitations to join a glorious gang, whether the Nazis or the 'righteous', by an appeal to the spirit than by mere rhetoric, or even brute force."
—Lynn Picknett and Clive Prince, *The Stargate Conspiracy*

Introduction

VOLTAIRE WAS NO FAN of organized religion. Thus his declaration (or simply *observation*) that, "Each one marches gaily off to crime under the banner of his saint."

With all due respect to Voltaire, and much respect indeed is due, his statement seems to indict *all* believers, or at least the self-appointed shepherds of those believers as being with "criminal" intent.

Voltaire doth paint with overbroad strokes.

Not all believers are fools. Nor are all shepherds of said believers criminally inclined.

For in contradiction to Voltaire's declaration, we could not counter with the oft-quoted proverb that "crime does not pay." It most certainly *does* pay. Most criminals commit *dozens* of profitable ventures before they are—inevitably—caught.

If crime truly did not pay, then why are cult leaders so often so prosperous?

In 2006, "*Atlantic Monthly*'s 100 Most Influential Americans"[171] included three cult leaders:

- #52 was Joseph Smith, described in the article as "The founder of Mormonism, America's most famous homegrown faith."

---

171. Cleveland Plain Dealer, December 24, 2006.

- #74 was Brigham Young. His bio: "What Joseph Smith founded, Young preserved, leading the Mormons to their promised land."[172]
- #86 was Mary Baker Eddy, founder of the "Christian Science" cult.

So, yeah, maybe crime *does* pay or, at the very least, starting your own "cult" sure as hell pays!

And let's not forget the "fringe benefits."

Joseph Smith had twenty-three wives while here on earth and is now a "god" of his own planet somewhere out in space![173] In fact, The Church of Jesus Christ of Latter Day Saints, better known as "the Mormons," once proclaimed a "cult" by orthodox Christianity but gaining more "respectability" even as we speak, teaches that Jesus and Lucifer were brothers[174] and that every *man* can become a god and rule over his own planet with many *wives*.[175]

Sounds like good work if you can get it. And what's to stop you from getting it?

It's not like you have to have any actual discernible skills; there's no required educational background, no age, sex, or proof of citizenship needed for *anyone* to start their own religion.

You're not even required to send a donation to that Universal Life Church out in California for "credentials." Fact is, you can print up your own and they're just as valid as if you went to seminary for four years.

We're talking (1) *a wide open field* with (2) *no racial, age, or gender restrictions* where—drum-roll, please—(3) *people give you free money for talking bullshit and telling them what they want to hear!*

I'm thinking "dream job" with no "downside"?

Down through history many people—male, female, and quite a few "undecided"—have started their own cults.

Of course, "cult" is what the big religion calls the little religion, so some of those hearty souls who decide to hang up their own cross, crescent, or

---

172. No mention was made of Young giving his blessing to the Mountain Meadows Massacre, where Mormon "Death Angels" slaughtered an entire wagon train of men, women, and children.

173. See "Secrets" in *Power of Prophecy* (Volume 161).

174. So does Islam, by the way.

175. See "Secrets" in *Power of Prophecy* (Volume 161).

decapitated chicken over the doorway to that dilapidated storefront and call it "The First Church of Bring Your Wallet" just might survive long enough—including surviving IRS audits and coup attempts by equally ambitious (read: "*greedy*") lieutenants—to win their respect as a true "religion."

So if you should decide starting your very own cult, or secret society for that matter, is the way to go, you're in good company:

> Behind a pale lie
> Behind a Yale tie
> Behind a palmer's collar:
> 'Tis two things for certain
> Hide behind The Black Curtain
> to poach a soul
> or depocket a dollar! (Finders' ditty, circa 1777)

In 1954, the Church (some say "cult") of Scientology was founded in Los Angeles.

A scant few years earlier, the cult's founder, former science-fiction writer L. Ron Hubbard, had confided to fellow sci-fi writer Lloyd Eshbach, "I'd like to start a religion. That's where the money is."[176]

It's called "Propheteering." Being a prophet for profit. The scam has been around since the first caveman (a weaselly-looking, little no-hunting-ability type) talked the other cavemen into giving him a mastadon steak in exchange for doing a song-and-dance to make Bad-Assed-Thunder-God-in-Sky stop hurling his lightning bolts.

Not much has changed since Og started that first "cave cult."

Today, especially since the advent of the Internet, it's so easy to start your own cult, even the U.S. government's getting into the act. First, because of cults' possible ties to dangerous "militant religious factions," and also for the potential of using such cults against our enemies:

> It is known that the security services have long taken an interest in such cults . . . seeking explanations for how such beliefs originate and spread, for reasons that are entirely understandable. For example, quasireligious cults and small but subversive political groups have the potential for great social

---

176. See *Over My Shoulder* by Lloyd Eshbach (1983).

unrest and worse—the Nazis started small, after all—and they are often used for criminal and anti-social purposes, such as drug-trafficking or gun-running. . . . Another reason for official interest in such belief systems is their possible use in psychological warfare. One can imagine, for example, the wealth of possibilities in introducing cult beliefs into an enemy country in order to seriously destabilize it or to ensnare and covertly influence susceptible politicians. One of the main purposes of the intelligence community is specifically to investigate the origins, structure and spread of belief systems. (Pickett and Prince, *The Stargate Conspiracy*)

Pickett and Prince go on to examine U.S. government involvement in "cult-creating" experiments in Mexico in 1956.[177]

By now you've undoubtedly realized that cults aren't only an American, or even a Western phenomenon. It might interest you to know that the world's fastest-growing Asian "cult" is the Chinese *Falun Gong*, whose members number in the millions inside China alone. And the cult—teaching a hodgepodge of Far Eastern meditation and philosophy—is spreading throughout the rest of Asia and to the West.

The Communist Chinese government—no fan of religion in general— is reportedly trying—unsuccessfully—to check the cult's growth.

Don't forget, there are still remnants of the *Aum Shunri Kyo* killer cult operating in Japan . . . and beyond?

Korea gave the world Moon's Unification Church, while India gave the world Bhagwan Shree Rajneesh, the Hare Krishna movement, and a hundred other cults—all of which seem to have found their way to Western shores.

From the Middle East, we have the eclectic *Bahai* faith, thriving despite Iranian Islam's genocidal attempts to wipe it out.

And there are cults who worship anything "Ancient Egypt," and Islamic spinoff cults like the Nation of Islam (showcased at the end of this section).

Cult is what the big church calls the little church.

In general, when we think of "cult" we think of a small group of fanat-

---

177. See Lynn Pickett and Clive Prince, *The Stargate Conspiracy* (1999).

ics and/or misfits desperately clinging to a wild-eyed Manson-like character. And half the time we're right!

But cults come in many shapes and sizes.

In general, a cult breaks away from a larger church body because someone gets a "revelation"—usually resulting in them writing a new "Bible"—or else they "discover" a new interpretation of existing scripture not accepted by entrenched church leaders.

And so the "cult" breaks away from the larger body.

Other times, followers will begin to "collect" around some charismatic person who makes them feel good by making them feel special.

Those disciples tell their friends and families, and before you can say "Which way to Waco?" a new cult is born.

It doesn't matter if this new cult is centered around a reinterpretation of existing scripture, or scripture handed to "the Master" by space aliens—all that matters is that the followers believe.

Pay attention now, here's the *key*: It doesn't really matter what the scripture or what spiel "the Master" spits and spins because, in a "cult," the followers are *not* devoted to the teachings, *they are devoted to the teacher!*

And so you have to become that teacher.

And although for the purposes of this study we focus on *religious* cults, don't think your cult has to be "religious" in nature, *per se.*

Cults come in all *denominations*—fives, tens, twenties, Visa, and Master-Card! (Sorry, old preacher's joke.)

Many gangs and cliques—including Al Qaeda—qualify as "cults," especially when they are centered around one charismatic "focus figure"—like Osama bin Laden.

Which brings up another important point: You don't have to be the *overt* leader of your cult. You can always set up a "front man," a naïve "true believer" whose strings you pull behind the scenes, who's available to take the fall if (when) the time comes. (See the chapter entitled "The Eleventh Commandment.").

> *"A man prefers to believe what he prefers to be true."*
> —Sir Francis Bacon

> *"All religions are founded on the fear of the many and the cleverness of the few."*
> —Stendhal

THE NATURE OF THE BEAST

"Oh, the nature of the beast,
born it West or born it East?
Sport a collar, wear a robe?
Matters naught, to cover globe.
Is it fast or is it feast?
You'll care no bit in the least,
When your pocket weights with gold,
from the sacred soul so sold!"
—Finder's ditty, circa 1777

Before getting down to the specific tactics that will allow you to recruit members to your new cult and, more importantly, turn them into slavish dogs salivating at their "Master's" feet, tails wagging time to your every word, content with the bones you throw them . . . before all that, you need to decide on your overall strategy for establishing your cult.

You have two options: Manipulate or Manufacture.

1. Manipulate somebody else's cult.

You join an existing church or cult and slowly subvert the members to your way of thinking.

David Koresh did this . . . brilliantly.

Briefly: Koresh (then called Vernon Howell) joined the already-existing Branch Davidian cult, a breakaway from the Seventh-Day Adventists (who, ironically, are still themselves considered a "cult" by mainstream Christianity).

After seducing the current sixty-five-year-old cult leader, televangelist Lois Roden, and surviving an actual Wild West–style gunfight with Roden's son, George (whom everyone expected to take over for his mother), Vernon-now-"David Koresh" succeeded in seizing control of the Branch Davidian's Waco compound.

From the day he became Lois Roden's *handyman*[178] to the day he became

---

178. Reportedly, in more ways than one!

the undisputed leader of the Branch Davidians, had taken David Koresh eight years.

"King David's" reign at Waco would last barely five years. . . . Better to burn out—literally!—than fade away.

You can also remain a loyal follower of the original cult founder, learn all their tricks, and peacefully succeed them upon their death. Should you get impatient, more than one "Master" has died of "suspiciously good health."

Brigham Young (1807–1877) inherited the Mormon cult after its founder-prophet, Joseph Smith, was lynched in 1844.

Likewise, Louis Farrakhan wrestled control of the Nation of Islam (NOI) cult from W. D. Muhammad, son of cult founder, Elijah Poole, after the latter's death.

Of course, it didn't hurt Farrakhan any that Malcolm X—whom everyone knew was slated to succeed Elijah Muhammad, died in a hail of gunfire in 1965 (and who do you think was the hands-down favorite suspect for having engineered said assassination?).

2. Manufacture your own cult.

Start from scratch after you receive that "divine revelation"—*God* spoke to you, *aliens* took you aboard their craft, whatever.

Or, you can mix-and-match elements to create an eclectic bricolage of bits and pieces stolen from various sects and different religions.

HOW TO RECRUIT CULT MEMBERS

Let's face it, a cult ain't much good without a bunch of fanatical followers at your beck and call.

What kind of followers? And how many? Depends on your agenda—*the Dollar*, or *the Diabolical*? Or both?

If your motivation for starting a cult is purely monetary—*the Dollar*—then you first need to do a little math:

Up front decide how much money a month you can live comfortably on—minus cult operation overhead.

So long as you've taken the time to file for federal "nonprofit status," then you don't have to worry about paying taxes. So it's all pure profit after overhead.

Let's say you decide you can live comfortably on $10,000 a month: $120,000 a year.

You could aim at building a cult with 10,000 members, each of whom would be *required* to tithe $1.00 a month.

But 10,000 followers is way too unwieldy, especially if you're trying to (1) keep your cult out of the papers and (2) stay under the radar.

If you're only looking to make $10,000 a month, 10,000 followers are a lot to keep track of, with all kinds of additional overhead costs inevitably cutting into your profit margin.

Ten thousand people sounds too much like work!

Five thousand followers, each contributing $2.00, would get you to your goal with only half as many "troubled" (and *troublesome*) souls to worry about.

Two thousand five hundred devoted followers 'fessing up $4.00 apiece a month would get you to the same goal.

One thousand followers kicking in $10.00 a month starts to look doable.

One hundred followers dropping $100 dollars apiece every month into the collection plate or, better yet, 50 followers turning over $200.00 a month will literally get you to the church on time!

So, the first thing to determine is (1) how much money you want (not need—*want!*), and (2) what's the least number of followers you'll need to accomplish that goal?

That is, if your goal is the all-mighty dollar—or *the All-Mighty's* dollar, as the case may be!

If, on the other hand, you've got some kind of *"diabolical"* agenda for starting your own cult—a vehicle through which to reap revenge on your enemies,[179] or taking over a small (or not so small) African nation, something along those lines—then there may be no limit to the number of followers you'll need to stuff up under your wing.

As you can see, doing "diabolical" is a lot more work than just "propheteering" for the dollar.

Even so, in both instances you still need to know how to pull in the

---

179. See section on "Hannibal's Five Rules for Revenge."

right kind of followers. To do that, you need to get good at both "The Pulling" and "The Culling."

Chance, Dance, and Trance

Chance. They say "Chance favors the prepared mind." Never was this truer than in the "cult" business.

Different times spawn and support different types of cult movements.

In Germany after World War I, cults sprung up all over the place—fueled by (1) a continent-wide *economic depression*, as well as (2) the *cultural depression* of the German people as a whole for having just been humiliated in "The Great War."

Many of these German cults, like the infamous *Thule Society* and *The Vril*, were a bizarre and volatile mixture of ancient occult hoodoo and the racial supremacy politics of the time.

Adolf Hitler and a half-dozen other "cult" leaders thrived in this atmosphere. . . . Hitler just thrived a little more ruthlessly than the rest!

In the countercultural 1960s, not just in America but around the world, we likewise witnessed cults of various kinds spring up, all at least giving lip service to the pervasive "peace and love" message so popular at the time—with just enough "Free Love" and free drugs thrown in to catch and keep a youngster's short attention span.

These "hippie" cults ranged from well-meaning Jesus Freaks and Bo & Peep's "love-bombing"[180] message, to the darker end of the spectrum where lurked David "Moses" Berg's *Children of God* cult and Charlie Manson's Spahn Ranch Devil-spawn.

After the British rock-and-roll invasion of the early sixties came the Far Eastern invasion of gurus, Maharishis, and Zen Masters in the late sixties.

The sixties—up through the seventies—were a good time for cults, up until Jim Jones went all catiwhompus in 1978. (It only takes one mass suicide to mess it up for everybody!)

---

180. "Love-bombing" refers to a cult overwhelming a new recruit with expressions of "love," "belonging," and "family." The formula is to give your followers understanding and attention to get them standing at attention!

After the figurative and then *literal* helter-skelter of the sixties and seventies, cults in the eighties discovered infomercials and started selling "self-help"—but remained cults nonetheless. Tagging along close behind came "channelers" and "ghost whisperers."

The eighties also saw an upsurge in the Christian fundamentalist "traditional values" movement, which, in turn, spawned several "Fundie" cults like *The Promise Keepers.*

The eighties also saw the emergence of those *"Fags must die! AIDS is God's punishment!"* placard-carrying "family cults," usually centered around a sexually repressed, possibly incestuous patriarch.

By the nineties, truly out-of-this-world UFO cults like the Raelians and Heaven's Gate began taking off. In the case of Heaven's Gate—literally!

The point? In each decade, there are wily propheteers who "catch the wave" and cash in—figuratively and literally—on the spiritual angst of the times.

Carpe diem. Timing is important in all things. Timing is simply seizing chance by the 'nads!

For example, cults often recruit on college campuses during exam time, when they know students are under stress and looking for a way out—*any* way out. A soothing empowerment message, a mojo prayer or fetish to help them pass a final, and you've got their interest long enough to draw them in.

Cults also recruit heavily in prison—where men and women have far too much time on their hands to read the tons of *free* cult writings that flood into prisons because prison officials are afraid to step on prisoners' "religious rights."

Of late, authorities are seeing more cult activity—especially from fringe Islamic groups—aimed at inmates.[181]

There are presently three million prisoners in United States prisons.

Many of these previously abused, ignored, and otherwise marginalized outcasts from society are willing and eager to accept *any* praise from outside prison walls.

Cults know this.

---

181. See "The Prison Connection" in *666 Devilish Secrets of Islam* by Baughman and Black (Only Publication: 2010).

Since the time of the Quakers, religion has been given a wide berth for ministering to prisoners.

During the sixties, various cults, as well as militant and racist gangs masquerading behind the Black Curtain of "religion," fervently recruited inside U.S. prisons.

By his own admission, while in prison Charles Manson suckled at every cult teat possible, from Crowleyan black magic to Scientology—much of which he later incorporated into his own "cult-speak." For example, Manson often bragged of having become a "Clear," the highest level of personal development within Scientology, and "borrowed" freely from the Christian book of *Revelation* for his "Helter-Skelter" end-times scenario.

Likewise, Malcolm X was recruited into the racist *Nation of Islam* (aka "Black Muslims") while in prison, as were several members of the violent 1970s *Symbionese Liberation Army* terrorist "cult."

Three of San Francisco's bloodthirsty "Death Angels" *Zebra Killers* had also joined the Black Muslims/Nation of Islam while serving time at San Quentin.[182]

The Zebra Killers were part of a Black Muslim splinter group calling themselves "Death Angels" that required the murder of "blue-eyed devils" as a form of initiation. In 1973 to 1974, fifteen whites were killed and another eight whites were wounded or raped by these "Death Angels."[183]

Former street gang members of Chicago's infamous *Blackstone Rangers* "converted" to Islam en masse in the late 1960s, transforming themselves into the "religious group" *El Rukn* ("rukn," Arabic for "stone" after the black stone worshiped by Muslims at Mecca).

You might recall that several members of El Rukn were indicted in the late seventies for taking money from Libya's Muammar Kaddafi in return for the assassinations of Libyan expatriates in the United States.[184]

The tradition of cults and killer cadre recruiting prisoners continues.

Since Nine-Eleven, U.S. prisons have become major breeding grounds for Islamic terrorist recruiters.[185]

But long before Nine-Eleven there were warnings of such recruitment:

---

182. See *The Encyclopedia of Serial Killers* by Michael Newton (2000).

183. Ibid.

184. See *666 Devilish Secrets of Islam* by Baughman and Black (Only Publication, 2010).

185. See *Report: Prisons breeding ground for terror* in *USA Today,* September 19, 2006, 3A.

In early 1986, Iran began approaching and ultimately recruiting prisoners while they were still incarcerated. Iranian-supported front organizations made contact with disgruntled black Muslim prisoners in all the major prisons in America. (Yossef Bodansky, *Terror! The Inside Story of the Terorist Conspiracy in America*)

So whether your cult plans are "The Dollar," or "The Diabolical," don't overlook the possible recruitment of prisoners.

Prison officials are often hard-pressed to find enough things to keep their charges occupied. "Religious services" are one way to remedy that problem.

Prisons thus provide a "captive audience" for your cult recruiting.

Convicted felons are no strangers to scheming after "the Dollar," and many of your convict converts will undoubtedly not be averse to adding their "expertise" to any "Diabolical" plans you might have. Pesky "morals" be damned.

The advent of the Internet literally opened up a world of possibilities—hence a world of possible cult recruits.

Who said your cult members have to live within driving distance of your physical church? You never heard of electronic wire transfer? Online credit card purchases?

Start a blog, or a church website. Express your "cult" revelations online. Run your "beLIEfs" up a flagpole and see who salutes—or bows.

So take a chance! Next comes . . .

Dance. As in "the ol' song-and-dance."

Before setting out to round up some *cattle* into your cult, you need to write down your basic line of *bull*.

Every cult leader needs a good (1) simple, (2) attractive, and (3) entertaining—spiel. You're free to "borrow" this line of BS from already existing "holy" writ, or you can make up your own. Or you can mix-and-match and pretty much make it up as you go along—you know, like Monty Python.

The trouble with borrowing from holy writ—say, the Bible, for instance—is that everyone knows the darn thing inside and out so, if you should stumble over a verse or otherwise misquote, you could end up undermining your credibility. (There is an exception to this. See "The Culling" that follows on what to do when you are "challenged.")

Folks have been translating and reinterpreting the Bible since it was first put together 1,500 years ago—and that's just the *New* Testament. Don't get me started on the Old Testament!

Being eclectic in nature, the Bible lends itself to differing interpretation so. . . . Have at it! Seems everybody else has!

Of course the same could be said of other "holy books." That's what cults do best—they reinterpret what already exists.

You can also mix-and-match East and West to create a "Universalist" hodgepodge philosophy impossible for anyone to refute—since no one has any idea where to start!

"Revelations" from on high seem to be more and more common.

Whether your muse is that wee-small voice within, or some god all a'thunderin' up on the mountaintop, either way, you're sure to get enough "revelations" to literally fill a book . . . or rather, a "Bible."

And don't feel guilty about putting words in God's mouth. At one time or another every cult has been accused of a little "gospel doctoring". . . . Okay, out-and-out *rewriting*!

Jehovah's Witnesses are still castigated for sticking "Jehovah" (their obvi-ous-to-everyone-but-themselves misinterpretation of the Hebrew "Yahweh") into *their* version of the Bible in order to give it a false impression of conti-nuity from Old Testament through New.

Word has it *The Book of Mormon* (first published in 1830) was either pla-giarized from an earlier 1823 religious book or else adapted from an unpub-lished—stolen—novel.[186]

The Aquarian Gospel of Jesus the Christ (first appearing in the nineteenth century, a beloved "Bible" of *New Agers*) was supposedly used as the tem-plate for the new "Koran" used by the *Moorish Science Temple* cult (reluctant progenitor of Elijah Poole's "Nation of Islam").

And, speaking of the Koran: Muslims themselves disagree on how their holy book came to be. Some maintain it descended from heaven already written, handed to Muhammad by the Angel Gabriel.

Other Islamic sects claim Muhammad (an illiterate man by all account) copied it from a mystical book Gabriel allowed him to view.

Still others opt for the more logical explanation that the various chapters (suras) of Koran were collected *after* Muhammad's death.[187]

---

186. Wilson (2000).

187. See Baughman and Black's *666 Devilish Secrets of Islam* (Only Publication, 2010).

Of late, numerous "UFO Bibles" have been beaming down—each a little more "out there" than the next.

If *they* can do it, why can't *you*? If you *write* it, they will come.

Early on in your cult creation, don't "obsess," carving the rules and regulations of your cult into stone (that only worked once, and only because nobody had invented Commandment Post-it Notes yet!).

It's better to *keep your cult philosophy as vague as possible in the beginning*. This gives you plenty of wiggle room later on.

Learn to improvise. And always have a backup plan. Any good "backup plan" includes knowing where the back door is! (More on this in the chapter "The Eleventh Commandment.")

Job One at this stage is to get those wallflowers up on to the "dance floor," get them moving, *fill them pews*.

It's a law of physics that "objects in motion tend to stay in motion." And it's a proven fact that the more time a person invests in a cult, the more time they *will* invest (further) in that cult. In for a penny, in for a pound (of flesh).

To get 'em on the dance floor, use a tune they are already familiar with (e.g., the Bible), before stepping up the tempo, changing the beat—just a little, at first.

Once you've got them stepping lively to your new tune, they'll never go back to their old arrangement.

Show them new and exciting ways to reinterpret their old faith. Convince them they're the most vital link in the "new" religion. They're *special* . . . becau . . . *you* need them, *God* is calling them!

Show them how interesting and exciting their boring lives can be and they'll follow you anywhere. (Middle-aged "empty nesters" lead "boring" lives, right?)

How you gonna keep 'em down on the farm once they've seen gay Par-ee?

Trance. In the same way a snake charmer entrances his pet cobra by both tapping his foot and by gently swaying back-and-forth,[188] so too your

---

188. What? You thought it was that boring flute music that "hypnotized" the snake? No, the music is just a distraction for the suckers watching the show.

"swaying" must first attract and then entrance (i.e., hold the attention of) your prospective recruits.

Congratulations. You've caught their attention, piqued their curiosity, and peeked behind the oh-so-proper *mask* they show everyone else. You've succeeded in making an entrance into their lives. Now, how do you keep them hooked and keep them coming back for more and, more importantly, keep them bringing their *money* back with them?

Use your *entrance* to *en-trance*.

Slowly, inexorably, you replace *their* needs with your needs, slowly replacing their old life with the "new" and "exciting" life you've chosen for them.

Start slowly, giving them hints and glimpses of possibilities, of things they can do to change their lives, to make their lives more exciting and *meaningful*.

Do this in small increments, because *change scares people*.

If people joining a cult *today* could envision what they'll actually look like and be acting like *a year from now*, the change would be so radical it would scare them off. This is the insidiousness of the cult experience—the way it slithers up into your soul, inch by inch, until slowly strangling your will and individuality from within. Ooh, creepy, huh? But only if you're on the receiving end. For "the Master" it's just another day at the office . . . counting *receipts*.

Begin with simple cult involvement: Get the person *listening* to what you or your strategically placed disciples are saying as you work next to them, then get them to read some of your cult literature.

Later, out of curiosity, they'll log on to your website . . . only to discover *their name* mentioned in a good light.

Ultimately, you talk them into coming to a meeting—just one meeting couldn't hurt, "just to see what we're all about." At that meeting you "love-bomb" them out of existence.

Another way to insinuate your cult in a person's life is to persuade them to volunteer for "community" events and projects, never suspecting the event is being sponsored by your cult.

Many cults use front organizations and sponsor events behind various organizational blinds and banners. The people and *politicians* participating in these "ecumenical" and "non-partisan" get-togethers never suspect the actual cult sponsor behind the event. Think "photo-op."

The Church of Scientology has been tried and convicted in the Court of Public Opinion of being experts of this kind of operation, as has the *Dahn Yoga* group (of which, more below).

Another ploy is to plant your recruiters in already existing "self-help" groups, including those sponsored by other churches: drug and alcohol therapy groups; troubled teen groups; groups for abused women; and sexaholics meetings—anywhere and everywhere "damaged" human beings might need a helping hand and a friendly shoulder.

Such small group settings are perfect for dropping "advertisements" (verbal and printed) for *your* meetings, and for your *agents provocateur* (working separately or as a team) to "testify" to how *your* group helped them "get it together."

Always offer to pick up and drive anyone interested in coming along to the next cult meeting. Bus the old folk.

Provide daycare for bored and lonely mothers needing a break . . . and a sympathetic ear.

Once your cult is up and running, host your own such self-help groups, all designed to spot and shepherd prospective recruits in your direction. Always *reward* self-help group members who bring friends and family—or complete strangers!—with them.

People who unknowingly volunteer to help with one of your (secretly) cult-sponsored community improvement projects will be pleasantly surprised when they learn your group is sponsoring the event—"But I thought you people were a crazy cult?" Pleasantly surprised enough to come to your next meeting?

Do "community improvement" work as a way of putting a helpful, friendly face on your cult.

At one point Jim Jones was appointed chairman of the local California Housing Commission, hobnobbed with local politicians, and was shown in one of his prized photos (photo-op!) shaking hands with activist-politician "Former Presidential Candidate" Ralph Nader.

The goal is to get recruits to do more and more for your cult, to spend more time "servicing" your cult. The more of their time you can occupy the better, until they have no life of their own and are coming to you every night for their next day's schedule.

Lures: "The Pulling"

The cult leader's craft is first and foremost the art of reading people.

Before you can get *what you want*, you have to figure out *what they need*.

The cult leader isn't a "taker" (at least not at first), he's the *worst* kind of "giver." He gives his disciples exactly what they want.

Nowhere is the warning "Be careful what you wish for!" more timely than when dealing with a sinister cult recruiter.

We all have our individual desires. And Buddha warned that *unrealistic desires* is where all our problems start. For the up-and-coming cult leader, Buddha's observation holds great promise—and potential profit!

Not only does each potential recruit have individual wants and needs the cult leader can exploit, but three are also general needs—and desires— all human beings share:

Offer them freedom. This works especially well on younger cult recruits who are eager to experience the "adult" pleasures of life without paying the costs. Free sex, drugs, and rock-and-roll works wonders on these kinds of recruits. Gangs know this.

This "freedom" ploy also works on middle-aged recruits.

For example, for middle-aged men going through a midlife crisis (trying to recapture some of their "glory days"), send your young female disciples to them to "show them around" and show them a "good time."

David Berg's seventies Children of God cult was notorious for their sexual escapades and molestations. The cult sent teenage girls called "Hookers for God" out to seduce men into the cult.

This is one of the oldest of cult lures, there are even examples in the Bible, but Charlie Manson summed it up nicely when he explained, "If I control the women, I control the men!"

And don't forget those now middle-aged women who married young, suppressing their own goals and desires. Their children now grown, these women would now like to "experience" a little of what life has to offer. Offer them an "adventure," make them feel young and desirable again, and they will follow you to the ends of the earth. Too busy to do the dirty deed yourself? Sic one of your young, studly "Personal Bible Tutors" on them. (Can you say "cougar"?)

Offer security. Offer security to those looking for discipline, those desiring to live a drug-free, anxiety-free life.

Offer security to the homeless family who's fallen on hard times. Kindness—whether sincere or sinister—is always the best grease.

Opening a soup kitchen or "mission" in a depressed part of town is an excellent way to pull in recruits. Granted, you probably won't be recruiting many "high-end" (i.e., wealthy) disciples off skid row, but what recruits from this part of town lack in out-of-pocket donations they often more than make up for in gratitude and devotion.

Offer sanctuary to the abused wife. Clothe the naked, feed the poor. Minister to their stomachs as well as their souls, and your cult will grow.

What's that old saying? "Win their hearts and minds . . . and their asses will follow!"

When offering security, offer *"The 4 F's"*:

No Financial Worries. All their future material needs will be provided for them by the cult—just as soon as they "donate" all their present material goods to the cult!

No Family Worries. *We* are your family now. It takes a village to raise a child, and a cult to raise *your* children to become future cult members. (Gotta love that *polygamy* thing, where you can "grow your own"!)

No Fucking Worries. On the one lubricated hand, our "Vow of Celibacy" relieves you of all that sexual "pressure to perform" you feel out in society—the "responsibility" to find a mate and satisfy that mate.

On the other hairy palm, should you "need" a mate, "the Master" will—after much "prayer"—choose a mate for you.

Recall how Reverend Sun Myung Moon of the Unification Church randomly chooses members to be wedded, officiating over mass marriages where thousands of his followers are joined in "holy" matrimony to people they've only met a few moments before.

For those male disciples showing especial devotion and/or chosen for special . . . delicate and messy tasks, "special companions" may be assigned to these agents and warriors to ease their burden and as "rewards" for dealing with difficult problems discreetly

Lest you get to thinking cult masters using sex to entice, control, and motivate followers is something new. . . .

The medieval Islamic Cult of the Assassins (Hashishins) were notorious for drugging recruits to sleep before placing them into a specially prepared "pleasure garden."

Upon awakening, the still woozy recruits would be convinced they had magically been transported to heaven for a glimpse of what awaited any "martyr" who died in the service of the Assassin Grandmaster. The recruits would suddenly find themselves surrounded by seventy-two (who can count when you're high?) beautiful *virgins* (yeah, like you can tell *that* when you're high!). These beauties would satisfy the recruits' every lust.

After a time, these recruits would again be unknowingly drugged and would reawaken "back on earth" in the Grandmaster's castle—eager to kill and to die a martyr, having already had a glimpse of what awaited them upon death.[189]

If you keep up on accounts of modern-day Islamic suicide bombers, you'll realize little has changed in the past seven hundred years. Seventy-two virgins is still seventy-two virgins!

No Final Worries. Heaven (or at least a nifty ride on a really cool space-ship!) awaits the faithful who show their love and devotion to God (or the aliens) by serving "the Master" here on earth.

Offer special and secret revelations.

Your cult is the sole (pun intended!) recipient of the All-Mighty's wisdom in this particular corner of the universe.

Your cult has "The Sacred Word" and/or "The Secret of the Universe"—the real spiritual meat any true seeker will gladly sell their soul to feast on. Feed it to them one morsel at a time in order to keep 'em hungry (and then hooked!) for as long as possible.

Offer power and revenge.

Offer this to those who desire both.

Assure your flock they will come out the "winners" at the end of time, sitting on that golden throne laughing at all the poor, roasting nonbelievers.

Play to any xenophobia and/or racism in your recruits. (Hey, it worked for Hitler and Elijah Muhammad.)

Give your loyal—albeit *grudge-holding*—disciples the power to strike

---

189. See *Assassin!* by Dr. Lung (Citadel, 2004).

back at their real and imagined enemies—"power" that comes with *your* strings attached.

Likewise, feed their need for "revenge"—just make sure you keep *the videotape* safely tucked away in case your dog ever decides to turn on you.

WHO TO RECRUIT

"Most religion is based upon the passive attitude. We are helpless puppets in the hands of fate. We are swept along by forces that are far bigger than we are. And if we happen to be religiously inclined, then we look for an organization in which we feel comfortable, surrounded by other believers. Most of us are natural followers."
—Colin Wilson, *Rogue Messiahs*

So when setting out to fill your pews, whom should you target—uh, recruit?

Anyone is fair game—some are just more fair, and some much more game than others.

We have the common stereotype of cult members being losers, of their being "drugged-out hippie types"—we can thank Charles Manson for that one.

Or we think of cult members as literally UFO-worshiping space cadets like Heaven's Gate and the so-called Nation of Islam.

The "garbage into gold" scenario (again thanks to Charlie) is that cults seek out the discarded, the disaffected, and the disenfranchised of society. The underlying idea being that the more worse off someone is (i.e., the more desperate), then the more susceptible they are to recruitment and, subsequently they are more fanatical (i.e., "kill crazy") when "saved" by a savvy and sinister cult leader.

It's true racist cults like the Nation of Islam *do* make their money by targeting those too often marginalized by society.

However, Charlie Manson's followers were college students, as were many of the students pulled into Berg's *Children of God*.

Jim Jones's cult was comprised of primarily hardworking middle-aged adults—hardly "wild-eyed dopers."

Heaven's Gate people were computer geeks and techno-mages. And recall how the Aum Shunri Kyo cult deliberately recruited scientists and technical advisers—unfortunately, just the kind of recruits who knew how to manufacture Sarin nerve gas!

As far back as 1955, L. Ron Hubbard's Scientology made a special effort to recruit movie stars, sports celebrities, and business and government officials.[190]

As previously alluded to, all of us have basic psychological needs that grow out of real physical concerns for sustenance and security—basically the base of Maslow's pyramid.

Beyond these basic "animal" needs, we humans have a need to belong, to be part of a tribe. This may grow out of our animal pack–mentality of safety in numbers. But (1) we also want—*need*—to find the *meaning of life*[191] and (2) we need to feel we have some influence over our destiny (à la Nietzsche's *Will to Power*).

Belonging to a cult can give us all of this: a meaning to life, a purpose, a feeling of family.

In return, often *without consciously realizing it*, we become dependent on the cult—especially the cult leader—for our new identity. In exchange, we overlook any "inconsistency" in our savior's philosophy or actions, and become fiercely protective—paranoid!—of our new "family," guarding it against any "outsiders" who threaten our newfound sense of purpose:

> The psychology of discipleship is just as bizarre. It is basically the psychology of wish fulfillment. In the skills of self-deception disciples are, if possible, even more adept than their masters. (Wilson, 2000)

Yes, all of us are fair game when it comes to cult recruitment. I know what you're thinking, "I'm too smart to ever get involved with a cult!" Heh-heh-heh.

Each minority and subgroup within a society has its own needs, and so cults adapt different strategies when recruiting from each of those groups.

It seems each of us have something unique to bring to the table—or at least to the collection plate:

The Young. Youth wants (needs) to prove itself through "rites of passage." Youth wants to be accepted into the adult world with all its vice.

---

190. See *Rolling Stone,* March 9, 2006.
191. See Vicktor Frankl's *Mans' Search for Meaning.*

Gangs know this. So do cults.

In the 1980s, White Supremacist Tom Metzger single-handedly created the racist Skinhead movement in the United States, a nationwide cult still numbering in the thousands. In turn, the American Skinhead movement influenced similar Skinhead movements worldwide.[192]

Today, thanks to Metzger, when we hear the word *skinhead* we instantly conjure up a picture in our mind of violent, racist street thugs. But prior to Metzger's involvement, most North American Skinhead "crews," centered mostly in Michigan and Toronto, were *non-racist and multi-ethnic* followers of a form of Jamaican music known as "Ska."

Disillusioned with the "old guard" of American White supremacists, Metzger revamped his WAR (White Aryan Resistance) organization to actively recruit and "turn" young, white, non-aligned Skinheads.

To accomplish this, Metzger hosted "Whitestock," a racist rip-off of Woodstock, inviting racially oriented heavy metal bands from all over the country. Metzger used Whitestock and similar WAR events to spread his Aryan gospel. Giving these young thugs the attention, and validation they so badly craved, WAR convinced previously unaligned Skinheads to turn racist.

Credit where credit is due, no matter how dubious that credit. Because he astutely recognized what those youth needed, within a short period, Metzger had succeeded in "breeding" the next generation of White supremacists, in effect, creating a nationwide Skinhead "cult."[193]

FYI: Metzger was eventually found liable in a civil suit of inciting (or at least inspiring) the beating death of an Ethiopian immigrant in Seattle. The punitive damages levied against Metzger bankrupted WAR. And, while it appears the Skinhead movement may have waned of late, those "cult members" Metzgers "converted" are still out there—adults now.

The Elderly. Older people often see themselves as closer to the grave. This makes them prime candidates for cult recruiters' "Do you know where you are going to spend eternity?" spiel. And all those cult people are "so nice," nice enough to come pick them old folks and shut-ins up in that big church bus and take them to church meetings. This, in addition to sending

---

192. See *The Skinhead Combat Manual* by Dirk Skinner (Only Publications, 1992).
193. Ibid.

"helpers" over to their homes to keep them company, tidy up, and help them cash their monthly Social Security checks.

According to a 2007 survey of people over the age of fifty, a full *87 percent* self-identified as being "a spiritual person" while 82 percent also agreed with the statement "I am a religious person."

Given the fact that "Baby Boomers" don't seem to be in any hurry to shuffle off this mortal coil, opportunities for sinister cult leaders recruiting the elderly looks very promising—at least from the cult's perspective.

Women. According to the most recent studies, women are more susceptible to religious conversion and more likely to be**LIE**ve in the paranormal.

Overall 52 percent of the people answering a Baylor University poll said they be**LIE**ved in prophetic dreams and more than 40 percent be**LIE**ve it's possible to be haunted.[194]

Gender differences came to light when more women admitted they be**LIE**ved dreams could foretell the future (58.9 percent) than did men (49.9 percent).[195]

Another significant number of people—again, more women than men—expressed be**LIE**f in UFOs, in the existence of "lost" civilizations such as Atlantis, and in the possibility of talking with the dead.[196]

So if you're a cult leader who can read minds and talk to the dead thanks to your alien friends from ancient Atlantis, there's a pretty good chance you'll have your *hands full* of *female followers*. Heh–heh-heh.

And don't forget how Charlie bragged, "Control the women, control the men."

David Koresh often seduced followers' wives in order to control their husbands. So did Jim Jones.

But it goes deeper than just getting to the husband through his wife.

Mothers bring their children to church with them. And, in many families, wives are responsible for paying household bills and so control the family *purse strings*. (Welcome to the Church of *Cha-Ching!*)

The woman who "confesses" an affair to her priest (or cult leader) places potentially damaging—blackmail—information in his hands. Good thing the confessional is "sacrosanct."

---

194. See *USA Today,* September 12, 2006, 7D.

195. Ibid.

196. Ibid.

Affairs within cults are commonplace . . . especially when the Master encourages one of his ever-ready studs to "help out" an obviously "frustrated" female follower. . . .

Black or White. Most cults tend to follow racial lines. It's just easier to convince people they belong to the "Chosen People," "Original Man," the "Master Race" if everybody looks alike to begin with.

Openly racist cults, like Farrakhan's *Nation of Islam* and the *Aryan Nations* (originally known as *"The Mountain Church"*), recruit along purely racial lines in keeping with their avowed racial separationist "be**LIE**fs."

A notable exception to recruiting along racial lines was Jim Jones's *People's Temple.* Jones's congregation was overwhelmingly black, as were most of those nine hundred who committed suicide alongside "Father."

Religions that teach universalism, "Come one, come all!", are color-blind, in order to sell a more lucrative *green* message . . . that has *nothing* to do with saving the environment.

When arranging those mass marriages, Moon's Unification Church went out of its way to deliberately mix couples racially, another way to break down individual ego and identity (in this case, racial identity), in order to more easily replace it with a new cult identity.

The Whole Family. Many cults spread by word of mouth, and the first people you run to, to run your mouth to about anything new, are your family and friends.

As just mentioned, mothers bring their children to church, and they browbeat hubby till even he gets up off the couch and comes to "Okay, just *one* service!"

Middle-aged couples, especially those experiencing "empty-nest syndrome" after the kids all move out, are especially vulnerable to cult recruitment. They need to still feel useful, and they want to share their wealth of rich life experiences.

So cults encourage them to "share the wealth" . . . the *real* wealth!

In *Rogue Messiahs*, Colin Wilson describes how a middle-aged couple felt when joining Jim Jones's cult:

> Suddenly they were "in," part of a warm and friendly environment in which they felt perfectly at home. It was like being back in the womb. (Wilson, 2000)

By the way, shortly after the People's Temple committed mass suicide in Guyana in 1978, this particular middle-aged couple was found tied up and shot to death in their California home.[197]

> *"The superstitious man is to the rascal what the slave is to the tyrant. There is more: the superstitious man is dominated by the fanatic, and becomes one."*
> —Voltaire

THE CULLING

Once you've "pulled" a few followers in, you'll need to start weeding your garden—identifying potential troublemakers and culling them from the herd.

Ideally, this culling process should take place while you're still scouting out potential converts.

Most secretive groups (secret societies, cults, etc.) are comprised of (1) an *Inner Circle* (sometimes occupied by the cult leader alone, or reserved for him and a few trusted lieutenants, those who are privy to the cult's true agenda), (2) a *Middle Circle,* where potential Inner Circle lieutenants are trained, and 3) the *Outer Circle,* where the general population of followers, contributors, and others "out of the loop" reside.

This concentric hierarchy is designed to provide "insulation" to the cult leader, sitting like an insatiable spider, *safe* at the center of his web.

So what do you do when a follower dares try to peek behind the Black Curtain at the "all-powerful Oz," daring to challenge your unique interpretation of scripture or, even more alarming, actually makes a move against your divinely sanctioned throne?

If it's just a disgruntled follower (pissed because he just found out you secretly "initiated" his wife behind his back and—maybe . . . his *daughter* too!—to "enlightenment" by way of forbidden *Tantric* sex [forbidden to all but "the Master," that is!]), and he's trying to make you look bad in front of *your* congregation, you can always attack *his* "lack of faith." Castigate him for causing a disturbance, for not coming to you privately, and either cast him

---

197. Colin Wilson, *Rogue Messiahs* (2000).

from the church—"Get thee behind me, Satan!"—or else hold a prayer session-slash-*exorcism* right then and there to "free him" of the contentious "demon of distrust and distraction" that has *obviously* taken possession of this poor man's soul!

But what if it's a more serious challenge to your leadership—in effect, a *coup* attempt?

First off, successful cult leaders are all "Alpha" males—even *female* cult leaders.

And, as everybody knows, there can only be *one* Alpha male leading the pack. All other males must remain subservient to *The* Alpha.

On the one hand, "Palm Open," if you're only after "the Dollar" then—depending on your greed—you might be satisfied with a smaller cult, running a "one man show," so long as it gets you all the money *and honey* you need.

On the other hand, "The Iron Fist," you might be the really ambitious "Diabolical" type, determined to expand your cult till it dominates this quadrant of the galaxy.

It's a conundrum. In order for your Diabolical cult to grow, you have to promote other Alpha males, but you can never show weakness or they'll turn on you. It's a *Klingon* thing.

If you get rid of every Alpha male, your cult will be weak and you'll have no one to watch your back. But if you surround yourself with equally competitive (and equally *sinister!*) Alpha males (the only kind!), then instead of having someone watch your back, you've got them all trying to stab you in the back!

David Koresh is a perfect example of this. He was an Alpha male who, if you recall, beat out another Alpha—the original ailing cult founder's son—to become Grand Poobah of the *Branch Davidians.*

Unfortunately, fearing a challenge to his own rule, Koresh then surrounded himself with sycophant yes-men. Predictably, with no one to warn him when he was out of control . . . he went out of control! Recall Hitler made the same mistake?

A small "Dollar" cult leader can afford to exile other Alphas.

But an ambitious cult leader, one of those "Diabolical" ones, needs other Alphas in order to branch out. Ah, there's the key phrase: "branch out."

Train and send your other Alphas out to start branch "churches" in *your name,* keeping the Inner Circle to yourself, keeping your "missionaries" dependent upon *your* resources.

There are too many examples of Alphas bumping heads in history. (Is it okay if we actually *learn* from the past, Mr. Santayana?)

Cain and Abel. Peter and Paul. Hitler and Ernst Rohm. Farrakhan and Malcolm X. Martin and Lewis. These things seldom turn out well.

WHAT'S THE BUZZ?

"What's the buzz? Tell me what's a'happening."
—*Jesus Christ Superstar*

To keep your cows happy, you need the right bull.

Cults all claim to have the inside track when it comes to scriptures faxed straight from God, rituals guaranteed to please God, ministrations and meditations designed to open your "third eye"—while blinding your other two eyes to the fact your pocket's being picked!

Before getting down to the specific *tactics* for controlling your cult, you have to decide on your overall *Strategy* for teaching "your children":

Teach the similarities.

Start by teaching the similarities between your cult and some already existing philosophy or religion.

People are naturally fascinated—and suspicious—of new things. You don't want to scare off potential cult recruits by confusing them with too much too soon, or by shocking them with too radical a departure from what they were (1) raised with and/or (2) still beLIEve in.

Offer a small twist-and-tweak on something comforting and familiar—the Bible, for instance.

Even "weirdo" New Age cults use some recognized "user-friendly" philosophy or premise when approaching potential recruits: Yoga, Zen, meditation, etc. Recall how *Dahn* added "yoga" to their name to make themselves more "user-friendly" to Americans.

Teach the differences.

But do so only after you've caught their attention.

Perhaps you casually mention an obscure scripture or a subtle interpretation on a well-known scripture.

They've got a sore back so, instead of offering them an aspirin, you put a little "yoga hand-warmth massage" on them.

Pique their attention with little differences at first: "Your church celebrates Jesus' birthday on July 4th? Why is that?" they ask. Congrats! They've taken the bait.

Now use that hook to reel them in.

Over time, as the person becomes more "invested" in your cult, you slowly begin to magnify what at first were subtle differences—eventually driving a wedge between the person's former be**LIE**fs and the be**LIE**fs you're *now* filling their head with!

> *"If you keep saying things are going to be bad, you have a good chance of becoming a prophet."*
> —Isaac Bashevis Singer

Two faces are better than one.

In keeping with your two-step teaching strategy, you always show one face to the public, and another face to your followers once you've slipped back behind the Black Curtain.

Being privy to this kind of mischief makes your follower(s) feel *special* and *superior*—they know something "outsiders" don't. As you give them more and more glimpses of your true agenda—slowly drawing them further away from their previous be**LIE**fs, they *unconsciously* begin to pull themselves away from the outside world, away from their former friends and their former self.

They now have *two faces* too!

Don't get high off your own supply.

People always wonder if cult leaders actually be**LIE**ve their own line of bull. Some do. Some "religious leaders" start out being true be**LIE**vers, and ultimately get corrupted by "The 3-P's": Prestige, Power, and . . . Sex.

Some cult leaders get in the business simply for the Dollar but, after having so many people kiss their ass, finding they suddenly have *sex* (and sundry assassination!) at their beck and call, start to think "Maybe I really am *The Chosen One!*"

That's what drug dealers call, "Gettin' high off your own supply," a warning that all the profits from your illegal (and/or immoral) activities are either going up in smoke (literally) or else straight up your nose. Either way—you're not taking care of business.

What's that old saying about "religion [being] the opiate of the people"?

CULTS AND SEX: FROM TANTRA TO POLYGAMY

In your cult, will sex be forbidden or *ridden*? To *stain* or abstain, that *is* the question.

Sex has always been a big problem for religious leaders. Look at how many Old Testament rules center around sex—from not coveting your neighbor's *ass*, to how many sheep you gotta pay to get away with rape. Lot, David, Solomon . . . none of them could keep it in their pants . . . uh, robes.

"Cults and sex" are linked in people's minds. That's because everybody *outside* a cult always thinks *everybody* inside a cult is screwing everybody else in the cult. Yeah, kinda like prison . . .

But the historical fact is many cults have preached total—abstinence—and worse! The most nefarious example of this was the Skoptzy cult of eighteenth-century Czarist Russia, which made male followers castrate themselves and female followers mutilate their breasts and genitals. And, believe it or not, this was a *popular* cult at the time!

Things like that still go on. Recall how Heaven's Gate members reportedly cut off their . . . well, members. Other cults force young girls to endure painful cliterodectomies, mutilating their genitals for life as a way to prevent infidelity.

So far as sex is concerned, cults range from one extreme to the other—some abstaining completely, others indulging shamelessly.

Polygamy always seems popular with cults—especially with *male* members.

Celibacy allows sexual energy to build up, tension that can be directed toward cult activities, or toward the personal search for enlightenment. It's called "Tantra."[198]

Cult leaders know that sex *is* an energy straining to be expressed.

When a cult leader reaches the level (or sinks to the level?) to where he can control his followers' sexual habits, he's literally got them by the short-hairs.

Example: The Unification Church has a sexual ritual called "pikarume" (blood-cleansing) during which "impurities" are believed to be removed from the follower simply by having sex with Reverend Moon or by having sex with a cult lieutenant who's already been "purified."[199]

Sex proves who's the boss. In pride or pack, the Alpha gets laid first and frequently. If any of the rest of the pack gets any, it's only with the blessing of the Alpha. So too in your cult.

Sex as reward. As cult leader, you decide *who* gets some, *when* they get it, and *with whom* they can do it—but only after *you* have gotten a "taste" of the merchandise first. Big dog eats first.

And anytime a lowly follower gets to have sex with "The Exalted One" himself (or herself) that *is* a reward!

Be especially good and the Master will let you have sex. This *is* a good *way* to keep an ass-kissing contest going among your followers, to see who can (literally) suck up to "the Master" the best.

Sex as punishment. The Master tells your wife not to give you any until you "come around" to the cult's way of thinking.

Sex as blackmail. During "confession," you tell the Master about that time in college you and your roommate got a little high and decided to . . . "experiment." Congratulations. You've just given someone a stick to beat you with.

Conversely, cult leaders often convince followers to experiment with sex—same sex, animals, even underage children—acts that will later be used to blackmail those followers should they consider defecting and/or testifying.

---

198. For a complete course on Tantric sex yoga, see *Mental Domination* (2009).

199. Stoner and Parke, 1977:38.

Berg's *Children of God* were notorious for using underage kids in their sexual escapades.[200]

Sex as an ego-breaker. Gay sex, and any number of other sexual "perversions," are forced upon confused cult members, only later to be used as "blood ties" to further bind them to the cult.

The cult leader always assures the humiliated member that he/she is still loved by the cult *but* (and here comes the threat), "Non-cult members just wouldn't understand *if this ever got out.*" . . . "They don't understand *our* ways."

Sex as bonding. For the short time that polygamy was allowed in the Mormon church, it allowed a few men to quickly father scores of children each, increasing the number of cult members at a breakneck pace. Today, the benefit of that polygamy "experiment" is that many high-ranking Mormons can trace themselves back to common ancestors—a strong, *unifying* cult bond.

On the more toxic side, Jim Jones freely engaged in sex with both women and men in his cult, "binding" the congregation together in a twisted way.[201]

Anyone into S&M will be glad to explain the difference between a "bonding" and "a binding."

> *"Above all take care not to establish a cult for rascals who have no merit but ignorance, hysteria and dirt, who may have made a duty and a glory of idleness and mendacity."*
> —Voltaire

THE TEN COMMANDMENTS OF CULT CONTROL

So what's the real secret for getting your cult members eating out of the palm of your hand and shittin' out donations?

Obey "The Commandments"!

---

200. Wilson, 2000:240.
201. Ibid., 48–49.

I. Control the setting.

"Your refusal is dictated by insufficient knowledge of your surroundings. You find yourself in a place strange to you, a place to which no clue can lead your friends; in the absolute power of a man—myself—who knows no law other than his own and that of those associated with him."
—*The Hand of Fu Manchu*

It's just like basic training boot camp in the military. As much as possible, take your recruits out of their familiar element, the same way you draw an enemy off familiar ground in order to ambush him.

Ideally, you get them to come to your church for a meeting. Maybe spend an all-expenses-paid, "stress-free" weekend at your cult retreat.

Create a reality within a reality—a peaceful place where the person can relax, far from the distractions of the day.

The Church of Scientology early on set up "Celebrity Centers," secretive retreats and hotels where high-profile members (movie stars, sports figures) could come and relax and study, far from the prying eyes of the public and the paparazzi.

Likewise, you should provide a place for your recruits to get away from the world—literally. Get them away from friends and family (who might question their choices), away from the comforting surroundings of their everyday life.

The goal is to get them to come to rely more and more on you and your cult as a place of peace and refuge, where they can leave all their worries behind, dropping their "worldly" identity at the door, allowing someone else to "be in charge" for a while. (Yeah, kinda like an S&M parlor!)

Restrict communication coming in and out of your "retreat."

You provide all the information your recruits need. And the only "news" they need is "the good news" about how wonderful you and your cult are!

This is the first step in what *is* known as the *Six Degrees of Cult Doom:*

You begin by (1) *Denying Access*. You're like that announcer on *The Outer Limits*: "We control all that you see and hear."

Like guerrillas dynamiting rail lines and bridges and tearing down telephone poles, you also stop the steady, orderly flow of information coming into your cult from the outside world. Soon their thoughts are in (2) *Disarray.*

Without any information other than what *you* are spoon-feeding them, their preconceptions—even their conception of time itself—begins to unravel.

> *"Contradiction" confusion, and continual change—Masters have always used these techniques with their disciples. They create receptivity, and openness to seeing things as they are, as they break habitual patterns."*
> —Gordon

They begin to (3) *Doubt* everything they've previously known. Ultimately, most importantly, they begin to doubt themselves. (4) *Dread* takes root that, left unchecked, *leads* to (5) *Debilitation,* as they are unable to decide for themselves anymore.

Finally, they have no choice but to give in to (6) *Dependency,* now looking to you and your cult for all the answers.

FYI: The same six steps are used in military *brainwashing.*

II. Separate the "Chosen" from the "Frozen."

Convince them they've been "chosen" for a higher purpose. Where others "less worthy" remain "frozen" in place, they have proved themselves worthy (by accepting your message) and now have been chosen to be promoted to an even higher station within the cult, chosen to learn the "special," "divine," and secret message revealed to only a few . . . through you.

Because of this new exalted position, the normal rules of "sin" and social order (e.g., lying, sex, even killing) no longer apply to them. Stand by for further orders. . . . See Commandment VIII below.

III. Give them the "Pure Cure."

Your cult teachings and your cult teachings alone will lead them to salvation. Only your guidance (which often requires nudity!) will "purify" them for the task to come.

No matter what they have done in the past, they need only confess it . . . to you, and all will be forgiven. And, once "purified," no matter what they may do in the future (especially in the Master's name) this will earn them brownie points in heaven.

The only "impurity" at this stage, the only "sin," is not obeying the Master's every word.

Scientology calls this being a *"Clear,"* having come to terms with all your inner demons, having freed yourself from the past, having been "born again." FYI: Charlie Manson claims to have reached the exalted level of "Clear" by studying L. Ron Hubbard's *Dianetics* while in prison.

What secrets *haven't* you told us? You can never be completely free until you free yourself of your hidden burden. (Back to Commandment III for you, backslider!)

Cults (and secret societies) often use this "cleansing" and "purifying" stage to subject the initiate to bizarre rituals and secret "shamings" (e.g., shaving the anus, fetish sex rituals, etc.), all of which can then be used later for blackmail. In other words, the cult first "cleanses" the initiate of past indiscretions . . . before then giving him a whole new set of things to feel guilty about!

IV. Use the "Confession Session."

All your once secret sins and hidden fears are now cult property. But you not only must "confess" *your* "sins," you must also reveal anything you know about your family and close friends.

Can you say "Blood Ties" and "Blackmail"?

Think about it. What does your wife (worse yet, your ex-wife!), close family members, your best friend, or that sixteen-year-old you've been texting know about you that you wouldn't want broadcast on the six o'clock news?

A "Cutting at the Edges" ploy: What might your wife, friends, or other family members be "confessing" about *you* to *their* cult master right now?

V. Use conscience and *"con-*science."

You are now initiated into the "secrets" of the cult; cult "history" stretching back to ancient Atlantis or to the moon 66 trillion years ago.

The Master's teachings are never to be questioned. If something *seems* like a contradiction to you, *the fault is your own,* you weren't paying close enough attention.

Obviously, you still have some "unresolved conflict," and an "impure understanding" because you are not yet completely "pure" yourself.

To *question* the Master's orders and revelations is to *doubt* the Master. Somebody needs a time-out. . . .

VI. Use semantics antics.

So it seems your native tongue isn't sophisticated enough to pronounce, let alone translate, our cult's sacred text correctly. That means you'll be required to spend hours a day learning a foreign language.

Let's think about this a minute: If *your native language* isn't "good enough," that must mean it is *"inferior"* to the language (and culture) of our foreign "Master." After all, God chose to send down his sacred word in the language of the ancient prophet(s). This means *their* "sacred" ancient culture is superior to *your* "corrupt" modern culture. You should be honored (and humbled!) we even let inferior scum like you come in the front door!

We should learn *that* language—just to be closer to God. After all, God must speak *that* language, he wrote *his* book in *that* language. Man! We are so lucky our cult leader speaks *that* language or we would really be screwed! (Give it time. . . .)

And from now on, when you greet your cult brothers, you must greet them only in this new "pure" tongue, using the same words as our ancient prophet(s) used.

A cross between a parrot with Tourette's syndrome and Pavlov's salivating dog, they instantly spit out the proper greeting, requiring instant response, lest you show lack of faith and disrespect to the ancient prophets.

Cults love to play word games: "Don't trust the library, that's where 'Lies-are-buried'!" and "Mankind" is only a "kind of man," only we are "the true man"!

Collectively known as "cult-speak," these are specially crafted words and phrases that (1) identify cult members to one another, (2) give cult members a feeling of possessing superior knowledge, and (3) help undermine a new recruit's former racial/cultural identity and his confidence in his "former life."

Cults constantly test their members, looking for doubt and weakness. They try to trip members up, listening for the least hesitation in vomiting up the proper response, in the proper "superior" tongue, to a coded greeting.

Cults also use Orwellian double-speak/double-think to further confuse both members and non-members: "Ignorance is strength! War is peace. We honor the creator of life by killing off his creations!"

VII. Teach "Selfless" and "Less Self."

Buddha once compared his teachings to a small boat one uses to ford a river. Once safely across the river, there is no need to keep carrying that boat.

Buddhism is the only religion that *expects* students to "move on" once they have used the Buddha's teachings to get their lives together.

Other religions—the more "cultic" especially—suffer from "abandonment anxiety," always paranoid that members will defect.

Once you're in a cult, you're in for life. To try leaving is an insult to the Master and the penalties *start* at harassment. . . .

Defectors have to be made an example of. *Just* ask cult leader Jeffrey Lungren. Oh, that's right, you can't. He was executed by the State of Ohio in October 2006.

FYI: Lungren, his son, and other lieutenants of his cult (a breakaway faction of the Mormons) killed five defecting cult members—an entire family—in 1989 in Kirkland, Ohio.

In a cult, the teachings are more important than any member. Doctrine always takes precedence over person.

You must sacrifice yourself to "the greater good."

We'll love you even more if you become a "martyr." Every fledgling cult needs at least one good martyr early on, someone they can write songs about and hold up as a shining example to recruits.

Often there is no need for cults to overtly manipulate recruits. Many willingly sacrifice themselves.

Some do it because they are looking for meaning. Others are loyal to the cult because the cult actually helped them get off drugs. Such ex-addicts are scared to death of falling back into their old life and so often become the most fiercely loyal (i.e., fanatical!) of cult members: "I must save the Master at all costs because he saved me!" goes their thinking.

The idea that people somehow "accidentally" fall into the grasp of a cult and, once "caught," can never escape isn't always accurate.

More often, folks voluntarily join a cult. Of course, it might not be a "cult" when they initially join.

As already mentioned, the cult might truly have "saved" the individual (from drugs, an abusive marriage, etc.). Afraid to fall back into that painful life, these "saved" individuals remain loyal to the cult—eventually to the point where they begin ignoring obvious faults in both the teachings and the teacher.

Having invested so heavily, emotionally, and perhaps financially, having sung the praises of the cult to friends and family for years, such die-hard loyalists are loathe to leave the cult, even in the face of death.

And so we count 900 dead at Masada, 900 dead at Jonestown: murder and suicide and madness, all at the order of maniacal cult masters.

Worst-case scenario: Six million dead and counting, cult members feeding more bodies to their murder machine even after realizing the inevitable fall of your "cult." But rather than tuck tail, you redouble your (killing) efforts on behalf of a cult leader who's already dead! Heil Hitler!

And while we're on the subject of individual choice: Cults don't believe in democracy. Don't let them tell you different.

Oh, they'll *participate* in "ecumenical" discussions of "Your religion's just as good as mine!" and they'll praise and promote democracy all the way . . . until they actually attain political power.

And then let's see how many elections there are after that!

VIII. Decide who lives, who dies.

This *is* an extension of the mind-set planted at the "Chosen versus Frozen" stage.

Cults kill (and do other lesser crimes) because they literally answer to "a Higher Authority."

The "Laws of Man" mean nothing when measured alongside the "Law of God."

And since the Master is the ultimate arbiter and interpreter of the All-Mighty's will in this world, what the Master says, goes. *Who* the Master says, goes.

Anytime a leader can talk you into doing anything you feel "uncomfortable" with, or have misgivings about, the "cult mentality" has already taken root.

Cults justify illegal and immoral actions by convincing themselves they are dispensing justice: "We steal from the rich to feed the poor—us!" and "The heathen deserve to die as a warning to others not to follow the evil path!"

Cults use the same tried-and-true methods the military uses to "demonize" the enemy. If you think it's easier to kill people who don't look like you, imagine how easy it *is* to kill "demons"!

IX. Make 'em lose face.

Stay with a cult long enough and you lose face—literally, you lose your face, your very identity.

One day you take a look around only to discover to your dismay that that mildly curious person who first picked up that cult pamphlet, who agreed to come to "just one meeting," that person—*you!*—no longer exists.

That's because you've passed through the cult's "Dress and Duress Department," where they first change *how you look*, then they change your *outlook*, until you *overlook* what's really going on.

Before you realize it, the cult has changed everything about you:

- *The way you talk.* Still learning that new language, are you?
- *The way you eat.* Studies have found that cult diets and repeated mandatory fastings actually change a person's brain chemistry, making their body weak and their mind more susceptible to suggestion.
- *The way you dress.* Don't even think about trying to run in those sandals. And that long robe sure makes it hard to escape over that compound wall. It doesn't even have any pockets for your ID and wallet—confiscated by the cult when you entered the compound anyway!
- *Even your actual face looks different.* Look at yourself now, compared with a picture of yourself before you came into the cult—that is, if the cult allowed you to keep any pictures from your "past life." Where you used to be clean-shaven, now you have a face-distorting beard, one that makes you look like all the other men in the cult. They made you shave your head—sometimes even if you're a woman.

The "duress" part comes when you find your entire day dominated by cult requirements: mandatory prayers, arts and crafts, and other labors designed to fill the cult coffers.

X. Burn bridges.

Ultimately, the cult gets you to do some obscene or illegal act there's no coming back from.

If they don't make you actively commit a crime, they will connive to make you complicit—an "accessory after the fact," as John Law refers to it.

> *"Dreams are slow to die. The hard facts of reality are not always powerful enough to kill a dream."*
> —William Sargent, *Battle for the Mind*

THE "ELEVENTH" COMMANDMENT

> *"Disciples can create a sticky web in which the guru becomes trapped."*
> —Colin Wilson, *Rogue Messiahs*

As difficult—and dangerous!—as it might be for a disciple to try escaping a cult, it's even harder for a *cult leader* to try pulling up stakes, to abandoning his flock, taking the money, and running!

I know it's probably hard for you to squeeze out a drop of sympathy for some low-life cult leader who spends years sucking his followers dry and then—Surprise!—finds it almost impossible to leave when he wants.

You need to keep in mind that cults are all about *dependence*, i.e., the cult leader's intent is to make his followers as dependent as possible *on him*.

The cult leader may, indeed, have a revolutionary idea—some mumbo jumbo guaranteed to confuse, cajole, and ultimately corral followers. But even when the cult is going full steam, a wily cult leader is always careful to *never let the message overshadow the man*. In other words, you don't want to give your disciples a message that will outlive you . . . because there just might be a ram hidden amongst your sheep: Does the name *Judas* ring a bell? How about David Koresh?[202]

So long as *you are the message*, then the cult literally cannot survive without you. Ergo, the lower the chances some young, ambitious David Koresh/Judas will arrange your premature "martyrdom."

---

202. Who befriended cult leader Lois Roden, eventually beating out her son as her successor.

Conversely, when it comes time to cut-and-run, when even a blind man can read the writing on the wall, as cult leader all eyes are in you—literally.

The bigger your cult, the more eyes on you, the harder for you to call it quits.

To openly declare, "I'm outta here!" is to risk that the resultant confusion from your "resignation" quickly turns into indignation and then anger. FYI: You might want to lock the cult compound arsenal up tight before making any such declaration!

Some of your followers will feel "This is just a test. The Master is only testing us! He'd never *really* abandon us!"

Others might rationalize (with what little brain you've left them!) that somehow the Master has fallen under the sway of "evil spirits." First comes them duct-taping you up—"So you won't hurt yourself, Master"—followed soon thereafter by the probably painful "exorcism" that, if you survive, could just as soon thereafter be followed by the bonfire . . . and guess who the *wiener* is!

Ironically, the cult might just survive on your martyrdom alone.

On second thought, maybe slipping *quietly* unobserved out the back door for that extended "sabbatical" might be the better part of valor.

And, while you've been smart enough to keep the IRS at arm's length by never, ever even thinking about taking advantage of your Federal tax-exempt status for *personal gain*, you just found out the cult's trusted treasurer—Judas was Jesus' choice for treasurer, by the way—just absconded to his newly purchased villa in Brazil leaving you praying for a miracle—time to dust off that Groucho moustache and beat feet with *however much* you can stuff in your pockets!

Always keep your bags packed.

And always have at least one follower who bears a startling resemblance to you. So, in case of say . . . an accidental fire? . . . it might take them days to prove whether or not the charred remains are actually you.

(On second count, maybe that's the "Twelfth" Commandment!)

CULT CASE STUDY: THE NATION OF ISLAM

"Power corrupts, but its real corruption is among those who wait upon it, seeking place, jostling with rivals, nursing jealousies, forming expedient cabals, flaunting preferment, crowing out the humiliation of a demoted favorite."
—John Keegan, *The Mask of Command*

Some people came to America for freedom of religion . . . the rest of us, freedom *from* religion!

Along with all the sundry flotsam and jetsam landing on our shining shores, it's inevitable that the occasional cult should wash ashore, their tightly clutched bundles and baggage including tactics and techniques inherited—or else stolen!—from past masters of cult craft.

America's tolerance for "different" views (i.e., cults and crazies!) makes us "religion friendly" (i.e., suckers). And that handy tax-exempt status for "religious groups" is just added incentive for every Tom, Dick, and Charlie Manson possessing no other marketable skills to try starting their own cult.

Not surprising, over the years our toleration for the sanctity of religious beLIEfs (no matter how whacko!) has encouraged the creation of quite a few homegrown American cults: Mormons, Jehovah's Witnesses . . . Jerry Springer. (Heh-heh-heh)

Some of these cults are relatively benign, others downright belligerent, ranging from the helpful to the homicidal.

Still, all things being equal, this is still America, and even when our homegrown cults are 100 percent certifiably, Grade-A, USDA-approved meatheads . . . they're still *our* cults!

And in America, where we still applaud initiative and still reward stick-to-it-ive-ness, all a "cult" has to do is (1) *survive* (i.e., outlive its founder) and (2) at least *try to be entertaining,* and it earns the right to start calling itself a "sect" and eventually, even a bona fide "religion."

When examining how cults in America use Black Science to their advantage, we have plenty of cults and cult leaders to choose from, but, hands-down, the best example of a currently successful cult leader is Louis J. Farrakhan, head of the 80,000 member so-called *Nation of Islam* UFO cult.

Why a cult? Because NOI's bizarre and racist inner-core beLIEfs have changed little since its founding in Detroit in 1931.

The NOI is still mostly referred to as the "Black Muslims" because, despite Farrakhan's back-slapping photo ops with Middle Eastern dictators and potentates to the contrary, the cult has never been accepted by orthodox Muslims as a legitimate sect of Islam.

With racism and UFO-worship at its core, NOI remains too radical for even Muslim radicals!

Not good enough to be a "sect," too small to be a "religion" . . . that only leaves "cult."

Why a "UFO" cult? More on that in a minute.

If you still doubt whether the NOI meets the criteria to merit the appellation "cult," review "The Cult Craft" chapter in *Black Science* (2001) and *Mind Manipulation* (2002) and *666 Devilish Secrets of Islam* (2010).

Current NOI mythology has the cult being founded in 1930 by a shadowy Middle Eastern (possibly Turkish) rug salesman named "W. D. Fard" who gave NOI its racist underpinnings:

> The black people, [Fard] said, were gods; the white man was
> the serpent devil and would ultimately be destroyed. (Mead,
> 1975)

NOI followers would later claim this mysterious Fard character was Allah (God) come to earth in the flesh.[203]

FYI: In orthodox Islam, such a blasphemous claim is called *Shirk* (defined as saying anything about Allah that isn't true) and is enough to get your head chopped clean off in most Muslim countries!

Before vanishing in 1933, as mysteriously as he appeared, Fard passed leadership of NOI on to Elijah Poole (aka Elijah Muhammad, 1887–1975), who, upon his death in 1975, passed the torch of cult leadership to Louis J. Farrakhan (b. 1934), NOI's current leader.

Or so says the NOI's *official* party line.

But it is an inescapable law of science—and of cult creation!—that "nothing comes from nothing" and, while you'd be hard-pressed to find anyone in the present NOI to admit it, dig a little deeper and you'll find

---

203. Mead, 1975:63.

Elijah Poole was a disciple of a *true* Black Science adept calling himself "Noble Drew Ali."

Myths and Moors

"In most of their secret talks there is no good."
—The Koran

Volumes could be—and perhaps should be—written on Noble Drew Ali (born Timothy Drew, 1886–1929). Most know him as the founder of *"The Moorish Science Temple,"* a fraternity-cum-cult practicing an eclectic mix of Afro-centric esotericism.

But Ali's contribution to Cult America goes far beyond his founding Moorish Science.

Noble Drew Ali was the American Adam Weishaupt.

You call yourself a Black Science student and you don't know that Professor Adam Weishaupt, aka "Spartacus" (inspiration for Sherlock Holmes's nemesis Professor Moriarty), was the supposed founder of the 1777 incarnation of the *Illuminati*—from which all modern-day secret societies claim descent, and back to which every modern-day conspiracy theorist worth his salt must eventually make haj!

After studying with anyone and everyone, from Moroccan Muslims to Philadelphia Freemasons, Drew Ali gathered around him a dedicated core of disciples.

What elevates Ali to the level of Adam Weishaupt and Hasan ibn Sabbah (founder of the Cult of the Assassins) is that he wasn't so much interested in starting a singular cult as he was in teaching his students how to start cults of their own. We'd be safe in saying that Ali's aspirations fell somewhere between "the Dollar" and "the Diabolical."

Neither was Ali so shortsighted as to limit himself exclusively to either Islam or Christianity. He borrowed shamelessly from *all* cult masters who had come before him. Thus while cloaking his true agenda behind a thin veil of Arab-speak, Ali ravished Levi H. Dowling's *The Aquarian Gospel of*

Jesus the Christ to create a unique "Koran" for his Moorish Science Temple.[204]

As a result, Ali was responsible not only for guiding and goading his student Elijah Poole to found the "Islamic-oriented" Nation of Islam, but also for inspiring another of his disciples, George Baker, aka "Father Divine" (1877–1965), to establish the Peace Mission, a popular East Coast "Christian" organization in the 1930s.

Ali taught Father Divine . . . and Father Divine taught Jim Jones, White leader of the People's Temple, whose 911 members (mostly Black) committed mass suicide in Guyana in 1978.

Cult begets cult.

Like all Black Science adepts, Ali was a true master when it came to reading people, at distinguishing true friends from those wearing a false face. . . .

Thus, while helping Elijah Poole concoct the mythology for Poole's first Black "Islamic" temple that would one day fester into the NOI, Ali—whom, it appears, never really trusted Poole—convinced Poole that, since "nothing comes from nothing," Poole needed to create a fictional "prophet" whom Poole could then claim as the source for his (Poole's) "revelations" and "secret knowledge."

In true Obi-Wan fashion, Ali planted the name "Fard" in Poole's mind and Poole accepted it . . . never realizing that in English "fard" means "to paint the face, to wear *a false face*"—a not-so-coded warning from Ali to anyone owning a dictionary that Poole was *not* to be trusted!

Cults constantly reinvent themselves.

Down through the years NOI revisionists have gone to extraordinary lengths to verify the actual existence of the mysterious W. D. Fard (whom no one except Elijah Poole ever seems to have actually seen).

In keeping with their Arabic pretensions, NOI "scholars" use various spellings of "Fard," for example "Farad"—pronounced "fraud." (Talk about your Freudian *slips*!)

---

204. See *In the Name of Elijah Muhammad* by Mattias Garden (1996).

Fu Manchu and Flying Saucers

From Day One, the message of Elijah Poole's "Nation" was built on claims alternatively ridiculous and/or blatantly racist.

When crafting his cult's mythology, Poole followed the lead of his mentor, Noble Drew Ali, ruthlessly ripping rhetoric and writ from a slew of spurious sources—from Holy Scripture (Bible and Koran), to science-fiction novels:

First, the original people of Earth, whom Poole dubbed the "Asiatic Black Man," came from the moon *66 trillion years ago*.[205]

Next, as exposed in *The Autobiography of Malcolm X* (1999), NOI teaches that the blue-eyed devil White race is the product of an evil genetic experiment conducted millions of years ago by a "big head scientist" named Yakub, on the island of Patmos.

This Patmos is the same island mentioned in the Bible's Book of Revelation (1:9), a perfect example of cults using familiar scripture in new schemes.

As for Poole's source for his fanciful tale of evil genetic experiments, some speculate he stole the idea from H. G. Wells's *The Island of Dr. Moreau* (1896) and/or from the novels of Sax Rohmer:

> The story propagated by Elijah Muhammad and his disciples—of whites being created by the genetic engineering of a 'mad scientist' on an isolated island—has some striking similarities to the plot of one of Sax Rohmer's hugely popular— though deeply racist—Fu Manchu novels, The Island of Fu Manchu, published in 1941. (Stephen Howe, *Afrocentricism: Mythical Pasts and Imagined Homes*)

FYI: "Sax Rohmer" was the pen-name for A. S. Ward, a member of the nineteenth-century London/Paris *Order of the Golden Dawn*, which, like so many secret societies of the day, took pains to trace itself back to Adam Weishaupt's 1776 Bavarian *Illuminati*.

Poole elaborates on these genetic shenanigans in several of his own NOI writings. For example, in his book *How to Eat to Live*:

---

205. See *Handbook of Denominations in the United States* by Frank S. Mead (1975).

The hog was made out of the cat, rat, and dog, so Allah (God) taught me. The hog has not always been on our planet Earth. The hog was made for medical purposes, a few years after the making of the White race. He was made to cure the diseases that the White race attracts since they are physically weak, so Allah (God) who came in the person of Master Fard Muhammad. . . . (1972:28)

Did you catch that part about W. D. Fard (aka Fard Muhammad) being *Allah* incarnating on Earth? *Shirk!*

It gets better. In an article titled "The Final Exam: Entrance into the Kingdom of God," appearing in the cult's official newspaper, *The Final Call,* in 2003, Farrakhan himself has been exalted to a higher post:

We've been invited to enter the inner sanctum of God's counsel. But we can't realize this without special divine help, which has been provided by God and His Christ, in the person of Minister Farrakhan.

Finally, according to NOI mythology, there's a gigantic "invisible" spacecraft known *as* "The Mother Wheel" in Earth's orbit. According to Poole's own writings, this UFO *was* built through the "superior technology" of the NOI Asiatic Black Moon-Man.[206]

Not only does NOI qualify as a "cult," it also qualifies *as* a "UFO cult," you know, like that lovely *Heaven's Gate* bunch who committed suicide.

Technically, one might argue that Poole's "Mother Wheel" is only an "Unidentified Flying Object" to the rest of us since NOI members have secret knowledge of this UFOs true design and purpose!

BeLIEf in the reality of the Mother Wheel is one of the core inner teachings of the NOI—*never, ever* discussed with outsiders.

To find further proof that the Nation of Islam is indeed a "UFO cult," we need only glance at the articles and book selections found in every issue of the cult's official newspaper, *The Final Call*.

For example, *The Final Call* (January 6, 2004), carried an ad for the *NOI*

---

206. See Lung and Prowant, 2001:161.

book *The Mind of President Bush,* its cover picturing a gigantic UFO and/or nuclear explosion menacing the White House.

Another book advertised in the same issue, this one written by Farrakhan himself, entitled *Divine Judgment,* pictures a gigantic silver flying saucer hovering over what appears to be downtown Chicago.

By the way, Farrakhan himself claims to have been taken *aboard* the Mother Wheel in 1985.[207]

Information about Farrakhan being beamed aboard the Mother Wheel while visiting ancient pyramids in Mexico was announced to help squelch a challenge to his authority within NOI. Seems his being beamed aboard the Mother Wheel *was* taken as ultimate "proof" (at least to NOI cult members) that he was, indeed, Elijah Poole's successor.

While aboard the Mother Wheel, Farrakhan claims to have heard the voice of the *dead* Elijah Poole speaking.

Which brings us to the ad in *The Final Call* (2003) for the book *Is It Possible That the Honorable Elijah Muhhad Is Still Physically Alive?* by Jabril Muhammad.

This pulls the Black Curtain off the secret teaching and be**LIE**f within NOI that Elijah Poole has somehow been "resurrected" aboard the Mother Wheel (maybe with that "superior technology"?) and that, like W. D. Fard, Elijah Poole was actually *Allah come to Earth in human form.* Shirk! (Where are all those scimitar-swinging Islamic fundamentalists when you need them?)

This "deification" of Elijah Poole to god status is forbidden in orthodox Islam, further testifying to NOI's status as a "breakaway cult" of Islam. (Actually, having never been accepted by orthodox Islam, *NOI* can't technically "break away," huh?)

Related "UFO/NOI Cult" item: Former World Boxing Champion Muhammad Ali, himself a Nation of Islam "Black Muslim" in his younger days, claimed to have seen UFOs on several occasions in New Jersey and in New York's Central Park.[208]

Related UFO item Number Two: October, 2002. The Eatonton, Georgia, cult compound of "Professor" Dwight York, founder of *The United*

---

207. Ibid.

208. See *The UFO Encyclopedia* by Margaret Sachs (1980).

Nuwabian Nation of Moors is raided, and Professor York is arrested on charges of child abuse.

York, raised on NOI tales of "The Mother Wheel," was the founder of what one source described as "a mostly black religious group whose spiritual leader [York] claims to be an extraterrestrial. . . ."[209]

York's self-published cult "bible" contains elaborate illustrations of "the original Black race" of alien beings who came from the stars "trillions of years ago."

FYI: Inspirational portraits of both Noble Drew Ali and Elijah Poole Muhammad appear in the front of York's "bible."

Guess the fruit doesn't fall far from the tree.

The Power of the Dark Side

Once you're done laughing your ass off about "stealth UFOs" and "genetic experiments" conducted by "big head scientists," you need to remind yourself there's a potential "dark side" to *any* cult—to any organization that deliberately distorts its members' concept of reality.

And how many times have we seen the fiery rhetoric of secretive cults explode out into the real world to engulf innocent victims? When cult members conspire against one another, what chance have the rest of us "civilians" got?

Malik El-Shabazz (the man formerly known as Malcolm X) was gunned down by fellow members of the Nation of Islam after he openly challenged Elijah Muhammad's racist teachings. Speculation that Malcolm's assassination was ordered by someone "higher up" in the NOI has never been proven.

Farrakhan's alibi, by the way, was airtight. . . . He was seen picnicking on the grassy knoll at the time.

When Elijah Poole died in 1975, a power struggle ensued between Poole's son, Wallace Deen Muhammad, and his father's number-one lieutenant—you guessed it—Louis J. Farrakhan.

When the smoke finally cleared, the NOI had split, with Wallace Deen

---

209. *Orlando Sentinel,* July 1, 1999.

Muhammad openly repudiating his father's racist teachings and moving closer to orthodox Islam by founding The Muslim American Society:

> Black Muslim doctrine was modified and softened slightly in Elijah Muhammad's last year, then thoroughly under his son and successor, Wallace (Warith Deen) Muhammad. Beliefs in the imminent end of the white world, in whites *as* devils, in lunar origins, and so on, were dropped. . . . Not all accepted the moderated de-racialized new mode, however. Louis Farrakhan left Wallace Muhammad's movement in 1978, and his breakaway organization reinstated the old millennial and racial exclusivist beliefs. . . . (Howe, 1998)

The revised Nation of Islam, or *"Farrakhaners"* as they are sometimes referred to by *real* Muslims, still thrives today.

Farrakhan: "The Untouchable" Cult Leader

Credit where credit is due, Louis Farrakhan is all we can admire—and should *fear*—in a cult leader.

He is both cult leader *and politician*, having fashioned himself an "untouchable" niche that exists in the gray "Hands off!" zone between religion and politics.

Study him well. Farrakhan's NOI has something for everyone: His "black empowerment" message (inherited from Elijah Muhammad) still plays in the Black community, so much so that non-racist Blacks all too often *pretend* not to hear Farrakhan's underlying racist mnessage. (Can you say, "Germany, 1933"?)

Though NOI's message has become more subtle down through the years (discarding their more overtly vehement and venomous racism in favor of "cult-speak" catch phrases and codes), NOI publications still preach "the genetic inferiority of the white minority population."[210]

Still today on the final page of every NOI *Muhammad Speaks* newspaper you'll find Elijah Poole's original, now eighty-year-old message, calling for racial separation:

---

210. *Muhammad Speaks,* volume 6, number 2, 1989:7.

> We believe this *is* the time in history for the separation of the so-called Negroes and the so-called White Americans.

Still, few White or Black, dare openly challenge or condemn Farrakhan.

If you're White and you dare question Farrakhan's motives, you're automatically accused of being "racist." If you're Black and speak out against NOI, you're branded a "race traitor."

Farrakhan uses just enough Middle Eastern symbolism to keep up the impression of being an Islamic sect, just enough "religion" to attract the "spiritual-minded," and just enough hoodoo and pseudo-history to dazzle those easily hoodwinked by such trappings.

Most importantly, since it's a "religious group," NOI qualifies for tax exemption. And what about NOI qualifying for state- and government-sponsored vouchers for NOI "schools" where racial superiority and separatism *is* taught with the blessing of *your* tax dollars?

(Would-be cult leaders take note. Credit where credit is due. . . .)

For all his mouthings of peace and Million Man Marches, Farrakhan *is* still a cult leader who rules by racism and fear. As already mentioned, he remains the hands-on favorite for having masterminded the 1965 assassination of his rival Malcolm X. And the NOI still maintains a private security firm/militia known as "The Fruits of Islam."

And like all cults, the NOI has spawned a myriad of jerk-off spin-offs, imitators ranging from the deranged to the even-more dangerous:

There's the esoteric-minded "Five-Percenters Nation" founded by Clarence Jowers Smith, aka "Clarence 13X" (1929–1969), who be**LIE**ve themselves to be "Gods." And there's Dwight York's Nuwaubian Nation. (Notice how that word "Nation" *is* real popular with cult leaders? Nation of Islam, Aryan Nations, etc.)

And then there's the 1970s "Death Angels," and the equally homicidal 1990s *Yahweh-ben-Yahweh* cult, both of which have roots in the Nation of Islam.[211]

After Nine-Eleven, for the first time, many of us noticed those Muslims living next door. (Oh! Like that makes us bad people!)

---

211. See *666 Devilish Secrets of Islam*.

Others started taking a long, hard look at Farrakhan, to see if his "Islamic" NOI poses a threat.

The answer is probably . . . no.

It's a well-known fact that long before Nine-Eleven, as far back as the mid-1980s, radical Middle Eastern Muslim organizations have been actively recruiting disgruntled African-American prisoners (not to be confused with NOI "Black Muslim" prisoners) in all the major prisons in America.[212]

But remember, most of orthodox Islam still does not acknowledge the NOI as "real" Muslims.

Thus, despite all Farrakhan's racist rhetoric and pre-Nine-Eleven rhetoric of "*Islam will destroy America!*", ultimately Farrakhan is too smart to screw up a good thing. (Again, if you're thinking about starting your own cult, take note.)

In other words, Farrakhan is more "the Dollar" than he is "the Diabolical."

Surviving conspiracy and coup attempts (and that's just within his own cult!) to ultimately craft himself an unassailable niche, ironically, Farrakhan is the perfect example of how a former calypso dancer can remake himself into a powerful homegrown American cult leader.

Who says this isn't still the "Land of Opportunity"?

> *"A casual stroll through the lunatic asylum shows that faith does not prove anything."*
> —**Nietzsche**

CONCLUSION

While it's true that "Cult is what the big church calls the little church," that doesn't mean every little church is a cult.

By the same token, just because a cult has a billion members, that doesn't make it any less of a cult!

> *"Pleads he in earnest? Look upon his face,*
> *His eyes do drop no tears, his prayers are in jest;*

---

212. See *Terror! The Inside Story of the Terrorist Conspiracy in America* by Yossef Bodansky (1994).

His words come from his mouth, ours from our breast.
He prays but faintly and would be denied;
We pray with heart and soul and all beside:
His weary joints would gladly rise, I know;
Our knees shall kneel till to the ground they grow.
His prayers are full of false hypocrisy; Ours of true
Zeal and deep integrity. Our prayers do outpray his;
Then let them have/ That mercy which true prayers ought
To have."
—Shakespeare, *Richard II*

A final thought on cults:

> Reason actually plays a fairly small part in human relations.
> There would be no point whatever in attacking Lundgren or
> Koresh or Jim Jones because what they taught was contrary to
> reason. We are surrounded by people who, by that strict stan-
> dard, ought to be in a madhouse. Our conviction of our own
> sanity may be no more than a prejudice. In the case of most
> religions, it certainly is. (Colin Wilson, *Rogue Messiah*)

In the end, we don't so much put our faith in God, or Gods, or even
spirits, so much as we—for lack of other options—put our faith in *men*,
putting our faith in the hope that the men who wrote or else unearthed and
then translated the "holy" writ we use to guide our lives and the lives of our
loved ones, are not lying to us. Worse yet, lying to us by way of first having
deluded themselves . . . or were—perhaps high-as-kite when receiving their
"divine revelations."

Remember:

- Only Abraham was there when God told him to slit his little son's
  throat.
- Only Moses saw what Moses saw on the top of Mount Sinai.
- Only Muhammad was there in that cave when the Archangel Gabriel
  started rattling off verses of the Koran.
- Only Joseph Smith was there when he dug up those ancient gold
  plates that would one day become the Book of Mormon.

- Only Louis Farrakhan was there that night in Mexico when he got beamed aboard the orbiting "Mother Plane" and heard the voice of the long-dead (or immortal?) Elijah Muhammad.

Again and again we place our faith not in the gods of Abraham, Moses, Muhammad, or Joseph Smith, but in the words coming out the mouth—and the quill—of these "prophets" themselves.

In lieu of our actually touching God ourselves, we put our faith in the word of our fellows when they testify to they're having been chosen—touched!—by the hand of God.

We put our faith in such men in the hope that we too might be so touched. Or, at the very least, that we might touch the hem of the garment of him who was himself touched.

To hope for such a boon does not make us bad people. Whether it actually helps make us better people, that is still up in the air.

So in the final analysis, *hope* is not so bad a thing. There are plenty worse things human beings can cling to . . . *hope* that we too might one day be found worthy of being touched by the hand of God, Gods, or even a friendly spirit or two, to finally be found worthy of notice in a universe most times too busy to notice stars colliding, let alone be bothered by the plaintive pleas and petitions of a few pitiful primates on some remarkably *un*remarkable planet on an fastly atrophying arm of a simple spiral galaxy that, even as we speak, is slowly being sucked down a voracious black hole that's only trying to work out its anger-management problem!

For the opposite force to hope and faith is *fear*: Fear that we are oh-so-alone in an oh-so-huge, cold, and uncaring universe where Elvis has left the building.

If history has proven naught else it is that, by putting our faith in, pinning our hopes on, the wrong person, taking up the sword of someone who *claims*—for we have only their word to verify—that he was first given that very sword by the Almighty Himself or Herself, that giving too much credence too quickly to such claims only leads just as swiftly to 960 dead cult members at Masada, another 900 dead cult members dead at Jonestown, and hundreds of thousands of cultists dead at a thousand Waco, Heaven's Gate, and Aum Shunri Kyo cult compounds around the world and back through time.

But, ultimately, unless we begger "Atheism," and perhaps even then, we have no choice but to place our faith—our fate—in the hands of those of our fellow man who have been "blessed" and "chosen" to be touched by the hand of God, or Gods, or Hoodoo hobgoblins.

For if it's true one man, or woman, can truly be touched by the hand of God . . . then there's hope that we all—or at least *me!*—can be touched by the hand of God.

So faith in our fellow man might not—necessarily—be a bad thing—unless our fellow man just happens to be named Savonorola, or Muhammad, or Manson, or Koresh.

Despite vehemently—sometimes cynically—warning us away from sinister cults and rogue messiahs, author Colin Wilson still seems to hold out hope (there's that word again!) that we as a species may one day find our path to enlightenment finally cleared of phony prophets and scandalous would-be saviors, those shameless "Propheteers" who have plagued mankind since that first cave became that first "church."

Wilson points to attempts by philosopher Auguste Comte[213] (1798–1857) to create a "Church of Humanity" based on "positive philosophy," espousing that humanity itself, what he called "The Great Being" was God.

Ultimately, this new "religion" would hold science in highest regard and rule man by reason, rather than by superstition.

Perhaps we should put our *hope* and *faith* in naïve dreamers like Comte and Colin Wilson:

> We may well feel that an updated version of Comte's philosophy is exactly what is needed to guide humanity through the next millennium. It would have to begin from the recognition that although the world's major religions are great humanitarian ideals, they are not divinely inspired, and that the world's sacred books are the products of the mind of man, not God. Then humanity would be ready to embark on the age of positive philosophy, and religions, as well as political messiahs would become a memory of the distant past. (Colin Wilson, *Rogue Messiahs*)

---

213. The man who coined the term sociology

CONCLUSION:

"How to Win by Failing"

WE TOAST WHAT COMFORT we enjoy today with wine viciously stomped from the grapes of wrath our victorious forefathers—be they beasts, badmen, or Buddhas—planted over the fresh graves of enemies less fleet of foot, less tactical of thought, enemies less-prepared when our forefathers' foresight and patient understanding of the past overran their enemies' paltry present on our forefathers' headlong charge toward a focused future those indolent enemies had already proven themselves unworthy to occupy!

Thus, we must refrain from judging too quickly, too harshly our forefathers' hard eye and heavy hand, lest the future use our own inflexible template to one day indict us just as harshly.

Often the truth and impact of a man's deeds are not fully revealed let alone recognized until time and distance allows for a fuller, more objective view, after all subjective wounds are healed (or at least bound up tightly), all bridges once put to the torch, rebuilt.

Without this luxury of time and distance, the line between success and failure always seems more clear than it really is.

For example, at first glance we might see only *failure* when hearing that:

- Hannibal died a suicide.
- Spartacus was killed in battle, his body never found.
- Yoritomo, despite all his accomplishments, died mundanely after a fall from his horse.
- Vlad Tepes was dethroned more than once, imprisoned, and finally assassinated . . . only to be further defamed, doomed to endlessly walk the earth—at least in fiction—as the demon Dracula.

Yes, has it not been said "Experience is what you get when you don't get what you wanted"?

Sometimes we really do win by failing.

To "win by failing" sounds a bit Orwellian. Yet, curiously, our modern English word "failure" comes to us from the Latin *fallere*, meaning "to deceive."

That some men might win fortune and fame by "deceiving" shouldn't come as any surprise.

In war, deception is *strategy*.

In commerce, *financial savvy and insight*.

In the bedroom, *seduction*.

So far as Hannibal, Spartacus, Yoritomo, and Vlad Tepes are concerned, perhaps their greatest success was in failure, i.e., "deception," deceiving their enemies into thinking they'd heard the last of them. It's called *legacy*:

- Hannibal "built" the Roman Empire by giving the Romans an enemy they had to scramble to stay ahead of and struggle to defeat.
- Spartacus then not only shook that empire, his slave revolt became the inspiration for future slave revolts, and for social revolutions up to our modern day.
- Shogun Yoritomo's iron hand and steel will set the standard for the Samurai ideal that would rule Japan for the next 1,000 years.
- Vlad Tepes held the line—often alone—against the invading Saracen horde, sparing European civilization from Islamization.

Given these examples, perhaps we would do better teaching our children to reach for "failure" than for success.

Perhaps we should wish departing soldiers a hearty "Failure!" than wish them "Victory!"

More realistically, we find a simple Taoist *yin-yang* meaning here: Within any plan for success—no matter how many times we dot the I's, cross the T's, there still exists the potential for failure . . . demanding we remain ever alert!

Conversely, no matter how abysmal appears our failure—or the failure of the Universe to recognize and reward our genius!—still, within that compacted compost of "failure" resides the seeds of success.

Let us not fail to become better gardeners.

SOURCES AND SUGGESTED READING

Bhagavad-gita (The Song of God) (miscellaneous translations).

Baughman, Robert D., and Black, C. B. **666 Devilish Secrets of Islam.** (OH: Only Publications, 2010).

De Beer, Sir Gauin. **Hannibal: Challenging Rome's Supremacy.** (NY: A Studio Book/The Viking Press, 1969).

Brandon, S. G. F. **Ancient Empires (Milestones in History).** (NY: Readers Digest Assn. Ltd. Newsweek Books. 2nd ed., 1973).

Chandler, David, ed. **A Dictionary of Battles.** (NY: Henry Holt & Co., 1987).

Clark, Jane. **"In the Shadow of Dracula."** (*USA Today*, 10.29.2010:5D).

Deacon, Richard. **A History of the British Secret Service.** (London, 1969).

Dhammapada (Sayings of The Buddha). (miscellaneous translations.

Florescu, Radu, R., and McNally, Raymond T. **Dracula: Prince of Many Faces.** (Back Bay Books, 1989).

Greaves, Richard L., et al. **Civilizations of the World.** (Harper Collins College Pub. 2nd ed. 1993).

Krippendorff, Kaihan. **Hide a Dagger Behind a Smile.** (Adams Media, 2008).

Lamb, Harold. **Hannibal: One Man Against Rome.** (NY: Doubleday & Co., Inc., 1958).

Ledeen, Michael A. **Machiavelli on Modern Leadership.** (Truman Talley Books/St. Martins, 1995).

Livy. (English translation by B. D. Foster. 1st printing, 1929).

Lowell, Thomas. **The Vital Spark: 101 Outstanding Lives.** (NY: Doubleday & Co., Inc., 1959).

Lung, Haha. **The Ancient Art of Strangulation.** (CD: Paladin Press, 1995).

————. *Ninja Craft*. (DH: Alpha Publications, 1997).

————. *Assassin! Secrets of the Cult of the Assassins*. (Paladin Press, 1997).

————. *Knights of Darkness*. (Paladin Press, 1998).

————. *Cao Dai Kung-fu*. (WA: Loompanics Unlimited, 2002).

————. *Assassin!* (NY: Citadel Press, 2006).

————. *Lost Fighting Arts of Vietnam*. (Citadel Press, 2006).

————. *Mind Control*. (Citadel, 2006).

————. *Mind Penetration*. (Citadel, 2007).

————. *Mind Fist*. (Citadel, 2008).

————. *The 99 Truths: Hannibal's Black Art of War.* (publication pending).

———— and Prowant, Christopher B. *Black Science*. (Paladin Press, 2001).

————. *Shadowhand: Secrets of Ninja Taisavski*. (Paladin Press, 2002).

————. *Mind Manipulation*. (Citadel, 2002).

————. *Theatre of Hell: Dr. Lung's Complete Guide to Torture*. (Loompanics Unlimited, 2003).

————. *Ninja Shadowhand: The Art of Invisibility*. (Citadel, 2004).

————. *Mental Dominance*. (Citadel, 2009).

————. *Mind Assassins*. (Citadel, 2010).

————. *Mind Warrior*. (Citadel, 2010).

Lung, Haha, and Tucker, Eric. *Nine Halls of Death*. (Citadel, 2007).

Machiavelli, Niccolò. *The Discourses*. (trans. Leslie J. Walker, 1929).

————. *The Prince* (1513).

Mahabharata. (miscellaneous translations).

Mao Tze-Tung. *On Guerrilla Warfare*. (miscellaneous translations).

Matthews, Robert. *Age of the Gladiators*. (2004).

Marr, Gerald. **"Japanese Women, Ancient and Modern."** (*Transactions and Proceedings of the Japanese Society*, 1920).

Miyamoto Musashi. *Go Rin No Sho (A Book of Five Rings)*. (1645, miscellaneous translations).

Omar, Ralph Dean. **"Ninja Death Touch: The Fact and the Fiction."** (*Black Belt* magazine, September 1989).

————. *Death on Your Doorstep* (Alpha Publications, 1995).

Ratti, Oscar, and Westbrook, Adele. *Secrets of the Samurai: The Martial Arts of Feudal Japan*. (Boston: Tuttle Publishing, 1973).

Sawyer, Ralph D. *The Seven Classics of Ancient China*. (Basic Books, 1993).

Seth, Ronald. *Secret Servants: A History of Japanese Espionage*. (NY: Farrar, Straus and Company, 1957).

Skinner, Dirk. *Street Ninja: Ancient Secrets for Surviving Today's Mean Streets.* (NY:Barricade Books, 1995).

Spencer, Robert. *The Politically Incorrect Guide to Islam.* (Regnery Publishing, Inc., 2005).

Strauss, Barry. *The Spartacus War.* (NY: Simon & Schuster, 2009).

Suetonius. *The Twelve Caesars.* (c. 79 A.D., miscellaneous translations).

Sun Bin. *Ping fa (The Lost Art of War).* (miscellaneous translations).

Sun Tzu. *Ping fa (The Art of War).* (miscellaneous translations).

Swartz, Stephen. *The Two Faces of Islam.* (Doubleday, 2002).

Timmerman, Kenneth R. *Preachers of Hate.* (2002).

Tokitsu, Kenji. *Miyamoto Musashi: His Life and Writings.* (Boston/London: Shambhala, 2004).

Turnbull, Stephen. *The Samurai and the Sacred.*(Osprey Pub., 2006).

Yoritomo, Taishi. *Influence: How to Exert It.* 1916 rendering by B. Dangennas (Kissinger Publications Co.)

Zen and Shinto: The Story of Japanese Philosophy. (CT: Greenwood Press, 1959).